AD

Travel Guide

Berlin

Potsdam and Schloss Sanssouci

Ulrike Krause and Enno Wiese

☐ Introduction

☐ Sights to see

☐ Services

Impressions of Berlin

The young wild one – glorious Renaissance of a fabulous capital city

'There is a reason for preferring Berlin to other cities: because it is continually changing.'

Bertolt Brecht

Berlin is a city with that certain something, a city of **contrasts**: you'll find elegant boulevards and counterculture scene sections, royal palaces and the dilapidated façades of housing in Prenzlauer Berg, hot nightlife in the inner city and idyllic lakeside scenery at Wannsee, elegant villas in Grunewald and streetwalkers in Oranienburger Straße, village life in Lübars and life in satellite settlements such as the Märkisches Viertel. Berlin is a city of tempo, temperament and turbulence. And Berliners are like their city. The *Berlin lip* is proverbial and modulation is virtually unknown here. 'Nobody's got anything on us' is what the locals say. And how could they, in this city

he rampages, where he romps. Berlin has always been quite impossible!

'Berlin is a continent rather than a city,' pronounced the poet Jean Paul. He should know. After all, he lived in Berlin in 1800/01. Even in his day Berlin was unlike other German cities. A **metropolis** of European stature. A city to which Schiller attested 'informality in bourgeois life' but a spot where you needed elbows even two centuries ago if you wanted to get anywhere. You had to be as tough as nails and had to be rude on occasion just to keep your head above water in Berlin – that was Goethe's experience and he was anything but squeamish. In Berlin everyone can be happy after their own fashion – Frederick the Great knew that and acted accordingly. And the famous *'Berlin air, air, air'* is great anyway!

Only a few pieces of the **Berlin Wall** and four border watchtowers recall forty

that is as strong as a bear? Yes, the **bear** is to Berliners what the little monk is to the people of Munich and the Hammaburg to natives of Hamburg – coat of arms and hallmark alike. But the bear stands for more than just that in Berlin. This is where

Top: *A view of Mt Olympus – The rotunda of the Altes Museum with statues of the gods*
Top right: *Flower-like dancers – a Korean dance group at the Carnival of Cultures*
Right: *Architects' heaven – the tent-shaped Philharmonie and Sony-Center top the Kulturforum roofs to overlook all of Potsdamer Platz*

years of partition. The bare Death Zone has long since disappeared. Construction cranes are still circling above the city; a skyline of stunning new architecture has appeared. Berlin, until 1989 an island in the Eastern bloc, then the interface between East and West, today has assumed the airs and graces of a capital. Since the Federal government moved to Berlin, the city has become an administrative and economic hub. Be it Pariser Platz or Friedrichstraße, Potsdamer Platz or the inner bend of the Spree, the new government and commercial buildings, shopping passages and designer hotels have changed the face of the city, lent it glitz and glamour which captivate with grand gestures and invigoratingly quirky eclecticism.

Unter den Linden and Alex

The best place to start exploring Berlin and acquiring more than a nodding acquaintance with it is the geographical and historical centre of the city, Mitte District. Here, on the great boulevard **Unter den Linden**, a bronze statue of Frederick the Great faces east to Lustgarten, where Frederick's official residence, the *Berliner Stadtschloss*, once stood. The palace was once the political centre of both the city and the state of Prussia. Like most of Berlin, it sustained severe damage in the Second World War but, unlike so many other historic buildings, was torn down in the early 1950s instead of being renovated. The *Palace of the Republic*, which the

GDR regime built on the site, has long ceased to have any political function and is scheduled for demolition in 2006. In July 2002 the Bundestag, the Federal lower house of parliament, proposed rebuilding the Berliner Stadtschloss and in August 2005 presented a concept for housing *inter alia* the Dahlem Museums, Humboldt University collections and a hotel in the Schloss.

The earliest Berlin settlements, Cölln and Berlin, were to the east of the Berliner Stadtschloss. Virtually nothing remains of old Cölln yet parts of old Berlin have been rebuilt in the **Nikolaiviertel**. The **Museumsinsel**, laid out by *Karl Friedrich Schinkel* in the early 19th century, is north of the Lustgarten. The **Altes Museum** housing the Antiquities Collection and the Egyptian Museum at the edge of the Lustgarten was designed by Schinkel to counterbalance the Stadtschloss: culture and politics confronting each other on an equal footing. Schinkel, who was the leading official Prussian architect for a quarter of a century, shaped the face of the historic city centre as no other has done before or since. He designed the **Neue Wache**, the **Schloss Bridge**, the **Friedrichswerdersche Church**, the Architecture Academy and a church on the site of the present **Berlin Cathedral**.

The world-famous collections on the Museum Island, including the **Pergamonmuseum** with the magnificent altar from ancient Pergamon and the **Alte Nationalgalerie** featuring Monet, Manet, Cézanne and many more greats of the 19th century, are a magnet for visitors.

Top: *Oh, Salomé – Strauss and the State Opera: all the world's a stage*
Centre left: *The Ku'damm often has its British moments*
Bottom left: *Really cool – Edward Kienholz's 'Art Show' at the Berlinische Galerie*
Right: *Everything at your fingertips – a heavenly beach and an island full of art: Museum Island and Beach Bar Mitte*

A few blocks on is **Alexanderplatz** with the **Television Tower** and the **Red Town Hall**. This vast square, which was last remodelled in the 1960s, is to be given a complete makeover that has been in the pipeline for years. For the time being it is undergoing extensive beauty treatment. Well worth exploring from here is the former **Scheunenviertel** with its **New Synagogue**. Enjoy a leisurely stroll through the inviting **Hackesche Höfe** with their Jugendstil façades, **Sophienstraße** lined with 1870s boom buildings and dip into the cafés and eateries in bustling **Oranienburgerstraße**.

Going down Unter den Linden from the Schloss Bridge towards **Friedrichstraße** and the dazzling new shopping malls, you pass the **Staatsbibliothek** (State Library), and the palaces built for the Hohenzollerns. The *Forum Fridericianum*, planned as a royal residence and now Bebelplatz, comprises **St Hedwig's Cathedral**, the **Staatsoper Unter den Linden**, **Humboldt University** and the **Alte Bibliothek** (Old Library).

Nearby is **Gendarmenmarkt**, one of Berlin's most beautiful squares. It boasts two cathedrals and the *Schauspielhaus* theatre designed by Schinkel.

Unter den Linden boulevard ends at Pariser Platz and the **Brandenburg Gate**. **Pariser Platz**, once dubbed the capital's 'drawing-room', has been rebuilt. The elegant *Hotel Adlon* reopened on its former site in 1997 and the new *Akademie der Künste* (2005) is not just an art academy but a contemporary art work. Other new buildings are stylistically attuned to the historic façades that used to line Pariser Platz.

Top: *Stage set with lady – a really successful production, with the Brandenburg Gate and the Reichstag playing the leading roles*
Bottom right: *Berlin has it all – stylish and all set for a day of fun at Grosser Wannsee*

Tiergarten and Ku'damm

Behind the Brandenburg Gate is the **Tiergarten**, Berlin's biggest inner-city park. Not far away is the **Reichstag**, surmounted by the unique glass dome from which visitors peer down into the workings of parliament. Since autumn 1999 the building has been the seat of the Bundestag. The **Bundeskanzleramt**, where the Chancellor has her offices, and parliamentary buildings such as the **Paul Löbe House**, have represented distinguished modern architecture at the bend in the Spree since 2001. The **Botschaftsviertel**, the Embassy Quarter, near the Tiergarten also boasts ultramodern architecture.

Potsdamer Platz and its immediate vicinity were Europe's biggest construction site for years. Late in 1998 the first complex of DaimlerChrysler-City, opened here, a quarter comprising nineteen city blocks. The Sony-Center complex followed in June 2000. The *Kulturforum*, with museums, and the **Philharmonie** are

nearby. To the east are some old government buildings that go back to the founding of the German Empire in 1871 and the Third Reich. The former Reich Aviation Ministry is now the **Federal Ministry of Finance**. The *Topography of Terror* documentation and the **Holocaust-Mahnmal** (2005), a sombre field of stelae, recall the atrocities committed by the Nazis.

A visit to the centre of West Berlin begins at the **Kaiser-Wilhelm-Gedächtniskirche**. A symbolic symbiosis between a war-ruined church and and 1960s architecture, it stands at the intersection of *Tauentzienstraße*, one of Berlin's busiest shopping streets, and the **Kurfürstendamm**. The Ku'damm, *the* boulevard for strolling in Berlin, is still the most elegant address as well as a lively commercial and entertainment section. Countless Cafés, restaurants, hotels, clubs, cinemas and glitzy emporia rub shoulders here.

Castles, lakes and museums

Schloss Charlottenburg is the only Hohenzollern city palace to have survived. Its fine **park** represents a successful synthesis of architecture, landscaping and natural beauty. Moreover, there are interesting museums in Schloss Charlottenburg itself and in the immediate vicinity,

including the **Museum Berggruen**, full of masterpieces by Picasso, Matisse, etc.

Modern and contemporary masters also reign supreme in the **Neue Nationalgalerie**, the **Hamburger Bahnhof** and the **Berlinische Galerie**, which notably practises a city art concept. Old Masters are there to be admired in the **Gemäldegalerie** at the Kulturforum. Another must since it reopened in 2004 is **Schloss Köpenick**, which houses a superlative museum of the decorative and applied arts. The excellent museums at the **Museumskomplex Dahlem**, by contrast, feature ethnology and Far Eastern art.

Berlin also boasts a great many attractions outside the city. An excursion on the river **Havel** and a stop at the **Pfaueninsel** reveal the beauties of *Mark Brandenburg* – a landscape of rivers, lakes and sandy soil typical of the Berlin hinterland. The extensive **Stadtwald**, the forest between the **Müggelsee** and the **Müggelbergen** to the south-east, is a place to be returned to again and again. A boat trip to **Potsdam**, a visit to **Schloss Sanssouci** and **Schloss Babelsberg** provide further entrancing glimpses of this Prussian arcadia. Thanks to their superlative palaces and magnificent parks, Berlin and Potsdam were declared a *UNESCO World Cultural Heritage Site* in 1990.

The bear dances here at night!

Berlin's liveliest sections nowadays include Kreuzberg, Mitte, Prenzlauer Berg and Friedrichshain. **Kreuzberg**, home to a thriving counterculture, has moved back into the city centre thanks to reunification. **Mitte** is a magnet for the young with fringe galleries and clubs, trendy boutiques and crowds of pedestrians. The **Prenzlauer Berg** district, a refuge for artists and dissidents in the GDR era, today overflows with pubs, restaurants and unique shops. The Friedrichshain scene quarter is just super-cool. And of course the great Berlin **nightlife** still lives up to its legend.

This guide

This volume describes the sights to see in Berlin in 16 chapters. **City maps** make it easy for visitors to find their bearings. **Top Tips** specially recommend hotels, restaurants, etc. The **Travel Infromation** section contains practical pointers on shopping, events, nightlife, city tours, sports etc. Brief **essays** round off the guide book.

An outline of history, art and culture
From Brandenburg village to dynamic metropolis

ca 8000 BC Old Stone Age settlement.

ca 700 BC Early Teutonic settlement.

6th/7th centuries AD Settlement by West Slav tribes.

1134–70 Albrecht the Bear, first Ascanian Margrave of Brandenburg.

1197 First mention of Spandau in records.

1237 First recorded mention of Cölln as a town, followed by Wedding in 1251 and Schöneberg in 1264.

1244 First recorded mention of Berlin as a city.

1307 Fusion of Cölln and Berlin.

1308–19 Margrave Waldemar the Great.

1320 End of Ascanian rule.

1338 First use of Berlin Bear as seal on a council document.

1369 Berlin acquired the right to mint coins.

1376/1380 Large parts of the city destroyed in two great fires.

1415 Hohenzollerns invested with electoral principality of Brandenburg in fief: Friedrich IV Hohenzollern, now Friedrich I, Elector of Brandenburg, became new ruler of Brandenburg.

1443 The Elector Friedrich II, known as 'Iron Tooth', laid the cornerstone for the Hohenzollern castle.

1470 The Hohenzollern castle was made the elector's seat.

1539 The Reformation prevailed.

1576–1611 Plague years: chronicles of the Cölln city scribe recorded 4000 plague dead in 1576, 3000 in 1598 and 2000 in 1611. Around 1600 the city had a population of 10 000–12 000.

1618–48 Thirty Years War: the suburbs of Berlin burned down. 1648: population 6000.

1640–88 Reign of the Great Elector Friedrich Wilhelm. He laid the groundwork for the ascendancy of Brandenburg-Prussia.

1647 1000 limes (lindens) and 1000 walnut trees planted to form an avenue from the Berliner Stadtschloss to the Tiergarten, later called Unter den Linden boulevard.

Berlin architect:
Karl Friedrich Schinkel

1658 Berlin fortified.

1662–69 Friedrich-Wilhelm Canal built between Spree and Oder rivers as a direct link between Breslau and Hamburg. Berlin was established as port of reshipment.

1685 Edict of Potsdam: French Huguenot refugees granted asylum and settled.

1688–1713 Elector Friedrich III. in 1701 crowned himself in Königsberg as king of Prussia, calling himself Friedrich I. Friedrichstadt laid out.

1700 Prussian Academy of Sciences founded.

1709 Berlin, Cölln, Friedrichswerder, Dorotheenstadt and Friedrichstadt united to form the royal city of Berlin.

1710 Berlin reached a population of 60 000, including 6000 French, 5000 Swiss and 500 from the Palatinate.

1713–40 Reign of Friedrich Wilhelm I, known as the 'Soldier King'.

1717 Introduction of compulsory school attendance.

1740–86 Friedrich II, Frederick the Great, made Berlin a cosmopolitan European capital and a centre of the Enlightenment. Science and research, art and culture flourished.

1756–63 Seven Years War: Austrian and Russian troops occupied Berlin.

1786–97 Reign of Friedrich Wilhelm II, dubbed 'Fat Wilhelm'.

ca 1790 Berlin became a centre of German Romanticism.

1797–1840 Reign of Friedrich Wilhelm III.

ca 1800 Berlin was Europe's third largest city after London and Paris.

1806–08 Berlin occupied by Napoleon's troops.

1813 6000 Berliners volunteered for the Wars of Liberation from Napoleon.

1816 Karl Friedrich Schinkel, Christian Daniel Rauch and Peter Joseph Lenné designed the new Berlin after liberation from Napoleon. First German-built steamer plied the Spree. Onset of the Industrial Revolution.

1826 The first gasworks (an English one) provided Unter den Linden with gas lighting.

1838/39 Opening of Berlin–Potsdam railway and the first Berlin horse-drawn omnibus line.

1840–61 Reign of Friedrich Wilhelm IV. Berlin rated as a major European industrial city.

(from left to right) Frederick the Great – Soldier King Friedrich Wilhelm I – Reich Chancellor Prince Otto von Bismarck

1847 The first (united) Prussian Landtag (parliament) convened in Berlin.

1848 18 March: March Revolution broke out. 22 May: Prussian National Assembly (dissolved on 5 December). 23 August: 1st German Workers Congress.

1861–88 Reign of Wilhelm I, King of Prussia.

1862–90 Otto E. L. von Bismarck as Prussian Minister President, from 1871 Reich Chancellor.

1866 Berlin became capital of the North German Confederation.

1870/71 Franco-Prussian War.

1871 King Wilhelm I crowned German Emperor (Kaiser) at Versailles. Berlin (population 823 000) became capital of the German Empire.

1872 Meeting of three emperors in Berlin: Franz Joseph I of Austria, Tsar Alexander II of Russia and Wilhelm I.

1879 Werner von Siemens presented the world's first electric railway at Moabit trade fair.

1881 First telephones in operation with 45 parties. The world's first electric tram operated in Lichterfelde.

1888 Death of Wilhelm I, he was succeeded as Kaiser by his son, Friedrich III, who died after only 99 days. His successor was Wilhelm II (Kaiser until 1918).

1890 Reich Chancellor Bismarck dismissed.

1894 Reichstag inaugurated.

1900 Berlin had a population of 1.9 million.

1902 First elevated and underground railways from Warschauer Bridge to the Zoo.

1905 First public buses in operation. Max Reinhardt took over the Deutsches Theater.

1912 Bust of Queen Nefertete displayed at the Egyptian Museum.

1914–18 First World War (called the Great War).

1918 Revolution: on 9 November Philipp Scheidemann proclaimed Germany a republic from the Reichstag. Karl Liebknecht proclaimed a Soviet republic from the Eosander balcony of the Berliner Stadtschloss. Kaiser Wilhelm II abdicated on 10 November.

1919 Spartacus Revolt. 15 January: murder of Karl Liebknecht and Rosa Luxemburg, the two important Communist Party leaders.

1919 Friedrich Ebert elected first Reich President of the Weimar Republic.

1920 Kapp Putsch: Free Corps soldiers occupied government offices.

Night battle: March Revolution broke out on 18 March 1848

Berlin, 1903: view of (from l. to r.) the Altes Museum, the Schlossbrücke, Berlin Cathedral, and, in the background, St Mary's. The Stadtschloss (demolished in 1950/51) and the former national monument to Kaiser Wilhelm I abut Karl-Liebknecht-Straße (formerly Kaiser-Wilhelm-Straße)

from 1923 Berlin established as the cultural, economic and social centre of Germany.

1924 First radio exhibition.

1929 Economic depression in Europe and America: 600 000 jobless in Berlin.

1933 30 January: Hitler seized power. 27/28 February: Reichstag fire. 1 April: first boycott of Jewish shops. 10 May: book burning in Opernplatz.

1936 XIth Olympic Summer Games in Berlin.

1938 9/10 November: National Socialists destroyed Berlin synagogues during 'Night of Broken Glass'.

1939 Beginning of the Second World War; Berlin had a population of 4.3 million.

1940 First air raid on Berlin on 25 August.

1941 Beginning of mass deportation of Jews from Berlin.

1942 20 January: Wannsee Conference, at which organisational measures for the 'final solution of the Jewish question' were co-ordinated.

1943 Joseph Goebbels declared 'total war' from the Sports Palace. 1 March: first heavy bombing of Berlin. 21 March: unsuccessful attempt to assassinate Hitler in the Armoury.

1945 30 April: Hitler committed suicide. 2 May: Red Army marched into Berlin. 8 May: Unconditional surrender signed by the German Wehrmacht in Berlin-Karlshorst. Berlin had a population of 2.8 million at war's end. 32 % of all private dwellings were destroyed. Rubble estimated at 80 million cubic metres. In June the city, divided into four sectors, became the seat of the inter-Allied Control Council.

1946 13 August: the Allies promulgated a temporary constitution for Greater Berlin and announced elections; Berlin was made a city state.

1947 The Prussian state was disbanded by Allied Control Council law.

1948 Currency Reform in the three Western sectors of Berlin. 24 June: beginning of Soviet blockade of West Berlin and the Allied airlift.

1949 12 May: end of the blockade. 7 October: foundation of the GDR with East Berlin as its capital.

1950 1 October: (West) Berlin constitution came into effect.

1951 Inauguration of the first Berlin International Film Festival ('Berlinale').

1953 17 June: revolt in East Berlin and the GDR.

1957 Willy Brandt was elected governing mayor of West Berlin.

1958 Khruschev gave Berlin an ultimatum: he wanted Berlin to become a free, demilitarised city.

1961 13 August: building of the Wall began. The Wall was 161 km long, 45 km of it bisecting Berlin. 16 August: over a half million people demonstrated in front of Schöneberg Town Hall against the division of Berlin. About 60 000 East Berliners were cut off from their places of work in the Western part of the city.

1963 John F. Kennedy visited Berlin. 17 December: first agreement on border-crossing permits. After two years of separation West Berliners could visit relatives in East Berlin for the first time.

1967/68 Student riots in West Berlin. 11 April 1968: assassination attempt made on student leader Rudi Dutschke.

1971 The Four Powers Agreement signed: recognition of status quo in Berlin. Transit agreement between the GDR and FRG came into effect.

1987 Celebration of Berlin's 750th anniversary as a city.

1989 18 October: Egon Krenz succeeded Erich Honecker as head of state and party in the GDR. 7 November: the GDR government

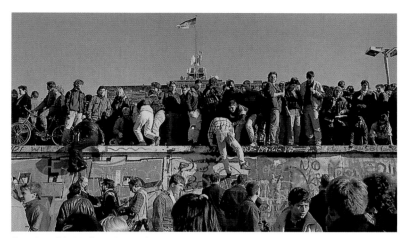

Opening of the Wall on 9 November 1989

stepped down. 9 November: opening of the Wall.
1990 3 October: the GDR dissolved by joining FRG; Berlin again Germany's capital. 2 December: East and West Berlin voted together for the first time; CDU and SPD form a grand coalition.
1993 West Berlin House of Representatives moved from Schöneberg to the former Prussian Landtag (Mitte).
1994 June–September: the Allied forces left Berlin.
1995 'Wrapped Reichstag' by Christo and Jeanne-Claude.

1996 Plebiscite against merging Berlin and Brandenburg into one federal state.
1999 Federal government and parliament moved from Bonn to Berlin.
2000 Berlin lead German cities for the first time with 10 million overnight stays annually.
2001 Prussian Year celebrated on the occasion of the tricentenary of the coronation of Friedrich III.
2004 Opening of the remodelled Olympic Stadium was celebrated.

2005 10 May: inauguration of the Holocaust Memorial by Peter Eisenmann, consisting of 2711 stelae. – 21 May: inauguration of the new Art Academy in Pariser Platz. – 13 August: Queen Nefertete moved to the Altes Museum, where the Egyptian Museum is housed until 2009. – 22 November: Angela Merkel (*1954) of the CDU (Christian Democrats) becomes the first woman to take office as Chancellor of Germany. She heads a grand coalition with the SPD (Social Democrats).

Ready for sports thrills and victories – modernisation of the Berlin Olympic Stadium was completed in 2004

*City-West with the Gedächtniskirche,
Breitscheidplatz and Kurfürstendamm*

Sights to see

From Pariser Platz through Unter den Linden Boulevard to Schlossbrücke – shades of Old Prussia

Pariser Platz and Unter den Linden boulevard were the 'reception room' and promenade of the German capital in the early 20th century. The extensive building operations of recent years have restored their former glory, while the Holocaust-Mahnmal field of stelae (2005) lends a sombre touch near Pariser Platz. A stroll from Brandenburger Tor to the Schlossbrücke bridge takes you past the highlights of the new metropolis such as the reconstructed Hotel Adlon and the new Art Academy straight into the centre of Prussian Berlin. Here Frederick the Great had his capital built to show Prussia as an emerging great power. You see the Prinzessinnenpalais and the Kronprinzenpalais, the enchanting residences of princesses and crown princes, and the Zeughaus or Armoury, before the splendid boulevard ends at the Schlossbrücke.

1 Brandenburger Tor

Monument to peace and victory, symbol of reunification – the city landmark.

Pariser Platz
S1, S2 Unter den Linden
Bus 100, TXL

Visible from far and wide, the Brandenburg Gate looms at the western end of Pariser Platz. Once the symbol of a partitioned Germany, it became the emblem of the *reunification* of the country in November 1989. Designed by Carl Gotthard Langhans, the gate was built of sandstone in 1788–91 to recall the awe-inspring entrance to the *Athens Acropolis* (Propylaea). The architect also borrowed a typical feature of ancient Roman public architecture – the **Quadriga**, a triumphal chariot drawn by a span of four horses. The Brandenburger Tor was once functionally the **city gate** but it also splendidly finished off Unter den Linden Boulevard. The Brandburg gate was opened to traffic on 6 August 1791.

The 5 m-high Quadriga driven by Victoria, goddess of victory, was designed by Johann Gottfried Schadow. It could not be put in place until 1795 because the figure of the goddess aroused a spate of controversy. Victoria – like her antecedents in classical antiquity – was to drive the battle chariot stark naked. Since she was to look towards the Stadtschloss, it is easy to imagine what travellers approaching Berlin from the west were faced with – a naked female posterior. Friedrich Wilhelm II, therefore, had a garment made to clothe Victoria decently.

The history of both gate and Quadriga has been turbulent. On 27 October 1806 **Napoleon** rode through the Brandenburg Gate to occupy the Prussian capital. As part of the victor's spoils, he had the Quadriga dismantled and sent to Paris packed in twelve crates. The *Wars of Liberation* during which Germany cast off the Napoleonic yoke brought the Quadriga back to Berlin in 1814. To commemorate the victorious struggle against the Napoleonic forces, Victoria was decorated with the Iron Cross, the Laurel Wreath and the Prussian Eagle.

In 1945 the Brandenburg Gate sustained severe damage that left the Quadriga lying in splinters. All that remained to show how it had looked were the 5000 unnumbered parts of a plaster cast made in 1942 and kept in the Western sector of the city. These plaster forms were used in 1957 to reconstruct the Quadriga. That was the sole **reconstruction project** on which East and West collaborated – they had no choice. SED head Walter Ulbricht then decreed that the Prussian Eagle and the Iron Cross could no longer be used as decoration. The Victoria of the GDR years was given a staff with an oak-leaf wreath to hold. The Prussian Eagle and the Iron Cross were not replaced until the second reconstruction after Germany was reunified in 1991.

After reunification, it was a matter of some dispute whether *car traffic* should again be allowed to flow through the Brandenburg Gate. Now the Berlin landmark, which is 20 m high, 65 m across and 11 m deep, is open to pedestrians and bicycles only. A total restoration of the grand monument was completed in 2002.

2 Pariser Platz

Reception room to the metropolis.
S1, S2 Unter den Linden
Bus 100, TXL

Until the Second World War, the square, measuring 120 x 120 m and incorporating the Brandenburg Gate and a number of palaces, was dubbed the capital's 'recep-tion room'. A wing of the former Prussian Art Academy and the ruins of the Adlon Hotel were all that survived the war. Since the **Berlin Wall** bisected the Branden-burg Gate, the square was left untouched during the GDR era, off limits except to groups of visitors. After reunification, Pariser Platz became a construction site. Today the rebuilt Hotel Adlon, the new Akademie der Künste (integrating the re-maining wing of the old Prussina Art Academy), the historicizing banks and the new buildings housing the British, French and the (upcoming) American embassies ensure that Pariser Platz is again one of Berlin's most attractive loca-tions.

Pariser Platz was laid out (along with the squares now called Mehringplatz and Leipziger Platz) in 1734, when Berlin was enlarged by the incorporation of Fried-richsstadt. At that time the square was used as a **parade ground** and a **forecourt** to the city gate, the first Brandenburg Gate of 1734. The area was also an elegant residential quarter on the outskirts of the city. As early as 1800 German officials and foreign legations resided here. Around 1840 the Baroque buildings surrounding Pariser Platz were remodelled in the Neo-Classical style of the Schinkel school. This is the formal idiom on which architects have modelled the present reconstruc-tion of the square.

The Berlin landmark and symbol of reunification – the venerable Brandenburg Gate viewed from the glass terrace of the Art Academy, which opened in 2005

The impressionist painter *Max Liebermann* lived in the **Max-Liebermann House** built in 1735 north of the Brandenburg Gate. He was president of the Art Academy in 1920–32 and from his house must have seen with misgivings the celebrations marking Hitler's accession to power on 30 January 1933. Destroyed in bombing raids, the house was rebuilt after plans by Josef Paul Kleinhues. Now *rotating exhibitions* are mounted and the 'Torgespräche' talks on culture and science take place here (Phone: 030/22 63 30 30, www.stiftung.brandenburgertor.de).

Until the end of the Second World War, the *Palais der Gräfin von Hagen* (No. 5), which had housed the **French Embassy** since 1860, also adorned the north side of the square. The new embassy was opened in 2002.

Palais Blücher, home to the **American Embassy** since 1930, was once adjacent to the south side of the Brandenburg Gate. The new official residence of the US ambassador is scheduled to open in 2007.

The **Akademie der Künste** (Art Academy, www.adk.de) is situated next to it, at 4 Pariser Platz. Founded in 1696, the Academy was at first housed in the Marstall (Unter den Linden). From 1907 it was here in the *Palais Arnim-Boitzenburg* that Eduard Knoblauch had remodelled in the

The reconstructed Adlon links up again with its glorious past as a luxury hotel

Neo-Classical style in 1857/58. During the Weimar Period leading intellectuals such as Heinrich and Thomas Mann, Alfred Döblin and Käthe Kollwitz met at the Academy. Only a side wing of the building survived the Second World War. The new Academy building with its austere glass show façade revealing slender columns inside, the trademark of its architect, Günter Behnisch, opened in 2005. It comprises exhibition rooms, a library, a sculpture garden, a café and a bookshop. The Hansa-Viertel academy branches [see p. 96] are to continue in use.

At the corner of Pariser Platz and Wilhelmstraße was a celebrity venue during the Wilhelmine Empire and the Weimar Republic: the **Hotel Adlon**. Lorenz Adlon had already made a name for himself in Berlin as a restaurateur and hotelier before being permitted by Wilhelm II in 1906 to demolish *Palais Redern*, a listed historic monument, and build one of the world's most luxurious hotels. The *haute volée* lost no time in flocking to the Adlon, which boasted 305 rooms to tempt the Rockefellers, Charlie Chaplin and Indian maharajahs. By a miracle the building survived the bombing raids of the Second World War unscathed, only to burn down shortly after the war ended. Since the Adlon reopened as the Kempinski in mid-1997, with a façade that is a faithful replica of the original and elegantly nostalgic retro interiors, it has been a magnet for tourists.

Nearby Wilhelmstraße 70/71 is the address of the stylish new **British Embassy** (2000), designed by Michael Wilford with a striking perforated façade.

3 Holocaust-Mahnmal

The Holocaust Memorial, a monumental field of stelae near Pariser Platz, commemorates the murdered European Jews.

Ebertstraße/Wilhelmstraße
Phone: 030/74 07 29 29, 030/200 76 60
www.holocaust-mahmal.de
Stelae field: daily 24 hours
Place of Information: daily 10 am–
8 pm, no admission after 7.15 pm
S1, S2 Unter den Linden
Bus 100, TXL

South of Pariser Platz and the Academy, the controversial Holocaust Memorial by US architect Peter Eisenmann was inau-

Thousands of stones tell the story of a country, its capital and innumerable victims – a view across the Holocaust Memorial to the Reichstag and the Brandenburg Gate

gurated on 10 May 2005. This **monument commemorating the murdered European Jews** is a field of stelae, a labyrinth for visitors to walk through consisting of 2711 grey concrete stelae of widely varying height (.20–4.70 m). It was composed to form a vast wavy surface when viewed from above. In addition, there is a *Place of Information*, a subterranean documentation centre.

The monument commemorates the 6 million European Jews who were victims of the Holocaust. Since its inauguration, thousands of visitors from all over the world, among them many young people, have flocked to the memorial. At the Place of Information, which attracts about 1800 visitors a day (waiting time up to 2 hours), there is also a database containing all the names, which was made available for research purposes by the Yad Vashem Memorial in Israel.

The monument goes back to a 1980s citizens' initiative. After much controversy, the Bundestag resolved to build it in 1999. Eisenmann's design has in the meantime been vehemently debated and has consequently undergone several modifications. At the inauguration, the architect refuted attempts at interpreting the field of stelae as a cementery or a wheat field.

He sees his work as a place of hope. While walking through the rows of stelae, visitors are supposed to listen to the victims' voices.

4 Unter den Linden

Boulevard with a past and a future.

S1, S2, S25, S26 Unter den Linden, U6 Friedrichstraße and Französische Straße, Bus 100, 200, TXL

Berlin's showcase boulevard is Unter den Linden. Here, too, building has gone on at a furious pace in recent years to restore its former glitz and glamour.

To think this was once a mere bridle-path! In 1575 a sand track was laid between the bridge spanning the moat to the Berliner Stadtschloss and the Tiergarten for the inhabitants of the Schloss to ride on. The Prince Elector Friedrich Wilhelm had **1000 limes** and 1000 walnut trees planted along it in 1647. The walnuts died but the limes (lindens) thrived to give the street its name. After *Pariser Platz* was laid out in 1734, Unter den Linden gradually grew into a boulevard. By 1800 hoteliers, merchants and purveyors of goods and services to the court were set-

Splendid architecture – Unter den Linden boulevard with the Crown Prince's Palace and the State Opera Unter den Linden from the Schlossbrücke

tling here. Intellectuals and officers alike thronged the *salons* und *cafés*.

The founding of the German Empire in 1871 brought an influx of bankers and speculators, who took over the palaces where the nobility had lived. **Public amusements**, including a waxworks in the Kaiserpassage near the Friedrichstraße intersection, provided robust entertainment in the early 20th century.

Nevertheless, Unter den Linden remained the *imperial boulevard*. It wasn't just that Kaiser Wilhelm I appeared daily at a window of the imperial palace to bask in the adulation of his subjects. No buildings could be changed without his approval.

Most of the palaces and emporia were destroyed in the Second World War. Buildings at what was once the *Forum Fridericianum*, now Bebelplatz, still attest to former splendour. The boulevard was divided into three sections in the GDR era. The area between *Wilhelmstraße* and *Glinkastraße* was reserved for embassies. Citizens of the GDR were not supposed to get too close to the border, which ran through the Brandenburg Gate. Shops settled in the area between Glinkastraße and *Charlottenstraße*. Prussian Berlin was reconstructed from Charlottenstraße to the *Schlossbrücke*. Among the reconstructions undertaken then were faithful replicas of the Crown Prince's Palace and the Princesses' Palace.

The turnaround in 1989 gave Unter den Linden a new look. The German Bundestag established offices there for members of parliament and former proprietors such as the Deutsche Bank returned to their old head offices. Some 'scandalously hideous' architecture was demolished and replaced by new buildings such as the elegant **Lindenforum** shopping mall.

If you walk up Unter den Linden from Pariser Platz, the first building to catch your eye is the **Russian Embassy** (Nos. 60–66), which was built in 1950–53 in the massive *Stalin Era* style. In 1800 the property was the site of a palace owned by the Princess of Courland, which became a fo-

cal point of Berlin society. In 1837 Tsar Nicholas I bought the building and had cartloads of Russian soil brought to the site of the planned embassy to provide his diplomats with a touch of home. In 1917 the Soviet government took over the building but it was destroyed in the Second World War.

The commercial buildings across the street, the former *Haus Wagon-Lits* (No. 40) and the old *Zollernhof* (Nos. 36–38), date from about 1910. They attest that Unter den Linden was then regarded as *the* address in the international business world. The only 1930s building remaining is *Haus der Schweiz* (No. 24), which was restored in 1993.

At the corner of Friedrichstraße is the **Westin Grand Hotel**, built 1985–87 on the occasion of East Berlin's celebration of its 750th birthday. It covers the site of what was once the Kaiserpassage. A 120-m-long covered passage built in 1873, the

Kaiserpassage housed cafés, cinemas and amusements. It was a popular attraction but went bankrupt in 1923 and had to close. Gutted by fire in 1944, it was demolished in 1950. This was the home of the celebrated *Café Kranzler*, where everyone who was anyone in Berlin congregated. The Kranzler was popular because it had a terrace from which one could observe the hustle and bustle of Unter den Linden. Although the terrace violated building regulations, the 'Kaisers' had a soft spot for the young officers who found it an ideal location for spotting future brides. After 1944 the Kranzler reopened on Ku'damm [see p. 111].

There are some prime examples of cosmopolitan hotels dating from 1900 not far down Unter den Linden. **No. 17** was the *Hotel Karlton*, built in 1902, it provided discerning guests with high-class accommodation. Across from it is the Hotel de Rome, built in 1865. Kaiser Wilhelm I, who lived in the nearby Altes Palais (Kaiserpalais) always had the hotel proprietor trundle a bath-tub across the street to his palace from the hotel once a week.

The *Deutsche Bank* is said to have paid a truly exorbitant sum to return to its old head office (Nos. 13–15), built in 1920. The **Deutsche Guggenheim Berlin** (Phone: 030/202 09 30, www.deutsche-bank-kunst.com/guggenheim, daily 11 am–8 pm, Th until 10 pm) was inaugurated in 1997 on the ground floor, a joint undertaking by the Bank and the Solomon R. Guggenheim Foundation. The bank building is a forum for world-class rotating exhibitions of modern and contemporary art. Next door the Baroque façade of the *Gouverneurshaus* (No. 11) dating from 1721 still graces the boulevard. Only a outer staircase, on the other hand, recalls the Netherlandish Palace, where Wilhelmine, mistress of King Friedrich Wilhelm II, lived. It was destroyed in 1943.

5 Denkmal Friedrichs des Großen

Still a magnificent equestrian, his radiance undimmed: King Frederick the Great

The Frederick the Great Monument with intellectuals under the horse's tail.

Unter den Linden
S1, S2, S25, S26 Unter den Linden,
U6 Friedrichstraße and
Französische Straße

The Frederick II Monument in Unter den Linden commemorates the great Prussian monarch of the Enlightenment. The 13.5 m-high **equestrian statue** was made by Christian Daniel Rauch in 1851. It portrays the king in his coronation robes, bearing a trident, a stick and wearing top-boots. The one hundred and fifty figures of distinguished Prussians adorning the base aroused heated debates after the monument was unveiled. After all, it was noted: the *military* were at the fore, with *artists* and *scholars* (including Kant and Lessing) huddled under the horse's tail! The GDR regime had a hard time coming to terms with the Prussian legacy and the Frederick the Great Monument was no exception. In 1950 it was moved to the park of Schloss Sanssouci and did not return to Unter den Linden until 1981.

The Frederick the Great Monument was restored a few years ago and was set up again in 2000 where it originally stood at the columned portal of the **Altes Palais** (Kaiserpalais), the residence of Kaiser Wilhelm I for fifty years. The Iron Chancellor Otto von Bismarck tendered his resignation here in 1890. Now the palace is part of *Humboldt University*, whose façade is currently being faithfully reconstructed.

Across from it is the former German State Library (No. 8), now the **Staatsbibliothek zu Berlin – Preußischer Kulturbesitz I** (Mo–Fr 9 am–9 pm, Sa 9 am–5 pm,

Friedrichstraße – new flair for the metropolis

Friedrichstraße has grown into a new magnet for visitors to Berlin-Mitte. With all its hotels, shops, theatres and establishments offering entertainment of all kinds, this street was a focal point of 1900s Berlin. The Second World War put an end to cosmopolitan urban life and the street was almost completely destroyed by the bombings. The GDR regime did try to link up with the old Friedrichstraße tradition by adding some new buildings, yet the **Friedrichstadtpalast** (1984), the **International Trade Centre** (1978), the Grand Hotel (1987), now the **Westin Grand Hotel**, and the Hotel Metropol (1977), now the **Maritim pro Arte**, looked somehow out of place. Friedrichstraße was in fact palpably the interface between East and West: One station, **Bahnhof Friedrichstraße**, was the sole link for intercity, urban and underground rail between the two parts of the city after the Wall was built in 1961. Now the station is once again an important travel junction. The adjacent old terminus building became a hall where events are put on and concerts are performed. Commemorating the fates of many affected by the partition of the city, it has been christened **The Palace of Tears**. Cultural events are also hosted in the **Admiralspalast** (Friedrichstraße 101) across the street but whether this will continue has long been under discussion. The builiding also houses 'Die Distel', a cabaret.

The metropolitan flair is today concentrated in the southern section of Friedrichstraße between Unter den Linden and Leipziger Straße. Here shop-

Vive la France! Shopping is a joy at Galeries Lafayette – this branch has opted for a conical décor

ping malls, department stores, stylish boutiques, offices and restaurants have opened in the new, luxurious emporia **Lindencorso**, **Hofgarten**, **Friedrichstadt-Passagen** and **Kontorhaus Mitte**, magnets for tourists and Berliners alike.

A major attraction is the **Galerie Lafayette** at the corner of Französische Straße 23 and Friedrichstraße – this elegant store is a branch of the celebrated Paris department store.

Phone: 030/26 60, www.staatsbibliothek-berlin.de). The echoes of the Baroque on its façade are deceptive since the building was only erected 1903–14. In the 17th century, the *Marstall*, the royal riding stable, was here. From 1700 it housed the Academy of Arts and Sciences. By 1939 the library owned nearly 4 million books but its stock has been reduced to 3 million (writings published up to 1956). The inventory of the State Library (I and II, see p. 102) comprises a total of 10 million volumes. Extensive restoration and rebuilding within the complex, including the addition of a new reading room after plans by HG Merz, are to be completed by 2008/2011.

6 Alte Bibliothek

The Old Library, an Enlightenment 'Commode'.

Bebelplatz 1
S1, S3, S5, S7, S75, S9 and
U6 Friedrichstraße,
Tram M1, 12, Bus 147

South of the Frederick II Monument is the *Forum Fridericianum*, jointly designed by Frederick the Great and Georg Wenzeslaus von Knobelsdorff. One of Berlin's most beautiful squares, it is now called **Bebelplatz**. While still crown prince, the young aesthete Frederick II wanted to create a new centre for 'his' Berlin. A new

Squiggles and scrolls whirling to the tune of a Viennese Walz: Berliners dub the Alte Bibliothek on Bebelplatz the 'commode'

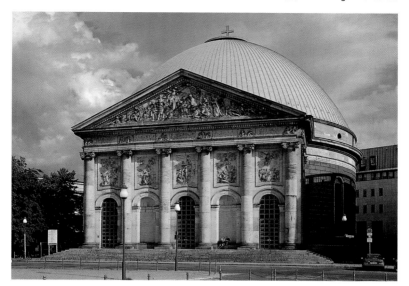

Bella Italia in Berlin: St Hedwig's Cathedral, the city's first Catholic church, was modelled on the Pantheon in Rome

royal palace was planned to rival *Versailles*.

The Alte Bibliothek (once the Royal Library) on the west side of the square was under construction from 1775 after plans by *Johann Bernhard Fischer von Erlach*, which were originally drawn for an annexe to the Hofburg in Vienna. The Old Library in the High Baroque style soon became a centre of the Enlightenment but its alternating concave and convex façade caused it to be dubbed the 'Commode'. In 1945 the library burned down but was rebuilt in 1967–69. It is now used by Humboldt University.

On 10 May 1933, in the square between the Alte Bibliothek and the Opera, a book-burning took place; roughly 20 000 works by authors who had fallen into disfavour with the Nazi regime were consigned to the flames. In 1995, the **Versunkene Bibliothek**, designed by Micha Ullmann, was inaugurated. The Sunken Library consists of a slab of plastic sunk into the cobblestones of the square, through which you can look down into a room below lined with empty book shelves. A memorial tablet quotes the poet Heinrich Heine: »[...] Where books are burnt, people are ultimately also burnt«.

7 St.-Hedwigs-Kathedrale

A Catholic church in Protestant Prussia.

Bebelplatz
S1, S2, S5, S7, S75, S9 and
U6 Friedrichstraße
Tram M1, 12, Bus 147

At the southern end of Bebelplatz stands St Hedwig's Cathedral with its impressively grand dome. It was modelled on the ancient *Pantheon* in Rome. The design sketches are from the hand of Friedrich II and the plans are by the court architect, *Georg Wenzeslaus von Knobelsdorff*. Building had begun by 1747 but was repeatedly interrupted by lack of money and the Seven Years War. In November 1773 St Hedwig's Cathedral, Berlin's *first Catholic Church*. was consecrated to the patron saint of Silesia. The church was regarded as a politically expeditious move on the part of Frederick II: after all, the Catholic congregation in Berlin had ballooned to roughly 10 000 following the Second Silesian campaign of 1745 when Frederick had conquered Catholic Silesia and incorporated it in Prussia. Consequently a signal of religious tolerance was called for – a Catholic church.

St Hedwig's Cathedral was gutted by fire during the Second World War but was rebuilt between 1952 and 1963. Since 1994 it has been the seat of the newly established archbishopric of Berlin.

8 Staatsoper Unter den Linden

Enrico Caruso sang here.

Unter den Linden 7
Phone: 030/20 35 45 55
www.staatsoper-berlin.de
S1, S3, S5, S7, S9, S25, S26 and
U6 Friedrichstraße; Bus 348

The Opera House across from the Alte Bibliothek was built in the Neo-Classical style in 1741–43 under the supervision of the architect *Georg Wenzeslaus von Knobelsdorff*. The opera house, the king's first large building project, made music history. The *premières* of Otto Nicolai's 'The Merry Wives of Windsor' (1849) and Alban Berg's 'Wozzeck' (1925) took place here. Celebrated conductors who have reigned over the orchestra here have included Giacomo Meyerbeer, Richard Strauss and Herbert von Karajan and the great tenor Enrico Caruso sang here.

Not much has survived of the original 'Linden Opera' building. By 1788 renovation was urgently needed. Because middle-class audiences were now also to enjoy the benefits of opera room had to be made to accommodate them. After a fire in 1843, Carl Ferdinand Langhans rebuilt the opera as it was; only the interior was remodelled on late Neo-Classical lines. The proscenium was built in 1910 and the wings were altered during renovations undertaken in 1926–28.

Even then Berlin needed a larger opera house but could not afford to build one after the First World War. In 1993 the State Opera celebrated its 250th birthday. *Daniel Barenboim* (*1942) was appointed general director responsible for the artistic agenda. Now he is lifetime chief conductor.

9 Prinzessinnenpalais & Kronprinzenpalais

Nursery of the Hohenzollerns.

Unter den Linden
S1, S2, S5, S7, S75, S9 and
U6 Friedrichstraße
Tram M1, 12, Bus 147

The **Prinzessinnenpalais** (No. 5), built in 1733–37 by Friedrich Wilhelm Diterichs, was the home of Friedrich Wilhelm III's three daughters. Also known as the *Opera Palace*, the building was completely rebuilt in 1961–63. Not even the old bricks from the original structure were fit for reuse. Made laboriously by indentured peasants, they varied too widely in quality. Today the Palais with its attractive garden houses the **Operncafé** [see p. 170] as a popular rendezvous. There are also a bar and two restaurants here.

An arched breezeway has joined the Prinzessinnenpalais with the **Kronprinzenpalais** since 1811. The history of the Crown Prince's Palace goes back to 1663,

A festive setting for great musical theatre – inside the State Opera Unter den Linden

Learning for life and forthcoming exams – about 39 000 students are immatriculated at Humbold University, Berlin's earliest institution of higher learning

10 Humboldt-Universität

Berlin's oldest unversity.

Unter den Linden 8
S1, S2, S5, S7, S75, S9 and
U6 Friedrichstraße
Tram M1, 12, Bus 147

when an important court official had a suitably showy building erected here in the immediate vicinity of the royal palace. It was given its Baroque façade when it underwent renovation under the supervision of Philipp Gerlach. King Frederick Wilhelm I, who had taken over the building, had it converted into a dwelling for the crown prince. Kaiser Wilhelm II, the last German emperor, was born here on 27 January 1859. The present structure is a reconstruction done in 1968/69 entirely from old engravings since the building was totally destroyed in the Second World War. The Crown Prince's Palace was used by the GDR government as a guest house for visitors of state. The building assumed political significance, however, when the **Unification Treaty** ending the separate existence of the two Germanys was signed here between the GDR and the Federal Republic of Germany on 31 August 1990.

The former Forum Fridericianum is bounded on the other side of Unter den Linden boulevard by Humboldt University. Frederick the Great had originally planned to build a new royal palace here but by the time he was ready to do so, he had become enamoured of Potsdam. Instead, a palace was built between 1748 and 1766 designed by court architect *Knobelsdorff* for Prinz Heinrich, a brother of Frederick's. After his death in 1802, his widow lived on in the palace. In 1809 the building was donated to the recently founded university. By winter term 1809/10 more than two hundred students were enrolled at the new institution of higher learning, which was then called 'Friedrich-Wilhelm-Universität'. In 1949 the university was given the name it now bears, after its founder, **Wilhelm Freiherr von Humboldt** (1767–1835). The polymath explorer, scholar and politician had been appointed head of the culture and education division of the Prussian Ministry of the Interior in 1809.

Although the building sustained severe damage during the war, teaching had begun again by 1946. Now Berlin's third largest university is the 'alma mater' of approximately 39 000 students.

11 Neue Wache

Schinkel's temple as a memorial.

Unter den Linden
U6 Französische Straße
Bus 147

The Neue Wache is easy to spot across the boulevard with its Doric portico modelled on ancient Greek architecture. *Karl Friedrich Schinkel* designed and built it in 1816–18. Originally planned as a guardhouse for the guards watching over the royal palace across from it, the New Guardhouse was converted to a **monument** commemorating the victims of the First World War in 1929. Yet every age honours different victims and therefore the building was turned into a Reich cenotaph during the NS era. After the fall of the NS dictatorship, the GDR regime built a cenotaph here to the victims of Fascism and militarism. On 14 November 1993, the day of public mourning, the Neue Wache was dedicated as a **Central Memorial of the Federal Republic of Germany**. Since then, a larger than life-size pietà statue of a 'Mother Mourning her Dead Son' by Käthe Kollwitz has stood inside the temple.

Behind the Neue Wache is the **Palais am Festungsgraben** (1751–53). The present façade of the former Ministry of Finance dates from renovation in 1861. The Prussian statesman and political thinker Karl Freiherr vom und zum Stein lived here between 1804 und 1807. The historic rooms are now used as a venue for cultural events. The *Tadshikische Teestube* (Tadjik Tearoom, see p. 168) with invitingly plush Oriental décor is the perfect place for a refreshing cuppa.

12 Deutsches Historisches Museum

History in Berlin's most significant Baroque building.

Unter den Linden 2
Phone: 030/20 30 40
www.dhm.de
Permanent collection closed until mid-2006; Armoury lobby, Schlüterhof and entrance to exhibition building by leoh Ming Pei daily 10 am–6 pm
S5, S7, S75, S9 Hackescher Markt
Tram M1, M2, M4, M5, M6

Berlin's first large building, once the **Zeughaus** (Armoury), is just before the Schlossbrücke. Built between 1695 and

A successful blend of old and new at the Deutsches Historisches Museum

A tour de force by the architect who made Berlin 'Athens on the Spree' – Neo-Classical sculpture in the Friedrichswerder Church designed by Schinkel

1731 by Johann Nering, Andreas Schlüter and other architects, the structure was used as an armoury until 1877, with infantry weapons and war trophies stored on the upper floor. In 1848 Berlin craftsmen stormed the building and armed themselves for the struggle for more democracy. The complex, measuring 90 x 90 m, was converted into a hall of fame for the imperial family when the Empire was founded in 1871.

The *façade* is articulated by cornices, balustrades and sandstone sculptures, most of them by Guillaume Houlot. Twenty-two masks of dying warriors in the *inner courtyard*, the work of Andreas Schlüter, warn of the ravages of war.

Until September 1990 the GDR Museum of German History, founded in 1952, was housed in the Armoury. It has become the Deutsches Historisches Museum. Apart from the permanent collection in the Armoury (reopens in mid-2006), there is a new building by leoh Ming Pei for rotating exhibitions and the virtual museum LeMo on the internet.

The historic section of Unter den Linden comes to a grand finale at the **Schlossbrücke** (1824), which boasts sculptures of Carrara marble, a total work of art by *Karl Friedrich Schinkel*. Its predecessor was a wooden bridge, called the 'Bridge of Dogs' because hunters used to assemble there with their dogs before setting off into the game parks just outside the city. During the Second World War the Schinkel statues were stored for safe keeping, in 1981 they were put back into place.

13 **Friedrichswerdersche Kirche – Schinkelmuseum**

A sculpture museum in a church.

Werderscher Markt
Phone: 030/208 13 23
www.smb.museum
daily 10 am–6 pm
U2 Hausvogteiplatz, U6 Französische Straße, Bus 147

A crowning touch to a walk down the historic section of Unter den Linden boulevard is a visit to the Friedrichwerder Church on the north side of Werderscher Markt. The church was built between 1824 and

Urban culture – the Deutscher Dom and the Schauspielhaus provide the right mood backdrop for open-air events at the Gendarmenmarkt

1830 in the Neo-Gothic style after plans by *Karl Friedrich Schinkel*. In his design, Schinkel drew on the simplicity and clarity of the North German tradition in ecclesiastical architecture. During the Second World War the church sustained severe damage and restoration work continued until the late 1980s.

Today the church houses the *Schinkel Museum*. Documentary material on this most important of Berlin architects supplements a collection of Neo-Classical 19th-century *sculpture*.

14 Gendarmenmarkt

Berlin's most stunning square, a dramatic setting with a theatre and the French and German Cathedrals.

U2 Stadtmitte, U6 Französische Straße
Bus 147, 148

Covering 48 000m², this square was laid out in the 17th century. It was named after the constabulary regiment (gens d'armes) which maintained a barracks, a guardhouse and stalls there between 1736 and 1782. The **Französischer Dom** built on the north side of the square in 1701–05 was used as a Protestant church by French Hugenots who came to Germany in the 17th century. The **Hugenottenmuseum** (Phone: 030/229 17 60, Tu–Sa 12–5pm, Su

11 am–5 pm) housed here is informative on the history of the French émigrés. From the 70-m-high church *tower* a console-operated, 60-piece Glockenspiel resounds daily at 12 noon, 3 pm and 7 pm. Ascending to the *observation platform* is a treat – since the 'Turmstuben' provides rest and refreshment including wine at an elevation of 20 m.

On the south end of the square, Martin Grünberg built the **Deutscher Dom** in 1701–08. Originally a simple church, the building assumed the grandeur of a cathedral under Frederick the Great, with the addition of a columned portico and a domed tower surmounted by a 7-m-high gilded statue of 'Conquering Victory'. By 1996 the severe war damage it had sustained was repaired. The façade was re-stored to its original appearance and the building houses an exhibition on the German Bundestag **Paths, Wrong Turnings, Detours. The Development of Parliamentary Democracy in Germany** (Phone: 030/22 73 04 31, Tu 10 am–10 pm, We–Su and hols. 10 am–6 pm, June–Aug. to 7 pm).

The French comedy theatre once at the centre of the square was replaced after a fire by Schinkel's Neo-Classical **Schauspielhaus** (1818–21). Destroyed in the Second World War, it was faithfully reconstructed between 1967 and 1984, when it reopened as *Konzerthaus* Berlin.

Excellent restaurants and chic shops have restored Gendarmenmarkt to its former elegance as a pivotal Berlin location.

The Spree Island between Lustgarten and Monbijoupark – Prussian pomp and circumstance

The way from Unter den Linden across the Schlossbrücke leads into one of Berlin's oldest sections. Unfortunately, Second World War bombs and the SED regime's passion for demolition have left their stamp on this part of the city. Historic Berlin is centred around the **Altes Museum** at the Lustgarten and the **Berliner Dom**. The cathedral façade is reflected in the **Palace of the Republic**, which is scheduled for demolition in 2006. This GDR showcase building was erected on the site occupied until 1950 by the *Berliner Stadtschloss*, the Hohenzollern palace. That historically and culturally important building could have been restored after the Second World War yet nothing – thus decreed the autocrats of the first German workers' and farmers' state – at the heart of the new Berlin was to recall Prussia's heyday. In the years to come part of the Stadtschloss is to be rebuilt and its Baroque façade faithfully reconstructed. The building is expected to house museums, libraries and a hotel. The former GDR **State Council Building**, which now functions as a campus for private universities, also covers part of the Schloss grounds.

15 Lustgarten

From kitchen garden to parade ground.

S5, S7, S75, S9 Hackescher Markt, U2 Hausvogteiplatz, U6 Friedrichstraße
Bus 100, 200

The name Lustgarten, pleasure ground, has remained although this square adjacent to the Schlossbrücke has changed its function numerous times. The Hohenzollerns had a **kitchen garden** laid out here near the palace in 1573. There a strange fruit from overseas was first planted in Prussia in 1649: the *potato*. That this plant was deemed an exotic is shown in the fact that the kitchen garden had already been converted into an ornamental garden by 1643. It was used for pleasant strolls but was turned into a parade ground during the 18th century in the reign of Friedrich Wilhelm I.

A lovely **park** was created here around 1830 by the landscape architect Peter Joseph Lenné. Only a century later this meeting place, popular with Berliners from all walks of life, was converted into a

forbidding square, used for parades and mass party rallies by the Nazis and then the SED. Now once again a green area, the Lustgarten is bounded by the **Altes Museum** [see p. 38]. The monumental *granite basin* (1827–30, Christian Gottlieb Cantian) in front of the outer staircase is known as 'Berlin's biggest soup bowl'.

16 Berliner Dom

The Cathedral houses Hohenzollern tombs.

Lustgarten
S5, S7, S75, S9 Hackescher Markt, U2 Hausvogteiplatz, U6 Friedrichstraße
Bus 100, 200

Berlin Cathedral (1894–1905) built by Julius Raschdorff looms on the east side of the Lustgarten. The church boasting a massive **dome** 74.8 m high, is modelled on St Peter's in Rome. Its lavish decoration is typical for architecture in the reign of Kaiser Wilhelm II – the era of Wilhelmine imperial Historicism provided a feast for the eyes. The Cathedral sustained severe damage in the war. While its exterior had been restored by 1974, the reconstruction of the **interior** was only completed by 1993. Noteworthy are the *imperial loggia* across from the altar, the *font* (1833) by Christian Daniel Rauch and the *chancel screen*, inspired by Schinkel. The numerous *sarcophagi* are particularly impressive since the Hohenzollerns were buried in the Cathedral. In the crypt and the nave there are about a hundred of these magnificent coffins dating from five centuries, including the tombs of the Great Elector, King Friedrich I and the Emperor Friedrich III.

The organ concerts given on summer afternoons in the Cathedral are an experience not to be missed.

17 Palast der Republik

The building in which the GDR People's Chamber used to convene is to be torn down in 2006. After that the celebrated Berliner Stadtschloss is scheduled for reconstruction.

Schlossplatz
S5, S7, S75, S9 Hackescher Markt, U2 Hausvogteiplatz, U6 Friedrichstraße
Bus 100, 200

The Palace of the Republic, in which the DDR People's Chamber (parliament) con-

venved from 1976, has been derelict for years. After the Wall went down, the Palace, a vast structure, 180 m long and 85 m wide, was supposed to be used as a *cultural centre* but too much asbestos was found in the building so it was closed in 1990.

Since then the debate has raged on whether or not to tear it down. After all, the Palace of the Republic was built where the **Berliner Stadtschloss**, the Hohenzollern royal palace, stood until 1950. From June 1993 until September 1994 a 'Palace curtain' the size of the original historic façade was draped across the front to show how the Hohenzollern palace had once looked. In July 2002 the Bundestag opted for demolishing the Palace of the Republic by 2006 and reconstructing the Stadtschloss. In August 2005 the Federal German government presented a concept for housing the ethnographic collections (now in Dahlem), the Humboldt University collections, the Berlin Central and State Libraries and a luxury hotel in the Stadtschloss. Completion of the comprehensive project has been tentatively scheduled for 2013.

The Berliner Stadtschloss was, incidentally, one of Europe's earliest royal seats. In 1443 the Prince Elector Friedrich II laid the cornerstone for the Hohenzollern palace. It continued to be enlarged and remodelled until 1716 so that the building,

The statues on Schinkel's Schlossbrücke line the street before the Berliner Dom, utterly unfazed by the modern Television Tower and the Park Inn Hotel at Alexanderplatz

which comprised roughly 1300 rooms, represented an eclectic blend of numerous period styles. Its last version measured 192 m in length and was 116 m wide. After 1918 the palace was used as a **museum** and also provided accommodation for fifteen households. On 3 February 1945, the palace was hit in the last large-scale air raid on Berlin but could have been restored. The important historic building was condemned by the decision of the 3rd SED Party Conference to raze it to the ground. By 30 December 1950 all that was left of it was Portal IV of the former GDR State Council Building.

18 Ehem. Staatsrats-gebäude

The former GDR State Council and present seat of elite institutions of higher learning incorporates a portal of the Berliner Stadtschloss.

Schlossplatz 1 (entrance Breite Straße)
S5, S7, S75, S9 Hackescher Markt, U2 Hausvogteiplatz, U6 Friedrichstraße
Bus 100, 200

The complex at the southern end of Schlossplatz was built in 1962–64 by Roland Korn and Hans-Erich Bogatzky as the seat of the GDR State Council. Erich Honecker had his office here. **Portal IV** (1710) from the north wing of the demolished Berliner Stadtschloss is incorporated in its show façade. The former palace gate was not, despite frequent assertions to the contrary, designed by Andreas Schlüter but rather by Johann Friedrich Eosander von Göthe. The columns and atlantes are the work of the great Dresden sculptor Balthasar Permoser.

Why was this particular portal of the Royal Palace saved? For the simple reason that, on 9 November 1918, Karl Liebknecht proclaimed the free socialist republic from its *balcony*, which ensured its status as labour movement memorabilia.

The Council building, used between 1999 and 2001 as the *Federal Chancellor's residence*, is used today as a campus for private institutions of higher learning. In September 2005 the *Hertie School of Governance* (of politics, economics and civics) opened its doors to students. It is to be followed in 2006 by an elite business school, the *European School of Management and Technology* (ESMT, www.esmt.org).

19 Breite Straße

Berlin's former high street.

U2 Spittelmarkt, Bus 147, 148

Breite Straße, which runs south east from Schlossplatz, was the elegant high street of the city of *Cölln* and of early Berlin as well until it was replaced by Unter den Linden boulevard.

Not much is left of the buildings which once lined it. At Nos. 36/37 Breite Straße stands the only early Baroque building left in Berlin, the **Alter Marstall**, the old royal stables, completed in 1670.

No. 35 is **Ribbeck-Haus**. Dating from 1624, it is Berlin's earliest Renaissance building. In 1960 the portal was replaced by a copy in the original cartilage Baroque scrollwork. The house was named after Georg von Ribbeck, who built it and was its first owner.

The Alte Marstall and the Ribbeck House are framed by the **Neuer Marstall**, the new royal stables, which were built in 1898–1900 but still boast Baroque elements.

Next door (No. 34) is the **Berliner Stadtbibliothek**, established in 1901. The wrought iron grille of the entrance to the Municipal Library incorporates one hundred and seventeen variations on the letter A.

20 Brüderstraße

Memorable Baroque dwellings.

U2 Spittelmarkt, Bus 147, 148

Running parallel to Breite Straße, Brüderstraße is notable for two Baroque dwellings. The **Galgenhaus** (No. 10) dates from the late 17th century. Its façade, however, was renovated in 1805 and Neo-Classical elements were added. The **Nicolaihaus** (No. 13) was named after Friedrich Nicolai, who owned it and moved into it with his celebrated *publishers and booksellers* business in 1787. Carl Friedrich Zelter, in his day an influential composer and a friend of Goethe, had the building remodelled in the 19th century. The *Baroque staircase* in the front building is original but the stair in the rear building, dating from 1830 and modelled on the Schinkel style, was incorporated in 1977. Plaques on the main *façade* explain the cultural and historical importance of the house and recall the distinguished people who lived here or stayed as guests.

Embraced by the Spree – the world-famous Museum Island looks like a ship drifting on the river with the hefty Bodemuseum as its rounded prow

Via Sperlingsgasse or Scharrenstraße you reach the **Spree arm**, which used to demarcate the old city of Cölln from Friedrichswerder to the west. Two bridges span the Spree here: the **Jungfernbrücke** (1798), which has retained the original drawbridge construction, and the **Gertraudenbrücke** featuring a statue of St Gertrude offering a drink to an itinerant journeyman – a bronze memorial to St Gertrude's Hospital, which was demolished in 1881.

21 Museumsinsel

World-class art centre and in 1999 declared a UNESCO World Cultural Heritage site.

Am Kupfergraben
www.smb.museum
S1, S2 Friedrichstraße, S5, S7, S75, S9 Hackescher Markt, U6 Friedrichstraße, Tram M1, 12 Am Kupfergraben, Tram M2, M4, M5, M6 Hackescher Markt, Bus TXL Staatsoper, Bus 100, 200 Am Lustgarten, Bus 147 Friedrichstraße

Between the Spree and Kupfergraben is the world-famous Museum Island, home to superlative art collections rivalling those of the Louvre in Paris, the Uffizi in Florence and the State Hermitage Muse-

um in St Petersburg. It will take years, however, for all the works of art which the war and subsequent partition dispersed throughout the city to be returned to their original locations, since some of the buildings on Museum Island are still undergoing extensive restoration.

Development of the Museum Island started at the **Altes Museum**. Schinkel built Berlin's first museum in the Neo-Classical style between 1825 and 1830, bequeathing in it one of his most important works. King Friedrich Wilhelm III used it to make art treasures that had until then been kept in palaces accessible to the public. Friedrich Wilhelm IV decreed in 1841 that the rest of the island behind the Altes Museum should also be dedicated to art. The **Neues Museum** was designed by Friedrich August Stüler, a pupil of Schinkel's and built between 1843 and 1855 The National Gallery, now the **Alte Nationalgalerie**, was built between 1866 and 1876. The *Kaiser-Wilhelm Museum* at the tip of the Island was inaugurated in 1904. Construction work began in 1912 on the **Pergamonmuseum**, situated between the Neues Museum and the Kaiser-Wilhelm Museum, but it was not completed until 1930. Wilhelm von Bode, head of all museums between 1872 and 1920, elevated the collections on the Museum Island to world-class standard. In

All roads lead to Berlin – modelled on the Pantheon in Rome, the rotunda of the Altes Museum is adorned with the deities of Greco-Roman antiquity

1956 the Kaiser-Wilhelm Museum was renamed **Bodemuseum** in his honour.

The museum buildings were 70 % destroyed during the Second World War. Since the art objects they contained were removed in time for safe keeping, most have been preserved, yet the partition of Berlin scattered them about the city. The process of reassembling the vast collections has been going on for years.

Altes Museum

Bodestraße 1–3 (entrance Am Lustgarten)
Phone: 030/20 90 55 77
www.smb.museum
Tu–Su 10 am–6 pm

Intended as a 'Royal Museum', the Old Museum was built between 1825 and 1830 to resemble an ancient Greek temple with a vestibule boasting eighteen Ionic columns. Severely damaged in the Second World War, the museum was rebuilt between 1960 and 1966. A particularly impressive feature of the interior is the **rotunda**. Reminiscent of the Roman Pantheon and decorated with Corinthian columns, it houses statues of ancient deities, mainly Roman copies of Greek masterpieces.

The **Antikensammlung** (Antiquities Collection), formerly on the Museum Island and kept in Charlottenburg until the 1990s, was reopened on the ground floor of the Altes Museum in 1998. It contains important Etruscan, Greek and Roman works of art, notably vases, jewellery and sculpture such as the 'Youthful Supplicant'.

Since August 2005 the **Ägyptisches Museum** and its papyrus collection, also from Charlottenburg, has been on the upper floor, where it is to stay until 2009 before moving to the Neues Museum (see below). The nucleus of the Egyptian

Museum collection was provided in the late 17th century by the Kunstkammer owned by the electors of Brandenburg. Today it affords an impressive survey of ancient Egyptian civilisation at its acme. World-renowned for its beauty is the elegant limestone and polychrome gesso **bust of Queen Nofretete** (Nefertete), excavated by German Egyptologists at Tell el-Amarna in 1912. The stucco head of her spouse, the monotheist *King Akhenaten* (both ca 1340 BC), is also from there. *A Walk in the Garden* and the *Noas Stele* depicting the royal sculptor Bak and his wife are also from the Amarna period. A *statuary group of a seated couple* dates to the 5th dynasty while the *seated statue of Hetepni* dates from the 6th (ca 2150 BC). The *Berlin Green Head*, named after the colour of its stone, is a Late Egyptian masterpiece (500 BC). The **Kalabasha Gate** was given by Egypt to the Federal Republic in gratitude for its help in moving Nubian temples threatened by the rising flood waters of the Nile when the Assuan High Dam was built. The reliefs of the gate portray the Roman Emperor Augustus as Pharaoh giving votive offerings to the Egyptian gods Isis, Osiris and Mandulis.

TOP TIPP

Neues Museum
Bodestraße
To open in 2009

The Neues Museum (1843–47) was the museum most severely damaged in the war and restoration work did not begin until 1986. It will not open its doors to the public for some time to come, probably in 2009. Then the *Egyptian Museum* collections (see above) will be housed here along with parts of *the Museum for Prehistory and Early History* collections based in Schloss Charlottenburg [see p. 122, 124].

Alte Nationalgalerie
Bodestraße
Phone: 030/20 90 58 01
www.smb.museum
Tu–Su 10 am–6 pm, Th 10 am–10 pm

The Alte Nationalgalerie was designed by Stüler and built between 1866 and 1876. After his death in 1866, the museum was completed by Johann Heinrich Strack as a Corinthian temple with a monumental outer staircase. The bronze equestrian statue of *Friedrich Wilhelm IV* (1866) above the entrance is the work of Alexander Calandrelli.

Egypt and antiquity – since August 2005 Nefertete has starred at the Altes Museum

The mummy of a young man (ca 130 AD) from Egypt at the Ägyptisches Museum

The dogmatically asserted National Socialist art theories wreaked more havoc with the Old National Gallery collections than the Second World War bombs. Outlawed as 'degenerate art', part of the collection was stored in various places or sold worldwide at bargain prices. Other works were later destroyed by fire in the Friedrichshain bunker where they were stored.

Specializing in **19th-century art**, the Old National Gallery reopened after a general overhaul in 2001. The collection features masterpieces by such celebrated Romantic artists as Caspar David Friedrich and Adolph von Menzel, works by such masters as Delacroix (Romanticism) and Courbet (Realism) as well as paintings by the Impressionists Manet, Monet, Degas and Lovis Corinth and that celebrated forerunner of Modernism, Paul Cézanne (Post-Impressionism).

Bodemuseum

Am Kupfergraben/Monbijoubrücke
Phone: 030/20 90 55 55
www.smb.museum
Coin cabinet: Mo–Fr 10 am–4.30 pm

The Bodemuseum (1897–1904) is a grand Neo-Baroque building ingeniously designed by Ernst von Ihne so that its ground-plan fitted the tip of the Museum Island, thus elegantly finishing off the architectural ensemble. A *basilica* modelled on San Salvatore al Monte in Florence is integrated in the museum. While all the museums are in the throes of restructuring, the Bodemuseum has also been undergoing extensive remodelling since it closed in 1999. In 2004 the Münzkabinett study room was established here. The rest of the collection is being housed in the Pergamon Museum and the Altes Museum for the time being. The entire museum will reopen in 2006, when, besides the Coin Cabinet, the **Sculpture Collection**, comprising works from the Middle Ages to the 18th century and the **Museum for Byzantine Art**, will be here again. The paintings, on the other hand, which used to be in the Bodemuseum, moved into the new *Gemäldegalerie* [No. 81] at the Culture Forum in 1998. The *Egyptian Museum* collections, which used to be in the Bodemuseum, are now on display at the Alte Museum and are scheduled to move into the Neues Museum in 2009 (see above).

Pergamonmuseum

Am Kupfergraben 12
Phone: 030/20 90 55 66
www.smb.museum
Tu–Su 10 am–6 pm, Th 10 am–10 pm

The Pergamon Museum at the centre of the Island was built between 1912 and 1930 in the Neo-Classical style after plans by Alfred Messel and Ludwig Hoffmann. The lobby dates from 1982. Restoration of the building, section by section, is to start

Top billing at the Alte Nationalgalerie is shared by Eduard Manet's 'In the Conservatory' (1879, centre) and Auguste Rodin's statue of a youth 'The Age of Iron' (1875/76, left)

Long live antiquity – looking and listening at the Altar of Pergamon, whose frieze, 113 m long and 2.3 m high, has been restored to all its former splendour (finished in 2004)

in 2008 but the collections are to remain open.

The highlight of the Pergamon Museum, which comprises three collections, is the superlative **Pergamon Altar** (2nd century BC), which the German engineer Carl Humann painstakingly excavated between 1878 and 1886. The altar came from Pergamon, one of the most important excavation sites of ancient ruins on the west coast of Turkey. The altar is adorned with a monumental frieze depicting the Battle of the Gods and the Giants. The dramatic composition and breathtaking movement of the figures reveal this altar as a prime example of Hellenistic architectural sculpture.

Other musts for admirers of antiquity are the *Market Gate of Miletus* (165 BC) in the antiquities collection, parts of the façade of the *Desert Castle of Mschatta* (8th century) from what is now Jordan in the Museum of Islamic Art and the *Ishtar Gate* and *Procession Street from Babylon* (7th/6th centuries BC) in the Near Eastern Museum.

Under the magnifying glass: a detail of the Altar of Pergamon, which was dug up and reconstructed in the late 19th century. The altar was dedicated to Zeus and Athene

From the Scheunenviertel to Chausseestraße – Berlin's back yard is blooming

Until the 1930s swindlers, gangsters, prostitutes and the poor peopled the Scheunenviertel, which is why it was also dubbed Berlin's back yard. About 50 000 East European Jews, who had emigrated to Germany after the First World War, also lived here. After the Nazi pogroms, all that was left of the Jewish shops, cafés, restaurants and synagogues were parts of the New Synagogue and what had been the White Elephant Inn. Today nothing recalls the barns and stalls that were here in the 18th century and gave the quarter its name. Still, it's well worth a visit – to get a whiff of that special blend of red-light district, art, lifestyle and East Berlin ambience. Incidently, many scenes from Alfred Döblin's legendary novel, 'Berlin Alexanderplatz' (1929), are set in the Scheunenviertel: The cemeteries, in what was once Friedrich-Wilhelm-Stadt to the west, tell a lot about Berlin's history and recall distinguished Berliners such as the philosophers Fichte and Hegel, the architect Schinkel and the playwright Brecht.

22 Volksbühne

The savings of the Free People's Theatre Association, founded in 1890, financed the building of Berlin's first modern theatre.

Rosa-Luxemburg-Platz
Phone: 030/247 67 72
www.volksbuehne-berlin.de
U2 Rosa-Luxemburg-Platz
Tram M2, M8, Bus 240

The Volksbühne theatre is at the heart of the Scheunenviertel, in Bülowplatz, which was laid out in 1906 and is now called **Rosa-Luxemburg-Platz**. In 1914 the city authorities thought they could clean up the sleaze by developing the area and building the theatre (architect: Oskar Hoffmann).

The name of the theatre derives from the *movement for a people's theatre*, which wanted to make contemporary theatre available to the working class. That this was not just a social-work project was revealed when the ensemble developed a cult following among devotees of the serious modern stage. Its first director (1915–18) was *Max Reinhardt* and a celebrated successor was (1924–27) *Erwin Piscator*.

The original auditorium, which seated 2000, was gutted by fire in 1943. Between 1952 and 1954 it was rebuilt on more simple lines to seat only 849. Under director *Frank Castorf*, the Volksbühne has made headlines as 'Germany's most exciting theatre' since 1992.

The north-east side of the square is occupied by the **Karl-Liebknecht-Haus** (1920), in which the Central Committee of the German Communist Party had its headquarters between 1926 and 1933. The building was reconstructed in 1949.

23 Hackesche Höfe

Interdependent cluster of dwellings and workplaces typical of late 19th-century industrialisation.

Rosenthaler Straße 40/41
S5, S7, S75, S9 Hackescher Markt

Hackesche Höfe is the largest court complex of its kind in Europe, covering an area of 10 000 m². August Endell submitted plans for these eight dwellings and commercial enterprises in 1906. Particularly interesting from the art historical standpoint is the first structure on *Rosen-*

A successful project to show the world – the splendid Hackesche Höfe Jugendstil façades

thaler Straße. Its colourfully glazed Jugendstil façade has listed historic monument status. The Hackesche Höfe Society e. V. was founded in 1991 to preserve existing structures and retain the functional interdependence associated with them. Now the cafés, bars and restaurants, art galleries and fashion boutiques are a magnet for chic Berliners. The **Chamäleon Varieté** [see p. 174], with an auditorium that seats 250, is a permanent fixture of the Berlin scene. It provides a regularly changing variety and cabaret bill. The 'Midnight Show', featuring surprise performances by a variety of entertainers, is particularly popular.

TOP TIPP

It's show time! Variety and cabaret are put on at the Chamäleon, a theatre in the Hackesche Höfe, which has been a Berlin institution for years

24 Sophienstraße

An intact group of houses from the boom phase of imperial industrialisation, with the first Spandau parish church, founded by Sophie Luise, third wife of Friedrich I.

U8 Weinmeisterstraße, Tram M2

Sophienstraße is one of the few 18th/19th-century streets to have remained virtually intact. The restored houses, small taverns and shops sporting their traditional guild signs, convey a good idea of the lifestyle and ambience of that period.

House **No. 18** was built about 1900 to provide a splendid headquarters for the Berlin Craftsmen's Association (established in 1844, it was forbidden between 1850 and 1859 as a hotbed of the labour movement after the 1848 Revolution). The front building dates from 1830–40. A noteworthy feature is the magnificent *double portal* with its terracotta decoration. The Neo-Gothic façade of house **Nos. 22/22 a** (1898/99, Gebert & Söhne) conceals *Jugendstil stairwells* in a superb state of preservation. Built around 1780, **No. 11** is the oldest house here.

The street is dominated by the **Sophienkirche**. Built in 1712 as a plain hall church, it was enlarged to incorporate two sacristies in 1834. The *belfry* (1732–34), one of only two original Baroque towers to have survived in Berlin, was designed by Johann Heinrich Grael. A notable feature of the interior, which was remodelled in the Neo-Baroque style by Adolf Heyden and Kurt Berndt in 1892, is the Ernst Max *organ*, dating from 1790.

25 Alter Jüdischer Friedhof

The Old Jewish Cemetery with the Moses Mendelssohn memorial tomb.

Große Hamburger Straße 26
S5, S7, S75, S9 Hackescher Markt

Where Sophienstraße and Große Hamburger Straße intersect was once the vibrant centre of Berlin Jewish community life. A memorial plaque commemorates *Moses Mendelssohn* (1729–1786) on the building at No. 27, once the **Jewish Community Boys' School**, of which he was a co-founder. Opened in 1778, the boys' school and the adjacent Jewish *Home for the Elderly*, which was destroyed in the war, were used by the Nazis as a detention centre, where 55 000 Berlin Jews were assembled before being transported to the death camps at Auschwitz und Theresienstadt. A group of statues in bronze form a *memorial* (1957, Will Lammert).

Behind the monument is the Old Jewish Cemetery, which was laid out almost synchronously with the establishment of the city's first Jewish congregation in

The past is no longer hiding its light under a bushel: façades of historic houses in Sophienstrasse and a vintage Trabi, an endangered species of car

1672. The cemetery was in use until 1827, when members of the Jewish community began to bury their dead in the Jewish Cemetery [see No. 48] at Schönhauser Allee. In 1943 the Nazis vandalised the Old Jewish Cemetery by ploughing up the 3000 graves, including the last resting place of Moses Mendelssohn, Enlightenment philosopher and friend of the enlightened German writer Lessing, as well as the grave of Veitel Heine Ephraim (1703–1775), banker to the court of Frederick the Great. Now only a lawn with a few gravestones in a green park is all that remains to be seen of the old cemetery. The Mendelssohn tombstone is even a replica. Twenty memorial *plaques* are set into the cemetery walls, including one over a century old in memory of Gumpericht Jechiel Aschkenasi, the first person to be buried here in 1672.

At the northern end of Große Hamburger Straße is **Koppenplatz** square, named after Christian Koppe, a wealthy Berliner with a keen social conscience. In 1705 he used one of his properties, at 59 Auguststraße, to endow a cemetery for the destitute and orphaned and later an *almshouse* (1708), which was converted into a hospital in 1739. A sandstone and granite *monument* depicting Christian Koppe was designed by August Stüler. It was donated by the city of Berlin in 1855 and set up at the corner of Augustenstraße and Große Hamburger Straße.

Soaring into the sky: the Sophienkirche boasts a graceful slender Baroque tower

in it only until 1757. Thirty years later the building was used to house art collections. The lodge was destroyed in the Second World War but its park has remained a much loved green oasis of peace in the pulsing life of the metropolis.

26 Oranienburger Straße

A fascinating street with an ambivalent ambience, a showcase popular with tourists, night owls and street walkers.

S5, S7, S75, S9 Hackescher Markt
S1, S2 Oranienburger Straße
U6 Oranienburger Tor

Oranienburger Straße is a hang-out for 'scene habitués' and tourists alike. It boasts a host of highly frequented restaurants, pubs and cafés, as well as the elegant New Synagogue.

Monbijoupark runs along the south side of the street – a recreation and leisure area with a small swimming pool. Here the *Lustschloss Monbijou* (1708), literally 'A gem of a royal lodge', designed by the grandly named *Johann Friedrich Eosander von Göthe*, once stood, surrounded by princely gardens. The Hohenzollerns lived

The grave of the Enlightenment philosopher Moses Mendelssohn in the Old Jewish Cemetery

Burnished bright – it took seven years to restore the Oranienburger Straße Synagogue. Now its glittering gold dome is once again part of the Berlin skyline

27 Neue Synagoge

A gem of architecture.

Oranienburger Straße 29–30
Phone: 030/88 02 83 16
www.cjudaicum.de
Su/Mo 10 am–8 pm, Tu–Th 10 am–
6 pm, Fr 10 am–5 pm, in winter until
6 pm, Fr until 2 pm, Sa and Jewish
hols. closed. Guided tours We 4 pm,
Su 2 pm and 4 pm
S1, S2 Oranienburger Straße

The restoration was a complete success: the *central dome* of the New Synagogue is resplendent in fresh gold. Minaret-like *side towers* underscore the Moorish style of the picturesque façade. Reconstruction of the house of worship, only part of which had survived, went on between 1988 and 1995 – just as long as it had originally taken to build it. Designed by Eduard Knoblauch in 1859, the synagogue was completed by Friedrich August Stüler in 1866 and consecrated with Chancellor Otto von Bismarck present. It was here that *Albert Einstein* gave a violin concert in 1930.

This was once Germany's largest synagogue and the second largest in Europe.

28 Kulturzentrum Tacheles

Art and Culture in the ruins of a department store.

Oranienburger Straße 54–56 a
Phone: 030/282 61 85
www.tacheles.de
U6 Oranienburger Tor

The Jewish community had had the magnificent building erected to symbolize German Jews' equality with Germans of other faiths. During the *Reich pogrom night* of 1938, the meeting-house was vandalised by the Nazis. Gutted by fire in 1943, the main synagogue was demolished in 1958. Reconstruction did not begin until the 50th anniversary of the pogroms.

In May 1995 the **Centrum Judaicum** was inaugurated to meet the needs of the Berlin Jewish community, which then numbered about 11 000 and continues to grow, along with the rebuilt New Synagogue. The Centre houses archives, a library and a *museum*, with a permanent exhibition documenting the history of the synagogue. In addition, there are rotating exhibitions.

Only a short walk away and just as eye-catching as the New Synagogue is the former **Post Office** (Postfuhramt: Oranienburger Straße/Tucholskystraße) – one of imperial Berlin's most dignified administrative buildings. Built between 1875 and 1881, it was designed by Carl Schwatlo. The handsome *façade* with its terracotta decoration boasts motifs representing the postal service and celebrated travellers down through history. The *courtyard* once had stables for 240 horses, sheds for mail coaches and rooms for drivers.

The Tacheles ('plain speaking') Culture Centre does honour to its Yiddish name. Built in the ruins of a **department store** established in 1900, the Centre provides plenty of art, culture and interesting fringe events.

The locale was originally a shopping passage built to make a profit: Franz Ahrens, who designed it, borrowed stylistically from Messel, the architect who designed the Wertheim Department Store in Leipziger Straße. The complex was commissioned by individual businesses in the hope of being able to compete with the large department stores if they were all under one roof. A serious error and one which would prove costly since the shops in the passage were forced to close, one after the other, due to lack of turnover and the building became dilapidated. Not a trace remains of the gigantic *dome* of the shopping centre, which was once 50 m high and boasted a diameter of 28 m.

Business once reigned supreme on the Tacheles premises in Oranienburger Straße – now a flourishing cultural centre has pride of place

The tract in Oranienburger Straße, now a listed building, was occupied by squatters in 1990. Since then an **artists' initiative** has become established here. For some time Senate funding made experimental theatre, music, cinema and art possible but nowadays the state coffers are empty and financing has to be provided through other chanels.

In the next few years an office, business and living complex, designed by Duany, a firm of American architects, is to be built on the property behind the department store passage although the date when construction is to begin has yet to be made known.

Across the street a bevy of cafés, restaurants, nightclubs and galleries invites visitors to enjoy a quirky new scene unparalleled for unconventionality even in Berlin.

29 Deutsches Theater & Kammerspiele

Both are renowned for theatre history and experimental theatre.

Schumannstraße 13 a
Phone: 030/284 40
www.deutschestheater.de
U6 Friedrichstraße and Oranienburger Tor

The Deutsches Theater (1849/50, Eduard Titz) and the Kammerspiele have pride of place among the city's innumerable theatres. They were already known for outstanding performances by the early 20th century when the Austrian director-manager *Max Reinhardt* (1873–1943) became head of the Deutsches Theater in 1905 and founded the Kammerspiele in 1906. Many celebrated German-speaking ac-

Girls, Girls, Girls: glitz, glamour and Gigi at the Kleine Revue in the Friedrichstadtpalast

Between Lido and Copacabana

Hard to believe that the broad façade of embellished preassembled framed units at 107 Friedrichstraße conceals one of Europe's most outrageously modern variety theatres – the **Friedrichstadtpalast** [see p. 174]. This splendid theatre, boasting ultra-modern stage technology, seats 1900. Not only are dance-hall shows staged here, even **underwater ballet** and **ice follies** are occasionally put on.

The beginnings of the Friedrichstadtpalast go back to the 19th century when Berlin's first covered market was built close by in 1865–68. Later used as a circus, it was converted to a theatre in 1919. The building was so dilapidated by 1985 that it had to be torn down. The new theatre was built somewhat to the north-east of the original site in 1985/86.

In the GDR era the Friedrichstadtpalast with its Revue Girls (›the longest line of showgirls in the world‹) drew aficionados of shows, musicals, variety and circuses. Only artistes with top billing performed here. After suffering a financial slump following German reunification, the Friedrichstadtpalast is once again what it always was: a blend of the Paris Lido and the Rio de Janeiro Copacabana.

Doing their bit for theatre – the reputation of the Kammerspiele and the Deutsches Theater has never lost its lustre

tors, including Elisabeth Bergner, Fritz Kortner and Käthe Dorsch, trod the boards here. Reinhardt, into experimental theatre and modern stagecraft, was associated with the two theatres for twenty-seven years. Although he owned them, he was forced to give them up in 1933 because he was Jewish.

To celebrate the centenary of the Deutsches Theater, the building was restored and superlatively refurbished in 1983. Particularly noteworthy is the original late 19th-century *dress-circle lobby* in the Italianate Neo-Renaissance style. The *Baracke* in what was once a stage for rehearsals next door is an experimental theatre attracting a young audience.

30 Berliner Ensemble

Renowned as the home theatre of Brecht and Max Reinhard.

Berthold-Brecht-Platz
Phone: 030/28 40 80
www.berliner-ensemble.de
S1, S2, S5, S75, S9 Friedrichstraße
U6 Friedrichstraße and Oranienburger Tor, Tram M1, M6, 12

The Berliner Ensemble is a theatre with an international cult following. Max Reinhardt came to it in 1903 as a reformer whose celebrated *revolving stage* made theatre history here. Built in 1891/92, the theatre was still known under Reinhardt's

The calm before a big storm: the historicizing auditorium of the Deutsches Theater is vintage 19th century and was designed in the Neo-Renaissance style

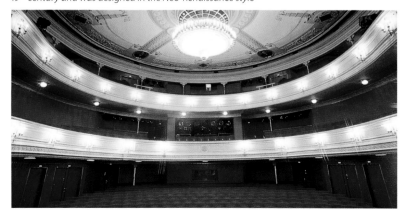

A 1996 burlesque Brecht production at the Berliner Ensemble – Einer Schleef's 'Herr Puntila und sein Knecht Matti' with Schleef as Puntila in a cutaway and lashings of jolly Mattis in sauna towels

tenure as the *Neues Theater am Schiffbauerdamm*. The brilliant première of Brecht's 'Dreigroschenoper' ('Threepenny Opera') was held here in 1928. Brecht returned from exile to the scene of his former triumphs in 1954 with a new Berliner Ensemble. After his death in 1956, his widow, Helene Weigel, managed the theatre until 1971. Performances of Brecht's 'Mutter Courage' and 'Der aufhaltsame Aufstieg des Arturo Ui' ('The Rise of Arturo Ui') created a furore worldwide. The Berliner Ensemble has continued to live up to its reputation. *Claus Peymann* was appointed managing director in 1999.

31 Charité

The famed University Clinic, nearby the former School of Veterinary Medicine with its Theatre of Anatomy.

Schumannstraße 20–21
S1, S2, S5, S75, S9 Friedrichstraße
U6 Friedrichstraße and Oranienburger Tor, Tram M1, M6, 12, Bus 147

The building on Luisenstraße that once housed the **School of Veterinary Medicine** (1839/40, Ludwig Hesse) has three three-storey wings surrounding a court.

Just behind it in a small park is the *Anatomy Theatre* of the school designed in 1789 by Carl Gotthard Langhans. The circular auditorium, notable for its steep tiers of seats, recalls an ancient theatre.

The news of an imminent plague epidemic made Friedrich I take the precaution of having a *plague hospital* built on the north-western fringe of the city in 1710. The plague failed to materialize but the rooms were used as an almshouse and workhouse. In 1726 the complex was enlarged into a hospital with the apt French name, Charité (Charity).

Incorporated in the University from 1810, the Charité was made one of Germany's most important hospitals by pioneering physiologists, scientists and physicians such as Robert Koch, Ivan P. Pavlov, Albrecht von Graefe and Ferdinand Sauerbruch, who worked there.

Between 1897 and 1913 Friedrich Althoff, a government minister, had the whole hospital and its grounds redesigned and rebuilt. Interspersed with green areas, the complex now incorporated separate specialised clinics in the Brandenburg brick Neo-Gothic style. The Charité had to be largely rebuilt after the air raids of the Second World War. The high-rise surgical centre on the east side of Robert-Koch Platz dates from 1981.

32 Hamburger Bahnhof – Museum für Gegenwart Berlin

Lots of Classical modern and contemporary art.

Invalidenstraße 50–51
Phone: 030/39 78 34 12
www.hamburgerbahnhof.de
www.smb.museum
Tu–Fr 10 am–6 pm, Sa 11 am–8 pm,
Su 11 am–6 pm
S5, S7, S75, S9 Berlin Hauptbahnhof
U6 Zinnowitzer Straße
Tram M6, M8, 12, Bus 147, 123, 245

Built in 1847, this terminus was no longer needed after only four decades. There were more conveniently located train stations in the city. The handsome late Neo-Classical station complex was con-verted into a museum for traffic, transport and building in the early 20th century. Destroyed by the bombs that rained down on it during the Second World War, it was not rebuilt until the 1980s under the supervision of the architect Josef Paul Kleihues.

Since November 1996 Hamburger Bahnhof and the new Berlin Museum of Contemporary Art it houses has been one of the most exciting forums for con-temporary art in Germany. The art lover *Erich Marx* gave his spectacular collec-tion, with works by such luminaries as Andy Warhol, Joseph Beuys, Roy Lichten-stein and Anselm Kiefer, to it on perma-nent loan. Moreover, the oustanding *Friedrich Christian Flick Collection*, on loan since September 2004, is to stay for seven years and be presented in rotating exhi-bitions. All major Classical Modern and contemporary styles and genres are rep-

Departed – Hamburger Bahnhof has long since gone off the rails and is now a gallery showing top works of international 20th and 21st-centuries art

In the best company – Schinkel's gravestone in the Dorotheenstädtischer Cemetery

resented, including numerous monumental Environments and projections and the œuvre of the American artist Bruce Naumann (* 1941).

Additional exhibition space has been made for the overspill from the New National Gallery collections, including some spectacular new acquisitions.

Media archives devoted to Joseph Beuys have also been developed.

33 Museum für Naturkunde

The world's biggest dinosaur skeleton.

Invalidenstraße 43
Phone: 030/20 93 85 91
Tu–Fr 9.30 am–5 pm,
Sa/Su/hols. 10 am–6 pm
U6 Zinnowitzer Straße
Tram M6, M8, 12, Bus 245

No need to go to the cinema to see dinosaurs when you can see the originals in the Natural History Museum, which possesses what purports to be the **world's biggest dinosaur skeleton**, a reconstructed Brachiosaurus brancai: 12 m high and 23 m long (removed for restoration until 2007). Apart from the palaeontology section, the museum complex houses mineralogical and zoological collections. In the open-air courtyard a monument commemorates Albrecht Daniel Thaer (1752–1828), Prussia's first scientific agriculturalist.

34 Dorotheenstädtischer Friedhof

Celebrities assembled for the long rest.

Chausseestraße 126
U6 Oranienburger Tor and Zinnowitzer Straße
Tram M1, M6, M8, 12, Bus 245

Small, romantic and packed with celebrities: the Dorotheenstadt Cemetery (1762, enlarged 1814–26) is the last resting place of **poets, philosophers and artists** who shaped German cultural and economic life. The august band includes the philosophers Johann Gottlieb Fichte († 1814) and Georg Wilhelm Friedrich Hegel († 1831), the industrialist August Borsig († 1854), the sculptors and architects Karl Friedrich Schinkel († 1841), Christian Daniel Rauch († 1857) and Johann Gottfried Schadow († 1850). Gravestones also bear the names of more modern celebreties: the writers Heinrich Mann († 1950), Johannes R. Becher († 1958), Anna Seghers († 1983), Arnold Zweig († 1968) and Heiner Müller († 1996); the composer Hanns Eisler († 1962), John Heartfield († 1968), inventor of the contemporary critical photomontage. Much visited are the austere graves of Bertolt Brecht († 1956) and his wife and fellow artist, Helene Weigel († 1971).

The last house in which Brecht and Weigel lived and worked (1953–71) abuts on the cemetery wall: the late Neo-Classical **Brecht-Haus** (Chausseestraße 125, Phone: 030/283 05 70 44, Tu–Fr 10 am–12 noon, Th 10 am–12 noon and 5 pm–6.30 pm, Sa 9.30 am–1.30 pm, Su 11 am–6 pm), which has housed the Bertolt Brecht and Helene Weigel Archives since 1978 and a *Brecht Memorial*. The artists' rooms are on view as they were during their lifetime. The building also houses a literary forum and a *cellar restaurant* (Phone: 030/282 38 43, www.brechtkeller.de, daily from 6 pm) featuring Viennese cuisine cooked to Helene Weigel's recipes.

Further east is **Friedhof II der Sophiengemeinde** (Bergstraße 29). The second cemetery of the parish of St Sophia is known as the 'Musicians' Burial Ground' because so many musicians, instrument makers and composers are interred here: Wilhelm Friedrich Bach († 1845) and Gustav Albert Lortzing († 1851), the piano manufacturer Carl Bechstein († 1900) and the composer Walter Kollo († 1940).

Between Alexanderplatz and Märkisches Ufer – art galore, pubs and more

In the area between Alexanderplatz and Märkisches Ufer visitors encounter an interesting cross-section of Berlin's municipal history: medieval buildings in Berlin-Cölln, the old royal seat; Rococo town houses once owned by the rich; grand administration buildings from the era of industrialisation; GDR prefab buildings and, in the Nikolaiviertel section, an attempt to revive something of Old Berlin. Nor is the visitors' physical well-being neglected on a sightseeing tour: numerous pubs and eateries invite them to linger.

35 Alexanderplatz

'Alex' – famed, notorious, beloved, is being refurbished.

S5, S7, S9, S75 and U2, U5, U8 Alexanderplatz, Bus 100, 148, 200, TXL

In the 17th century Alexanderplatz was arable land, then a wool and cattle market and later still a parade ground. Not until the *Stadtbahn*, the urban railway, was constructed in 1882, did the square grow into an East Berlin **traffic junction**: a station was built here to accommodate rail travel within the city and beyond as well as the underground, tram and bus lines. In 1929 *Alfred Döblin* commemorated the throbbing heart of the metropolis in the socially critical novel 'Berlin Alexanderplatz'.

Bombing during the Second World War turned 'Alex' into rubble. In the 1960s the East Berlin municipal authorities tried to evoke capital-city ambience round the square by putting up high-rise buildings, including the House of the Teacher, the House of Travel and the House of the Electrical Industry. Since then Alex has also been a *pedestrian zone*, with traffic flowing around it.

In 1993 the architect Hans Kollhoff drew up a **master plan** for future site development: it provides for twelve high-rises at least 150 m tall to house offices and flats as well as the demolition of the bleak GDR blocks except for the House of the Teacher and the earlier Behrens houses, which are listed monuments. Whether

The sins of urban planning redeemed: Alexanderplatz with the Television Tower and the World Clock, still just as popular as ever as an East Berlin venue, is undergoing a facelift

the plan will be implemented is, however, uncertain. Now beautification is on the agenda: by 2007 Alexanderplatz is to have new paving, steps for sitting on, benches, etc. Even the colourful folkloric **Brunnen der Völkerfreundschaft** (Fountain of Friendship between Peoples, 1969), previously scheduled for demolition, is to stay.

Alexanderplatz, named after Alexander I following a visit by the Russian Tsar in 1805, has also been a focus of Berlin history: here street fighting raged behind barricades during the bourgeois revolution of 1848. In 1918/19 pitched battles were fought between workers and the police and, on 4 November 1989, 500 000 East Berliners demonstrated here peacefully for a democratic restructuring of the GDR.

The **Behrens houses** on the south side of the square, the Alexander house and the Berolina house (1928–31), are late works by the architect Peter Behrens in the New Objectivity style. From 1895 the city landmark, Emil Hundrieser's wrought copper statue of 'Berolina', stood nearby. Removed in 1927, it landed on the rubbish tip, was set up again by the Nazis in 1933 and was finally melted down in 1944. Where it once stood, the steel, aluminium and enamel **Weltzeituhr** (1969) now tells the time round the world. The **Park Inn Berlin Hotel** (1967–70), 122 m high with 37 storeys, dominates the north side of the square.

Fernsehturm

At 365 m, Berlin's highest building and Europe's third-highest television tower.

Alexanderplatz
S5, S7, S9, S75 and U2, U5, U8 Alexanderplatz, Bus 100, 148, 200, TXL

Inaugurated in 1969 and popularly dubbed 'Telespargel', the structure looming for all the world like a giant spear of asparagus over what was once densely settled *Alt-Berlin* is Europe's only downtown television tower. The concept was developed by Hermann Henselmann and Jörg Streitparth. In 1965 Fritz Dieter and Günter Franke began to plan and then build it. Not an easy task since urban planners and technicians had had no previous experience of dealing with such high towers in inner-city areas. The glazed **sphere**,

32 m in diameter, weighs 4800 t. In it, on different levels, are an **observation point** (203 m) and the **Telecafé** (207 m). The sphere revolves round its axis every 59 minutes. When the visibility is good, you can see for 40 km.

The buildings at the foot of the Television Tower were not completed until 1973: **pavilions** for housing rotating exhibitions and gastronomic facilities. An open-air stair with fountains and lighting effects echoes the form of the pavilions.

In front is an open space with the 10 m high **Neptunbrunnen** at its centre. In designing it, Reinhold Begas drew on Bernini's 'Fountain of the Four Rivers' (Rome). Holding court from on high, Neptune, god of the seas, looks down on four female figures personifying the rivers Elbe, Weichsel, Oder and Rhine. The red granite fountain basin is 18 m in diameter. Originally set up in 1891 on the south side of the former Berliner Stadtschloss, it was moved to its present site after restoration in 1969

Berliner Rathaus
Rotes Rathaus

The mayor governs from the Neo-Renaissance Rathaus, known as the 'Red Town Hall' because of its red brick walls.

Rathausstraße/Spandauer Straße
U2 Klosterstraße, Bus 148

Since 1991 the Town Hall tower has flaunted a banner with the city emblem – the *Berlin Bear*. Since then, the **Senatskanzlei**, where the city senate convenes, and the mayor's office have been in the Rathaus, in GDR days the seat of the East Berlin municipal authorities and council.

In 1861–69 the city fathers had a structure designed by Hermann Friedrich Waesemann, architect to Friedrich Wilhelm IV, built on a square measuring 99 x 88 m. Its wings enclose three inner courtyards and a 74 m high tower, recalling the tower which houses London's Big Ben. The history of Berlin from the beginnings to the founding of the Empire in 1871 unfolds on a *relief frieze* comprising 36 terracotta panels.

By 1958 all traces of the severe damage sustained by the Rathaus had been effaced. At the entrance, two *bronze statues* (1958) by Fritz Cremer, 'Rubble Woman' and 'Reconstruction Helper', com-

Time for sunbathing while the mayor has to govern from the Red Town Hall: the ancient god of the seas and his playful retinue inhabit the Neptune Fountain

memorate the labours of rebuilding after the Second World War.

38 Marienkirche

St Mary's is Berlin's second-oldest parish church and a memento of the Middle Ages. It houses important treasures of Berlin and Brandenburg sacred art.

Karl-Liebknecht-Straße 8
S5, S7, S9, S75 and U2, U5, U8 Alexanderplatz, Bus 100, 148, 200, TXL

The Marienkirche, one of few remaining witnesses to medieval Berlin, is dedicated to three saints: the Virgin Mary, St Anne and St Maurice. Building began in 1270, when the city was being enlarged at the New Market. The Church of Our Lady was first mentioned in records dating from 1294. After a fire in the city, the elongated, three-aisled nave underwent restoration for the first time in 1380–1405. The **West Tower**, 90 m high, was designed by Carl Gotthard Langhans in 1789/90 after the

earlier tower had burnt to the ground. The present tower is an eclectic blend of the Gothic and Neo-Classical styles.

The furnishings and appointments of the Marienkirche are memorable. The celebrated *'Totentanz'* is a fresco 22 m long by 2 m high by an unknown artist. Probably painted after plague broke out in 1484, the 'Dance of Death' was painted over in 1730 and did not reappear until the transept was being renovated in 1860 by Friedrich August Stüler. The personification of Death is shown with representatives of the various estates in 28 scenes. Further attractions are a bronze *font* (1437) and the marble *Baroque pulpit* (1703) by Andreas Schlüter on a pier in the north aisle. The *organ* (1720/21) was built by Joachim Wagner. *Johann Sebastian Bach* played it on a visit to Frederick II, the Great, in 1747. The *Memorial Cross* at the main portal recalls the murder of provost Nikolaus von Bernau in 1325.

To the west of the Marienkirche is the former Marx-Engels-Forum – now **Rathausstraße**. Here there was once a densely

No tempest in a teacup – the AquaDom in the Radisson SAS is a superlative column of water with fish in psychedelic colours

settled medieval quarter that extended from what is now the Old Berlin side across the Spree to Alt-Cölln in the area between the Berliner Stadtschloss and

Tunnel vision – Sea Life Berlin provides memorable encounters with the denizens of the underwater world

the Lustgarten. However, starting in 1950, demolition of all buildings to make way for the remodelled socialist capital obliterated the structure of the old city.

The **Heiliggeistkapelle** (Spandauer Straße) adjacent to the Radisson SAS Hotel is all that recalls the Middle Ages. First mentioned in records from 1313, the Chapel of the Holy Spirit was once part of the *Heiliggeist-Hospital*, on the site since 1272 but demolished in 1825. Between 1655 and 1703 the chapel was the garrison church but was later used as a lecture hall by the Berlin Management Academy. Since it was restored in 1978/79, its deconsecrated interior has been a cafeteria, the Humboldt University **Mensa** – the students eat beneath a late Gothic stellar vault (1746).

The green space on the Forum boasts commemorative statuary unveiled in 1986 and portraying **Karl Marx and Friedrich Engels** – both, small wonder, gazing resolutely eastwards. One hundred and seventy-four photographs on double stelae document the history of the labour movement. A five-part *marble relief* wall with socialist scenes completes the ensemble.

At the **Radisson SAS**, part of the *CityQuartier DomAquaree*, things are a lot livelier and more colourful. The **Aqua Dom** (Spandauer Straße 3, Phone: 030/99 28 00, www.sealifeeurope.com, April–Aug. daily 10 am–7 pm, Sept.–Mar. daily 10 am–6 pm), the world's biggest freestanding aquarium, soars 25 m up from the hotel atrium. Visitors ascend in the lift through the underwater world of a coral reef and see schools of exotic fish gliding by. From there you go to the adjacent

The perfect place for a break: time seems to have stood still in the idyllic Nikolai Quarter with its Nikolaikirche

Sea Life Berlin, which documents riverine and marine flora and fauna from the Spree to the North Sea and the Atlantic in over thirty aquariums. Also stunning are the aptly named Schwarmring, a glassed-in circular room in which you stand amidst swarming schools of fish, and the Atlantic Aquarium, which you walk through in a glass tunnel with fish, eels and sharks darting around you.

39 Nikolaiviertel & Nikolaikirche

Historic Berlin quarter recreated on the drawing-board with St Nicholas' Church, the city's oldest listed building.

Between Spreeufer (Bergstraße), Mühlendamm and Spandauer Straße
U2 Klosterstraße, Bus 148

The Nikolai Quarter is one of *the* tourist attractions in Berlin-Mitte. Not just be-cause this was once the core of old Berlin, the eastern half of the double city of Berlin-Cölln. Visitors find something here which they would not expect to en-counter in the area: **Old Berlin ambience** with an abundance of inns, taverns, arts and crafts and souvenir shops. Although there was a settlement here by the early 13th century, the structure of this quarter today has nothing to do with organic ur-ban growth. The Nikolai Quarter was planned on the drawing-board by archi-tect Günter Stahn on the occasion of the city's 750th birthday and rebuilt from scratch. It is popularly dubbed *'Socialist Disneyland'*. A few old houses were there to be restored but most are historical re-constructions. In addition, historic monu-ments from other sections of the city were moved here.

The heart of the quarter, the **Niko-laikirche** (Phone: 030/24 72 45 29, www. stadtmuseum.de, Tu, Th–Su 10 am–6 pm), is still as it was. St Nicholas' is Berlin's old-

est parish church. It was also the scene of important events that shaped the *city's history*: The council and city of Berlin converted to Lutheranism here on 2 November 1539. The first Berlin municipal authorities were sworn in here on 6 July 1809. After reunification, the first democratically elected Berlin Senate convened here on 11 January 1991 to draft a constitution.

The *origins* of the church go back to the 13th century. About 1230 a cruciform basilica with three aisles was built here of unfinished stone. It was converted into a Gothic hall church about 1260/70. The present brick structure came to look as it does today with the addition of the 84-m-high *twin towers*. They were built in 1877–79 when Hermann Blankenstein of the municipal board of works renovated the church. In 1944/45 the structure was reduced to a gutted shell with the stumps of the towers, the dome collapsed in 1949. Reconstruction did not begin until 1981. St Nicholas' has housed a subdivision of the *Märkisches Museum* [see No.

47] since 1987: the medieval collection, under the heading *'Berlin between 1237 and 1648'* and sacred artefacts and sculpture. Also on view are what is left of the rich church furnishings and appointments, including a painted pewter *font* (1563), the *funerary chapel* (1725) of finance minister Johann Andreas von Krauth and the *'Portal of Death'* by Andreas Schlüter – an impressive monument to Daniel Männlich, goldsmith to the court.

Gotthold Ephraim Lessing lived at **No. 10 Nikolaikirchplatz** (the house is a reconstruction) between 1752 and 1755 while he was writing the drama 'Minna von Barnhelm'. Across from St Nicholas', where the priory used to be, is the historic Old Berlin inn **Am Nussbaum**, once frequented by Otto Nagel and Heinrich Zille. The inn was moved here from the Fischerinsel.

Just opposite stands a reconstruction of the medieval **Gerichtslaube**, the Court Arbour, which was torn down in 1871 and initially reconstructed in the park of Schloss Babelsberg.

The reconstructed Nikolai Quarter with the Nikolaikirche, the Red Town Hall and the foot of the Television Tower

Right on the banks of the Spree, in Burgstraße, stands a bronze equestrian statue of **St George**, designed by August Kiß in 1849. This is its third home since the work, presented by the artist to King Wilhelm I, stood in the first courtyard of the Berliner Stadtschloss from 1865 until 1950 and then in the Volkspark Friedrichshain until 1987.

40 Palais Ephraim

The finest 18th-century patrician Berlin town house – an architectural gem in the Nikolai Quarter.

Poststraße 16
Phone: 030/24 00 20
www.stadtmuseum.de
Tu, Th–Su 10 am–6 pm,
We 12 am–8 pm
U2 Klosterstraße, Bus 148

Palais Ephraim (1761–64) is the most important historic private dwelling in the Nikolai Quarter. This gem of Rococo architecture with its rounded corner façade was named after *Veitel Heine Ephraim*,

Take time for a good look: the Nikolai Quarter invites you to stroll through it and enjoy the reconstructed historic houses that make Old Berlin come alive

Anything as handsome as the Palais Ephraim in the Nikolai Quarter looks good up close, too. The 'golden' building houses an art collection from the Märkisches Museum

jeweller to the court of Frederick the Great and master of the mint, and designed by Friedrich Wilhelm Diterichs. The exquisite façade was demolished in 1935/36 to accommodate modern urban traffic. All 2493 parts of it were stored in West Berlin. The town house was rebuilt from these original building elements in 1985–87 but was moved 16 m into Poststraße.

The modern interior houses the *Märkisches Museum* prints collection [see also No. 47] and is also used for temporary ex-

hibitions. A copy of the *stucco ceiling* from the Wartenbergsches Palais designed by Andreas Schlüter in 1704 but torn down in 1889, adorns a reception room on the first floor.

A second Rococo house stands diagonally across from it at 23 Poststraße: the **Knoblauchhaus** (Phone: 030/23 45 99 91, www.stadtmuseum.de, Tu–Su 10 am–6 pm). Built in 1759/60, it is embellished with early Neo-Classical scrollwork dating from 1800. It belonged to the master needle-maker Johann Christian Knoblauch and was the meeting place of distinguished intellectuals, including Lessing, Wilhelm von Humboldt, Moses Mendelssohn and Freiherr vom Stein. Its twelve rooms house the permanent *Märkisches Museum* exhibition on 19th-century Berlin history focusing on 'Biedermeier Design and Lifestyle' [see also No. 47]. Many exhibits tell the story of the Knoblauchs, the Jewish family who owned the house until 1928.

41   Palais Schwerin

*Baroque palace with a
turbulent history.*
Molkenmarkt 1–3
U2 Klosterstraße, Bus 148

Molkenmarkt, meaning Dairy Market, is the point from which Berlin grew as an urban nucleated settlement: the first settlers lived here and here was the first town hall. Palais Schwerin is one of the few historic buildings still in their original locations. Built in 1704 by Jan de Bodt for minister of state Otto von Schwerin, the Palais was incorporated in the new *Reich Mint* in 1935 and the façade was set back. In the GDR era it was the Ministry of Culture. Now it houses various divisions of the municipal and state administration.

Above the windows on the main floor are lunettes with reliefs of putti. The façade also boasts a copy of the *relief frieze* (about 1800) by Gottfried Schadow, which was on the mint at Werderscher Markt until it was demolished in 1886. The original sandstone frieze, an important example of Berlin Neo-Classical sculpture, now adorns a house at 42–43 Spandauer Damm in Charlottenburg.

42   Altes Stadthaus

*A stately early 20th-century
administration building.*
Klosterstraße 47
U2 Klosterstraße, Bus 148

No sooner was the Red Town Hall [see No. 37] completed in 1869 than it turned out to be too small. An entire section of the city was torn down to make room for an additional administration building at Molkenmarkt. Designed by Ludwig Hoffmann, it was built between 1902 and 1911 to fulfil official representative functions.

Until 1990 the Alte Stadthaus was the official seat of the GDR Council of Ministers. Now it houses branches of various different ministries.

The original plans by city architect Hoffmann were based on a trapezoidal layout with four *inner courtyards*. Three elements are salient: first, the sculptural effect created by the high rusticated blind story of the façade, second the massive columns and, finally, the 101-m-high tower on the west wing. The tower echoes those by Gontard at Gendarmenmarkt.

In neighbouring Parochialstraße is the **Neues Stadthaus** (1937–39, Franz Arnous, Günther Starck). The Berlin municipal authorities convened here until 1948, when the SED staged a coup known as the Stadthausputsch. The consequences of the putsch: the West Berlin representatives moved out and an East Berlin municipal government was formed.

Close by is **U-Bahnhof Klosterstraße**, which still incorporates part of the Berlin *fortification walls*. Inside, tiles on the walls of the underground station concourse are a stylistic borrowing from the *Procession Street of Babylon* in the Pergamonmuseum [see p. 41]. And an old third-class underground carriage creates a bit of retro station ambience.

43   Parochialkirche

Berlin's oldest Baroque church.
Klosterstraße/Parochialstraße
U2 Klosterstraße, Bus 148

Berlin's first Baroque sacred building was begun in 1695 by Johann Arnold Nering, who modelled it on Dutch churches, and completed, with alterations, by court architect Grünberg. The Sophienkirche [see p. 44] and the Parochialkirche are Berlin's only remaining Baroque churches. From the bell chamber of the *tower* (1713/14, Jan de Bodt, Philipp Gerlach) the ringing of thirty-seven bells sounded for the first time in 1715. The church was gutted by fire in 1944 but the tower survived. The last mass until the present was held in 1961 in the main building, to which makeshift repairs had been done. In 1988 the roof was retiled and reconstruction work began in 1993 that will still take years to complete. In the **parish hall** to the right of the church, an attractive *model house*, the only one of its kind left in

Where celebrities were once sent to school: formerly a Franciscan monastery, the building is now an anti-war memorial

1966. By 1970 it had been restored to its original appearance.

Waisenstraße, one of the city's oldest streets, has retained some simple 18th-century houses called Traufen houses, which are aligned with the street rather than facing it. They were built on remains of the 13th/14th-centuries city wall, once about 4 m high. Extensive restoration took place in 1960. The building at Nos. 14–16 is a famous old inn: **Zur letzten Instanz** (Phone: 030/242 55 28, www.zur letzteninstanz.de, daily from 12 noon). A tavern was recorded on the site as early as the mid-16th century.

44 Ehem. Franziskaner-klosterkirche

Chruch ruins warn against war.

Klosterstraße/Grunerstraße
U2 Klosterstraße, Bus 148

Berlin dating from the period when the belfry was built, is on display.

To the left of the church, at 68 Klosterstraße, is **Palais Podewils** (1701–04), a Baroque building designed by Jan de Bodt. Severely damaged in the war, it was rebuilt in 1952 but was gutted by fire in

Until it was destroyed in the Second World War, the Franciscan Monastery Church was one of the most important Brandenburg brick Gothic buildings in Berlin. A basilica with low arcades and squat piers that are still Romanesque in style, the church dates from about 1300. The ruins – like those of the Gedächtniskirche – are a memorial warning against war. The monastery building on the north side, also damaged in the war, was demolished in 1968. It once housed

Cool beer has been foaming here for over four centuries! Popular artist Heinrich Zille used to frequent the 'Zur letzten Instanz' tavern, an authentic Old Berlin institution

Eclectic architecture: Gothic, Baroque and Jugendstil make this grand stairwell in Mitte District Court a successful blend of styles

Berlin's most famous secondary school, the *Gymnasium zum Grauen Kloster*, founded in 1574. Important people went to school here: Karl Friedrich Schinkel, Gottfried Schadow and Otto von Bismarck. Friedrich Ludwig Jahn, the father of gymnastics, was both pupil and teacher here. In the *park* there are two capitals from columns that once adorned the Berliner Stadtschloss.

45 Amtsgericht Mitte

A palatial court-house, the architectural model for others of its kind.

Littenstraße 13–17
S5, S7, S9, S75 and U2, U5, U8 Alexanderplatz, Bus 100, 148, 200, TXL

Amtsgericht Mitte was built between 1896 and 1905. Other Berlin court-houses in Moabit, Schöneberg, Lichtenberg and Pankow were modelled on this district court. Because Grunerstraße was to be widened, the north wing was torn down along with its grand *stairwell* in 1968/69. The impressive staircase, now in Littenstraße, is still worth seeing – an eclectic blend of Gothic, Baroque and Jugendstil

elements. The building housed the GDR Supreme Court until 1990, now Mitte District Court and Berlin State Court convene here.

46 Ermeler Haus

Once a gem of an interior.

Märkisches Ufer 10
S5, S7, S75, S9 and U8 Jannowitzbrücke, U2 Märkisches Museum, Bus 147, 265

Ermeler Haus (1760–62), another patrician town house that stood in Breite Straße until 1968/69 before being rebuilt on the Märkisches Ufer, was once celebrated for its furnishings. Since the Second World War only the *Banquet Hall* and a *bedchamber* attest to the graceful Rococo interior which the affluent Berliner Wilhelm Ferdinand Ermeler enjoyed when he moved into the house in 1824. In its new location, the Ermeler House has been embellished with an additional cellar and a outer staircase. However, the Neo-Classical stucco *façade* with its scrollwork and palmettes dates from 1805. There is also a restaurant in the building.

The **Michaelkirche** is several side-streets away to the south-east. Built between 1851 and 1856 by August Soller, St Michael's Church is still an impressive example of post-Schinkel Historicism despite being in rather dilapidated condition. Protestant Berlin's second oldest Catholic church after St Hedwig's Cathedral [see No. 6], St Michael's is a visible landmark in the Luisenstadt section of Berlin.

47 Märkisches Museum

Extensive collection surveying Berlin history from its beginnings to the present.

Am Koellnischen Park 5
Phone: 030/30 86 60
www.stadtmuseum.de
Tu, Th–Su 10 am–6 pm,
We 12 am–8 pm
S5, S7, S75, S9 and U8 Jannowitz-brücke, U2 Märkisches Museum
Bus 147, 265

The Märkisches Museum harks back to Brandenburg brick Gothic and Renaissance architecture. Built by Ludwig Hoffmann between 1901 and 1907, the build-ing resembles in part the Wittstocker Bischofsburg castle in Potsdam district and St Catherine's Church in Brandenburg. Before the entrance stands a copy of the statue of *Roland von Brandenburg* (1474).

Under the heading of 'Look at this City', the museum documents the history and cultural history of Berlin from the Middle Ages to the present. The thematic focus is on urban development, crafts, industry, the Enlightenment, science and scholarship, modern art, Berliners and the partition and reunification of the city. Some of the exhibits came from the former Berlin Museum. The Märkisches Museum is the headquarters of the **Stiftung Stadtmuseum Berlin**, comprising fourteen collections.

The building is at **Koellnischer Park**, covering a hectare of ground between Rungestraße and the south bank of the Spree. Here Heinrich Drake's bronze **Zille Denkmal** (1965, see p. 126) commemorates the Berlin 'scene painter' Zille, portrayed larger than life at his favourite pastime of sketching. At the opposite edge of the park rises the **Wusterhausener Bär** (1718), a round tower from the city fortifications. Once it stood on the bank of the Grüner Graben moat but was relocated here in 1893.

Ludwig Hoffmann quoted from all sorts of buildings when he designed the Märkisches Museum – it's far better than a handbook of Brandenburg architecture

Prenzlauer Berg and Friedrichshain – lifestyle in the old working-class quarters

Prenzlauer Berg, affectionately called '**Prenzl'berg**' by locals, is not only one of the most densely populated sections of the metropolis but also one of the liveliest (Kastanienallee is shown below): here the streets are still paved with cobble-stones and the stucco is still crumbling off façades but right next door there are also streets with splendidly restored 1900s houses, numerous cafés and pubs, some of them sleazy, frequented by students and arty types as well as the 'natives'. In brief – Prenzlauer Berg is, along with Kreuzberg, *the* **local scene**.

In the GDR era people who refused to vote and young political dissidents sought refuge by squatting in empty flats here – there wasn't much even the Stasi could do about it. Artists and young people created a little haven of freedom for themselves in the decrepit houses, lending the section the flavour of a '**Berlin Montmartre**'. After the turnaround many Kreuzberg residents and people new to Berlin discovered this unconventional section in the eastern part of the city, especially since rents were extremely low here.

The neighbouring section of **Friedrichshain** has shrugged off its dreary pre-fab ambience to emerge as a new scene venue. Creative people, youthful entrepreneurs and students have shaped the area around **Volkspark Friedrichshain** and **Karl-Marx-Allee** (www.kma-berlin.de/alleeverfuehrer). It was on Karl-Marx-Allee, in the early 1950s constructed on the Soviet model, that the revolt of GDR citizens against the SED regime broke out on 17 June 1953. Construction site workers formed into a protest parade and Russian tanks had to come to the aid of the regime. Ninety metres wide, the splendid boulevard is still lined with buildings in an eclectic style blending austere Schinkel Neo-Classicism and fussy Soviet gingerbread, inviting you to take an architecture walk. Further to the south-east the extensive landscaped park surrounding Baroque Schloss Friedrichsfelde was converted in 1955 into **Tierpark Friedrichsfelde**, a zoo still highly popular for the diversity of the fauna it harbours.

The façades of old buildings like these along Knaackstraße suit the casual lifestyle and designer image of the popular Prenzlauer Berg quarter

48 Jüdischer Friedhof

Berlin's second oldest Jewish cemetery.

Schönhauser Allee 23–25
Mo–Th 8 am–4 pm, Fr 8 am–1 pm
U2 Senefelderplatz

Nostalgic memories of distinguished 19th and 20th-century Berliners are reawakened at the Jüdischer Friedhof in Schönhauser Allee, Berlin's second oldest Jewish cemetery. Laid out in 1827 outside the city wall, it represents an ivy-covered 'stone' page in the chronicles of the city. Five thousand Jews were buried here. Unfortunately, many of the graves are now untended and, moreover, for several years now so vulnerable to vandalism that they must be protected. The illustrious Berliners buried here include the composer Giacomo Meyerbeer († 1864), the doyen of publishers, Leopold Ullstein († 1899), and his family, Gerson von Bleichröder († 1893), who was Iron Chancellor Bismarck's banker and financial adviser, and the painter Max Liebermann, who died in 1935.

49 Kollwitzplatz

Pulsing heart of Prenzlauer Berg.

U2 Senefelderplatz

Kollwitzplatz is at the heart of Prenzlauer Berg. The square is jumping, especially in summer. Its broad pavements provide plenty of space for the tables and chairs of a host of cafés, pubs and restaurants.

Since 1947 Kollwitzplatz has borne the name of a celebrated couple: *Käthe Kollwitz* (1867–1945) was a graphic artist and sculptor. During the Third Reich, her work was outlawed as 'decadent'. Her husband, *Dr. Karl Kollwitz*, had his practice where he ministered to the poor nearby at what used to be 25 Weißenburger Straße (now Kollwitzstraße 56 a/Knaackstraße 36). The house was destroyed by bombs towards the end of the war. The new house at the corner used to boast a copy of the Käthe Kollwitz limestone sculpture *'Mother and Two Children'* as a memorial to the socially committed couple but the sculpture was moved to the grounds of the local government offices at 17 Fröbelstraße. It was replaced by a larger than life-size bronze **seated figure** portraying Käthe Kollwitz, which Gustav Seitz created in 1956–59, modelling it on a self-portrait (1938) of the artist.

Not far to the south of the square on the *Mühlenberg* is a round **water tower**, the tallest structure in the area and another familiar landmark of this section of the city. It was planned in 1853–55 as part of the waterworks. Its nickname *'Dicker Hermann'* – a reference to fat Hermann Göring – and a memorial plaque are a reminder that political dissidents were detained in the cellar vaults and tortured there during the Nazi era. The former industrial facilities, now a listed building, have been divided up into flats.

Rykestraße to the north is just as steeped in history. The name of the street recalls the Ryke family, which provided Berlin with several mayors in the 14th century. In 1900 many Jewish families lived here: Johann Hoeninger, architect to the Jewish community, built a *synagogue* in the rear courtyard of No. 53 in 1903/04. Designated a **Temple to Peace** in 1978, the synagogue is one of only two in Berlin to have also retained its original interior. Although it was vandalised on the night of the 9 November 1938 pogrom, it was not set on fire. Following reconstruction work, the synagogue was reconsecrated in 1953.

Although a great deal of renovation work has been carried out here, some façades in the street still bear visible scars of war. In recent years at least the grand buildings dating from the boom period of the 1870s have been restored with Senate funding.

Husemannstraße, running north from Kollwitzplatz, exemplifies the GDR approach to restoration. In the mid-1980s the section between Kollwitzplatz and Sredzkistraße was faithfully restored to its original appearance on the occasion of the 750th anniversary of the founding of the city. It became the token example of urban renewal displayed to visiting dignitaries. Retaining the genuine *Bismarck-era boom ambience*, it boasts quaint shops selling handmade articles with forged wrought-iron guild signs, authentic 1900 Berlin tavern interiors – serving sour 'Yurken' (gherkins) and 'Buletten' (meatballs).

50 Prater-Garten

From beer garden to cultural oasis.
Kastanienallee/Oderberger Straße
U2 Eberswalder Straße, Tram M1, 12

Like Vienna, Berlin also has a Prater. In 1852 the fun started with a beer garden in what was then a suburb. From 1881 a horse-drawn tram ran along Kastanienallee, bringing increasing numbers of weekend excursionists to the Prater. A good excuse for the clever owners of the garden, Schneider & Hillig, to broaden the bill of fare in 1900 to include cultural events such as summer theatre, concerts

During the summer months the Berlin Prater is a much-frequented venue for open-air plays and concerts

Culture always on tap: Since 1991 plays, concerts, parties and exhibition have been in full spate on the premises of the old Schultheiss brewery

and operettas. Working men from the large blocks of flats nearby started using the Prater for political rallies. Ernst Busch (1900–1980) sang working-men's songs and SED Young Pioneers gave rousing choruses here.

There has been an **open-air summer theatre** for 'moving pictures' since 1960 and a few years later the *Kreiskulturhaus Prenzlauer Berg* was established as a cultural forum.

The Prater is still a green oasis for liquid and cultural refreshment. Prater balls are held here and the *Pratergalerie* puts on art exhibitions.

rant and the boiler-house but the new proprietors are concerned primarily with culture, gastronomy and entertainment. Franz Schwechten, the architect who designed the trapezoidal facility in 1891, could not have imaged the theatre productions and concerts, films and poetry readings, exhibitions and parties that would one day take place here.

Several years ago, some urban planners wanted to erect an office-building complex here to replace the multicultural centre – but to date only part of the old grounds has new buildings on it and the Culture Brewery is still going strong.

51 KulturBrauerei

Culture, culinary treats and nightlife.

Schönhauser Allee 36–39,
entrance: Knaackstraße
Phone: 030/44 31 51 52
www.kulturbrauerei-berlin.de
U2 Eberswalder Straße, Tram M1, 12

Culture in undiluted form has been served up on the premises of the **Schultheiss-Brauerei** since 1991. Beer is still on tap in the old brewery, in the beer restau-

52 Gethsemanekirche

Symbol of peaceful resistance.

Stargarder Straße 77
S8, S85, S41, S42 and U2 Schönhauser Allee, Tram M1

The Gethsemanekirche was a major nucleus of resistance against the SED regime. Not only did the congregation pray silently here for a turnaround; peaceful protest also emanated from the church.

The police countered the demonstrations with a show of force.

The red cruciform church building, faced with clinker, was built in the late 19th century after plans by August Orth. In the spacious interior stands an interesting 1920s *wood sculpture* by Wilhelm Groß representing 'Christ on the Mount of Olives'.

53 Zeiss-Großplanetarium

One of Europe's best-equipped planetariums.
Prenzlauer Allee 80
www.astw.de
S41, S42, S8, S85 Prenzlauer Allee

The universe is so near you can almost reach out and touch it: the large projection room at the Zeiss Planetarium, built in 1985–87, seats an audience of nearly 300 eager to learn about discoveries in outer space and the science of astronomy. Its modern special projectors and laser facilities make it one of Europe's best planetariums. The polished **outer dome**, 30 m in diameter, shimmers with a silvery sheen in the sun. The **planetarium dome** is 23 m in diameter. The core of the facility is surrounded by rooms for events, a cinema, a café and a library.

54 Fruchtbarkeitsbrunnen

The Fountain of Fertility (1920s/30s) is one of Berlin's most important monumental fountains of its era.
Arnswalder Platz
Tram M4, M10

Made of red porphyry, the Fountain of Fertility, a late work (1927–34) of Hugo Lederer (1871–1940), is as solidly impressive as the monument to Iron Chancellor Bismarck he designed for Hamburg. Lederer symbolised Fertility in the figures of a woman reaping, a fisherman, a shepherd and a mother and child. The central basin is 8 m in diameter and is flanked by two bulls. The heavy grandeur of the fountain has made Berliners dub it the 'Bull Fountain'.

55 Volkspark Friedrichshain

The biggest green area in East Berlin.
Am Friedrichshain
Tram M4, Bus 200, 240

From Prenzlauer Berg you should head for the public park named after the neighbouring section of **Friedrichshain**. The first spadeful of earth was dug by

Outside glossy, inside grand: the Zeiss Planetarium on Prenzlauer Allee tells you everything you ever wanted to know about astronomy

Not the Monkey House – Schloss Friedrichs-felde (17th/18th centuries), one of Berlin's finest historic buildings, is a museum and part of the zoo of the same name

workmen on relief in 1846 in the meadows in front of the excise and customs wall. Here a recreation park was to be laid out for the poor, designed as the eastern counterpart of the Tiergarten by the landscape architect *Peter Joseph Lenné*. Gustav Meyer, a pupil of Lenné's and gardener to the Potsdam court, carried out the plans, widening the area to include *Neuer Hain* (1874–76).

The war did not spare the 52-ha green oasis and its century-old trees were destroyed. The park was completely redesigned between 1969 and 1973. Incidentally, the Nazis left behind two *bunkers* in which some of the art treasures remaining in Berlin were stored. They were taken by the Soviet occupation authorities to Moscow and Kraków. The bunkers were blown up after hostilities ceased and filled in with rubble to create the **Kleiner Bunkerberg** (48 m) and the **Großer Bunkerberg** (78 m). From these artificial hills you can see a *Sport and Recreational Centre* (SEZ) covering 8 ha of ground east of Friedrichshain and on the southern edge the Kanonenberg and the *Cemetery honouring those who died in the March Revolt of 1848*. Incorporated in it is the Cemetery for those who fell in the November Revolution of 1918.

In the western part of the public park stands the semicircular (34 x 54 m) Neo-Baroque **Märchenbrunnen** (1913, Ludwig Hoffmann). The Fairy-Tale Fountain is a prime example of classic Wilhelmine architecture and all for show. Figures familiar from Grimms' fairy-tales pose on plinths in front of arcades about the basins – virtually everyone who is anyone from Cinderella to the (Seven) Dwarfs is present and accounted for.

Now, where are they going, wherever can they be going? – Even the youngest members of the Friedrichsfelder elephant family are as headstrong as they can be and sport pert hairstyles

56 Tierpark und Schloss Friedrichsfelde

A large landscaped zoo with a tiny Baroque palace.

Am Tierpark 125, entrances:
Bear Window and Schloss
Phone: 030/51 53 10
www.tierpark-berlin.de
April–Sept. 9 am–6 pm; March, Oct. 9 am–5 pm; Nov.–Feb. 9 am–4 pm.
Feeding the felines Sa–Th 3 pm, bathing the elephants Nov.–March Sa/Su 3 pm–3.30 pm
U5 Tierpark, S5, S7, S75 Friedrichsfelde, Bus 194, 296, 396

Tierpark Friedrichsfelde in the East Berlin district of Lichtenberg is a zoo created in 1955 as the counterpart of the West Berlin Zoologischer Garten [see No. 106]. Covering 160 ha, Friedrichsfelde is one of Europe's biggest landscaped zoos. The spacious grounds crisscrossed by some 23 km of paths are home to 9800 animals of 1072 different species. Anyone underway with children is advised to rent a wagon to pull them in at the Bear Window entrance. An absolute must is the *Alfred-Brehm-Haus* at the south-eastern edge of the grounds, where Siberian tigers, lions, leopards, panthers and other great cats can be observed. The neighbouring *Pachyderm House* contains African and Asian elephants as well as rhinoceroses, with the aquatic element represented by dugongs and manatees. Reptile aficionados can admire one of the world's biggest colonies of vipers and adders in the *Snake Farm*.

The historic core of the grounds is **Schloss Friedrichsfelde** (Phone: 030/ 24 00 21 62, www.stadtmuseum.de, guided tours Tu–Su 1 pm, 2 pm, 3 pm, 4 pm) in the north-western part of the park. The Prince Elector Friedrich Wilhelm had it built as a hunting lodge in 1682 after plans by Johann Arnold Nering and turned it over to Benjamin Raulé, Lord High Admiral of the Electoral Navy. The latter added land so Peter Joseph Lenné had space for laying out a landscaped garden in 1821, which would be converted into the Friedrichsfelde Zoo some hundred and thirty years later. The lodge was enlarged by Martin Heinrich Böhme in 1719 to accommodate three more windows on each side and a triangular pediment was added to the show façade. After the building had changed hands several times, the interior was redesigned in the Neo-Classical style in 1785. The double-L staircase with a handsome oak balustrade and the stuccoed banquet hall on the upper floor are original. Since 2002 a branch of the *Stadtmuseum* has exhibited antique furniture, porcelain, silver, etc from the 17th–19th centuries in the rooms.

Treptow-Köpenick – once industrial section, now a green lung

The 2001 merger of Treptow and Köpenick for administrative purposes created the district covering the biggest area in the city, 168 km² (area of greater Berlin: 891 km²). This section, bisected by the Spree, is enlivened by the contrast between an industrial landscape from the 1870s boom and a diverse urban recreational area. In the GDR era the biggest East Berlin industrial section, Treptow-Köpenisck is still full of derelict factories and industrial facilities. But it has been growing into a modern service and information sector area. The change is noticeable in **Adlershof**, where a university campus, a technology park and a media city make for a creative environment.

Extensive *parks* and *woodland* represent the other face of Treptow-Köpenick, exemplified by the spacious *Stadtforst* surrounding the *Müggelberge* (elevation 115 m). The district also boasts 165 kilometres of waterways and seven lakes inviting exploration by excursion boat. The banks of the Spree and **Müggelsee**, Berlin's largest body of water, are dotted with traditional inns where day trippers can eat Bockwurst and potato salad washed down with a 'Molle', vernacular for draught beer. The most rewarding of the fifteen sections of the district to visit is **Köpenick**. The Old Town boasts a Neo-Gothic town hall and the Baroque **Schloss Köpenick** palace, reopened in 2004, is a stellar attraction for art lovers.

57 Altstadt Köpenick

The Old Town of Köpenick is the setting of the world-famous Köpenickiade.

Alt-Köpenick 21
S3 Köpenick, then Tram 62, 63, 68 to Schlossplatz, Bus 164, X69, M69, 269

Köpenick was a town in its own rights for a long time. After all, it is nearly four centuries older than Berlin. In the 9th century Slav fishermen settled at the confluence of the Dahme and Spree. A prince named **Jaczo de Copanic** built a fortified keep there in the first half of the 12th century but it was soon razed by the Ascanians under Albrecht the Bear.

Cöpenick and its southern suburb of *Kietz* were first mentioned in records dating from 1209. It was incorporated as a town in 1232. Its economy was based on *fishing* and, increasingly, on tanning as well as wool and silk weaving, the latter

Köpenick Town Hall is an authentic gem of Brandburg brick Gothic architecture

*They shouted it from the rooftops:
'The Captain from Köpenick was fortunate
as a soldier but without bearing arms'*

The Captain from Köpenick

In spring 1906 **Wilhelm Voigt**, a fifty-seven-year-old cobbler from Tilsit with a record of petty crime landed in Berlin to seek his fortune. There he succeeded in pulling off a spectacular coup on 16 October 1906: purchasing the uniform of an imperial guards officer from a Potsdam flea market for 20 Reichsmark, he commandeered unquestioning soldiers at the Wedding Neue Wache and took them on a suburban train to Köpenick. At the town hall there, he invoked an urgent 'Cabinet decree' to have the mayor, Dr. Georg Langerhans, Senior Secretary of State Rosenkranz and Treasurer von Wiltberg arrested, helped himself to 4000 Reichsmark from the city coffers replete with a receipt and vanished without anyone lifting a finger to stop him.

Everyone was amused at the **escapade** because no one had ever made such a fool of the Prussian authorities so impudently. Ten days after the coup Voigt was arrested and sentenced to four years in prison. Pardoned by the Kaiser two years later, Voigt made money with his story. After publishing his **autobiography**, 'Mein Lebensbild' (1909), he travelled round the world with a circus as the 'Captain from Köpenick' before settling in Luxemburg to enjoy his earnings. However the galloping inflation after the First World War soon cost Wilhelm Voigt the fortune he had honestly earned. He died destitute in 1922 and is buried in a pauper's grave in the Notre Dame cemetery in Luxemburg.

The writer **Carl Zuckmayer** (1896–1977) made a popular vernacular play of the story. The 1956 film by Helmut Käutner based on it starred Heinz Rühmann in the title role as 'Der Hauptmann von Köpenick', immortalizing the poor cobbler who had masqueraded as a Prussian officer. The coup is re-enacted as the **Köpenickiade** in its original setting in front of Köpenick Town Hall every We and Sa at 11 am as a 20-minute piece of lively street theatre to the accompaniment of singing and some snappy Prussian goose-stepping.

trades introduced by the numerous Huguenot refugees fleeing persecution in France who settled here in the 17th and 18th centuries. Since there was no lack of water in Köpenick, it was 'Berlin's washhouse' in the 19th century, home to four hundred laundries, followed by dyers and dry cleaners. Not until 1920 was the independent little industrial city at the gates of the capital incorporated in Greater Berlin.

The Old Town of Köpenick is dominated by the **Rathaus** (1901–04). Built in the Brandenburg brick Neo-Gothic style, the town hall boasts a handsome, five-part decorative gable and a clock tower 54 m high. In 1906 the coup pulled off by Wilhelm Voigt, the self-styled Captain from Köpenick, made this town hall world-famous. Next to the entrance portal a life-size statue of the impostor Voigt (1996, Spartak Babajanan) recalls the *Köpenickiade*, as the escapade is called. In the former treasury room on the ground floor of the town hall, a permanent exhibition (daily 10 am–6 pm) is devoted to Köpenick's most famous person.

The **Köpenick Blues and Jazz Festival** is held in the town hall courtyard from June to August each summer. The little stage in the vaulted Ratskeller (Phone: 030/655 51 78, www.ratskellerkoepenick.

de) has made a name for itself among aficionados of jazz.

The alleys around the town hall entice visitors with the attractive **Kolonistenhäuser**, mostly single-storey houses dating from the 17th and 18th centuries. Huguenots living in them then were exempt from taxes and conscription into the army. After years of persecution in their native France, they could live in peace for the first time. The old street name, '**Freiheit**', refers to their new-found freedom. Paradoxically, the prison was in the courtyard of the old district court (now board of trade and commerce) at No. 16 Freiheit. From a small platform outside, you can look into the 'Captain's cell', in which Wilhelm Voigt was incarcerated. It has been recreated as a tourist attraction. A charming example of Frederician Rococo is the mid-18th-century **Anderson'sches Palais** (Alt-Köpenick 15). The restored building houses offices but is accessible to the public via the hall leading to the Jennrich ceramics workshop in the Hofgarten.

◁ *Music lovers are packed into the Town Hall courtyard during the Köpenick Blues and Jazz Festival*

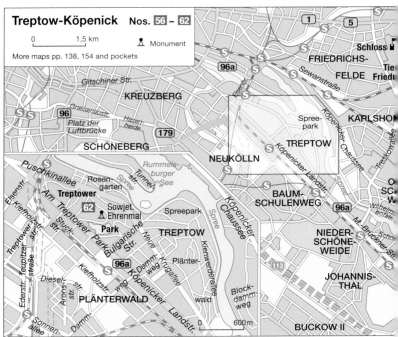

Treptow-Köpenick Nos. **56** – **62**

0   1,5 km   ⚔ Monument

More maps pp. 138, 154 and pockets

Gitschiner Str.

Gneisenaustr.

KREUZBERG

96

Platz der
Luftbrücke

Hasen-
heide

179

SCHÖNEBERG

Puschkinallee

Rosen-
garten

Rummels-
burger
See

Tunnel

Spree

96a

Eisenb.

Sewanstraße

FRIEDRICHS-
FELDE

Tie
Friedr

1

5

Schloss

Spree-
park

Köpenicker Chaussee

KARLSHO

TREPTOW

Köpenicker Landstr.

Spree

Treptowallee

NEUKÖLLN

Elsenstr.

Am Treptower Park

Treptower
str.

Teupitzer
str.

Stuck
str.

Bulgarische
Str.

Neue

Krugallee

Kiefholzstr.

Arons
str.

Köpenicker Landstr.

Diesel
str.

Treptower

62 Sowjet.
⚔ Ehrenmal

Park

TREPTOW

Spreepark

Plänter-

Köpenicker

Chaussee

Spree

Kiefholzstr.

Damm-
weg

Plänter-
wald

Block-
damm-
weg

96a

Kiefwerderallee

BAUM-
SCHULENWEG

96a

Wilhelm-
inenstr.

M. Brückenstr.

Schne

NIEDER-
SCHÖNE-
WEIDE

113

O
SC
W

JOHANNIS-
THAL

PLÄNTERWALD

Sonnen-
allee

Damm-

0   600m

BUCKOW II

Have a look at the oval stairwell with its curving carved wooden stairs.

At Alter Markt near the town hall, the **Heimatmuseum** (Phone: 030/617 23 35, Tu/We 10 am–4.30 pm, Th 10 am–6 pm, Sa 2 pm–6 pm), drawing on archaeological finds, maps, records and extensive photo and press archives, informs about the city's history. The meticulously presented collection is in a half-timbered house dating from 1665. Originally part of an urban manor, it was later used as a brewery, school and almshouse.

At Platz des 23. April on the Old Spree, a 6-m-high granite monument (1969, Walter Sutkowski) commemorates the **Köpenick Week of Bloodshed** in June 1933, when SA men captured and tortured more than five hundred opponents of National Socialism. Ninety-one captives died, twenty-three of them in this square.

The **Fischerkietz** section across from the Old Town boasts attractively restored streets full of old single-storey houses in which fishermen once lived. Here you can swim in the Dame at Berlin's oldest **River Baths** (Phone: 030/65 88 00 94) still in existence, where 50 m of man-made sandy beach, inflated crocodiles and boats for hire guarantee summer fun.

58 Schloss Köpenick

Baroque splendour with exquisite interiors.

Schlossinsel
Phone: 030/266 29 02
www.smb.museum
Tu–Su 10 am–6 pm
S3 Köpenick, then Tram 62, 63, 68, Bus 164, X69, M69, 269
S47 Spindlersfeld, then Tram 60, 61, Bus 167

Extensively restored since 1994 and re-opened in May 2004, Köpenick Palace boasts some of the capital's most magnificent Baroque architecture. A true **Wasserschloss**, it is in an idyllic setting on the Schlossinsel in the river Dahme to the south of Köpenick Old Town. A narrow wooden bridge joins it to the mainland. By the 9th century a moated keep stood here, which Joachim II, Elector of Brandenburg had replaced by a moated castle in 1558. It owes its present appearance to the Great Elector, who had it renovated as a **country house** (1677–90) for his son, who would become King Friedrich I. Its architect was Dutch, Rutger van Langervelt, who was also a painter. He

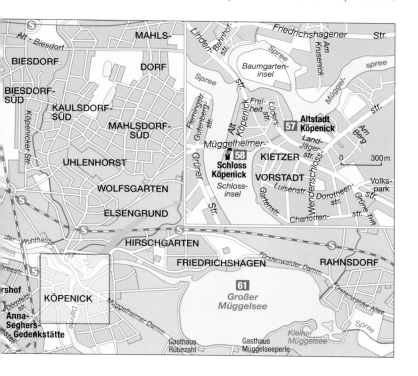

Since it underwent extensive alterations in 1677–90, Schloss Köpenick has exemplified the assured, massive Dutch Baroque style of architecture

designed a three-storeyed building with a frontispiece finished off by a round gable. In 1682–85 Arnold Nering added an impressive Baroque palace chapel.

The palace was later used by princes' widows as a dower house, changed hands several times and figured variously as a prison, student dormitory and, after 1945, housed the GDR folk art collections. In 1963 the Museum for the Decorative and Applied Arts (East) moved in. An exhibi-

Silver on show in the Schloss Armorial Hall

tion in the rooms on the *lower floor* surveys architectural and settlement history. The other rooms once again house a branch of the reunited **Kunstgewerbemuseum** although the main decorative and applied arts collections are at the Kulturforum [see No. 83].

Under the heading 'The art of the Renaissance, Baroque and Rococo Interior' the collection at Schloss Köpenick is presented in an exhibition of modern design surveying a cross-section of court and middle-class lifestyles and formal interiors from the 16th to the 18th centuries. Roughly 600 exhibits are distributed over 1500 m² exhibition space comprising twenty-one rooms sumptuously decorated with Baroque stuccowork. Painted ceilings, silk tapestries, beautiful chandeliers and sconces and especially the **panelling** and **wainscoting** are superb.

On the *ground floor* the formal Haldensteiner Prunkstube (1548) superlatively exemplifies the perfection attained in Renaissance art of intarsia. No less splendid are the panelling and wainscoting of the adjacent room from Schloss Höllrich in Lower Franconia. Medallions, some of them silvered, with armorial bearings are set into its coffered ceiling (1555).

The *1st Upper Floor* displays exquisite German Renaissance and Rococo furniture. Highlights include an Augsburg bureau-cabinet (ca 1650) of lustrous ebony decorated with gilt metal mounts and inlay. In the rooms to the left of the staircase, the lemon yellow *Lacquer Cabinet* (1740–50) from Palazzo Graneri in Turin, Italy, documents the chinoiserie craze that swept 18th-century Europe.

The *2nd Upper Floor* features the Baroque *cabinet of mirrors* (1724/25) from Schloss Wiesentheid in Lower Franconia. It boasts a sumptuously ornamental stucco ceiling and its walls and floors are decorated with ornate marquetry in pewter, mother-of-pearl, walnut, poplar and other hardwoods. Passing the magnificent sideboard from the Basle Saffron Guild, you reach the *Grand Silver Sideboard* (ca 1698); the nine sets of pouring vessels here were part of the Brandenburg-Prussian state treasure. The main room at Schloss Köpenick is the **Armorial Hall**, lavishly decorated in Baroque stuccowork by Giovanni Caroveri of the Ticino about 1685. Eighteen herms on pilasters articulate the rectangular room. The one hundred and sixty-piece *banquet service* (1767/68) from the Breslau Stadtschloss at the centre is its sole exhibit.

Other fine pieces of Frederician porcelain can be admired in the Study Collections in the *attic*. The collections also include glass, silver, pewter and brass. As an added attraction, the attic affords glimpses of the roof-truss construction and lovely views across the **Palace Garden**, which abounds in ornamental statuary. It was laid out on English lines about 1690, with rhododendrons and old trees fram-

Baroque forms also dominate the Köpenick Castle chapel, which is a later addition

ing the lawn. Venerable trees include an elm that is three hundred and fifty years old and a Black Walnut that has lived for one hundred and fifty years.

On the eastern shore of the island, the Baroque **Chapel** (Su 10 am mass), consecrated in 1685, was designed by Johann Arnold Nering (1659–1695), the leading exponent of Brandenburg Baroque. The exterior sports Ionic pilasters with sandstone figures of the four Evangelists. Memorable interior features include the richly carved pulpit and ceiling paintings by Giovanni Caroveri.

For urgent reasons of state

The **Royal Court Martial** convened in the Armorial Hall of Köpenick Palace on 28 October 1730 to pass sentence on Crown Prince Friedrich, who would become King Frederick the Great. His crime was having tried to flee the severe regimen imposed by his father, the 'Soldier King' Friedrich Wilhelm I, by escaping to England with Lieutenant Hans Hermann von Katte, who was presumably his lover. In a trial meant to set a **precedent**, the two young people were condemned to die. The king pardoned the crown prince but not von Katte. Frederick's punishment consisted in having to watch the execution of his friend.

59 Adlershof

Science and technology park.

www.adlershof.de
S45, S46, S8, S85, S9 Adlershof

The grounds covering 420 ha in the south-east of Treptow-Köpenick came from a manor established in 1754, with a plantation of mulberry trees whose leaves were to be used in the *breeding of silkworms* in what was then the suburb of Adlershof. The attempt failed and it remained quiet at the site until Germany's first aerodrome, **Motorflugplatz Johannisthal-Adlershof**, opened on 9 September 1909. Some of the old runways are now being converted to a nature reserve and landscaped park. The rest of the property has become the **Wissenschafts-**

A great place to be – a lakeside restaurant by the Müggelsee

und Wirtschaftsstadt Adlershof (WiStA) since German unification. The Adlershof Science and Commercial City is home to firms in the technology sector, supplemented by Humboldt University science departments, non-university research institutes and *Media City Adlershof*, where cinema films, TV shows and audiobooks are produced. Comprising 645 businesses, a workforce of roughly 10 000 and 7000 students, Adlershof is one of the world's fifteen largest science and technology parks.

The most striking building is the **Innovation Centre for Photonics** in Rudower Chaussee. A three-storeyed glass palace with coloured blinds, built in 1996–98, it was designed by architects Louisa Hutton and Matthias Sauerbruch. It is called the 'Amoeba' because of its fluid curvilinear form.

60 Anna-Seghers-Gedenkstätte

A piece of literary Berlin.

Anna-Seghers-Straße 81
Phone: 0 30/677 47 25
Tu/We 10 am–4 pm, Th 10 am–6 pm
S45, S46, S8, S85, S9 Adlershof

The street named after Anna Seghers (1900–1983) was still called Volkswohlstraße when the writer lived here from 1955. After her death, her flat was opened to the public as the Anna-Seghers-Gedenkstätte. Two rooms of the *memorial* contain simple 1950s-style furnishings, a Remington typewriter on the desk and a library of 9000 volumes attesting to the lifetime of demanding intellectual work led by this committed woman of letters. Her novel, 'Das Siebte Kreuz' ('The Seventh Cross') was one of the most internationally successful works of German exile literature and contributed substantially after the war to enlightening the world on National Socialism and its causes.

61 Müggelsee

Berlin's biggest bath-tub.

S3 Friedrichshagen or Rahnsdorf,
Tram 60, 61, 87, 88, Bus 161

Großer Müggelsee and its eastern appendage, **Kleiner Müggelsee** are the most popular places for a day trip in East Berlin and, after Wannsee and Tegeler See, the city's biggest *aquatic sports centre*. Fed by the Spree, the lakes cover an area 4.5 km long and 2.5 km wide between Köpenick and Rahnsdorf. The largely undeveloped shores of Großer Müggelsee are fringed with extensive stands of maple, alder and conifers.

A good place to start off on a steamboat excursion is the former spinning village of **Friedrichshagen**, where the Müggelspree flows out of the north-western tip of the lake. Excursion boats leave the Müggelpark quay for one-hour tours of the lake. From the Friedrichshagen north shore, pedestrians reach the western shore of the lake via the 120-m-long *Spree Tunnel*, built in 1926. Technology freaks will be interested in the *Museum im Wasserwerk* (Phone: 030/86 44 76 95, March–Oct. Tu–Fr 10 am–4 pm, Su 10 am–5 pm, Nov.–Feb. Tu–Fr 10 am–3 pm, Su 10 am–4 pm) on the eastern outskirts of Friedrichshagen. A Neo-Gothic brick building (1893) by Richard Schulze houses exhibits dealing with the history of the Berlin waterworks.

Rahnsdorf on the north-east shore of Müggelsee is still quite rural. The *village church* (1887) designed by Friedrich Adler forms the centre of the horseshoe-shaped settlement around a green. Canoeing through **Neu-Venedig**, a labyrinth of five narrow canals laid out in the 1920s and spanned by fourteen bridges, is fun. Weeping willows on the banks conceal idyllic waterfront properties with arbours and boat-houses. In the late 19th century, attractive *colonies of villas* in the country-house style were built on undeveloped land in Neu-Rahnsdorf (now Wilhelmshagen) and Hessenwinkel. Fans of swimming and sunbathing are advised to try the **Strandbad Müggelsee** (Phone: 030/648 77 77) that opened in 1912 on the Fürstenwald Embankment. Replete with beach umbrellas and basket chairs, the bathing area also has a section for nudists. The windsurfing is good here and there is also a *Surfing and Sailing School* (Phone: 030/648 15 80).

The gently rounded summits and wooded slopes of the **Müggelberge** 'range', Berlin's highest, rise to an elevation of 115 m above sea-level on the southern shore of the lake. From the Müggelseeperle and Rübezahl quays, each with restaurants, hikers can follow good paths to *Köpenick Heath* and the *Berliner Stadtforst* between the lake and the 'mountains'. A magnet for day trippers is the *Müggelturm*, a 30-m-high tower built in 1960 to replace one that had burnt down. The observation platform affords a sweeping panorama of the lake, the city and the countryside. When the visibility is good, you can see as far as Teufelsberg in the west.

The bronze soldier of the Soviet Monument ▷ is portrayed smashing a Swastika

62 Treptower Park

Green lung in the south-east with public observatory and Soviet monument.

Puschkinallee
S41, S42, S8, S85, S9 Treptower Park, Tram 87, Bus 161, S8, S85, S9 Plänterwald, Bus 166, 167, 177

This public park stretches for more than 85 ha from south-east of Treptower Park S-Bahn station to Bulgarische Straße and between the Spree and the road along Treptower Park. Through the northern third of it runs Puschkinallee, a road lined with plane trees.

Treptower Park was laid out from 1876 following a proposal made by the celebrated physiologist and physician *Rudolf Virchow* (1821–1902). The thick clumps of trees, playing fields and open meadow, flower beds and large carp ponds he loved are still there. Gustav Meyer, head landscape architect and a pupil of Lenné's, played a paramount role in designing the gardens in 1888.

Centrally located in the east of Treptower Park is the **Sowjetisches Ehrenmal** (1947–49). Designed in austere geometry by Jakov Belopolsky, an architect, and Yevgeny Vucheritch, a sculptor, the monumental Soviet memorial commemo-

An oasis of green – despite the extensive industrial facilities surrounding it, Treptower Park, Berlin's second biggest park, can be really idyllic

rates 5000 Soviet soldiers who fell in the Second World War and are buried here. Two portals with round arches lead to the area from north and south. Weeping birches and granite slabs bearing war scenes in relief line the main path. At the centre of the area a stair leads up to a marble cenotaph crowning a low hill. It is surmounted by a colossal statue of a Soviet solder, 11.6 m high and weighing 70 tonnes. A child nestles trustingly against his left shoulder while he shatters a swastika with a sword he is holding in his right hand.

Not far to the north is the **Archenhold-Sternwarte** (Phone: 030/534 80 80, www. astw.de, We–Su 2 pm–4.30 pm, guided tours Th 8 pm, Sa/Su 3 pm), Germany's oldest public observatory. In 1896 the astronomer *Friedrich Simon Archenhold* (1861–1939) first publicly demonstrated the movable telescope he had developed here. Twenty-one metres long and weighing 130 tonnes, it is still the world's largest telescope. Through a massive lens 68 cm in diameter, star-gazers can observe the heavenly bodies at a magnification of x 210. In 1959 a **Zeiss small planetarium** with an 8-m observation dome was added to it. A mirror telescope (500 mm) and a solar observation cabinet are among the facilities on the premises. The Big Zeiss Planetarium [see No. 53] in the Prenzlauer Berg district also belongs to the Archenhold Observatory. Incidental-

ly, the most famous visiting lecturer at the observatory was *Albert Einstein*, who spoke to a packed auditorium here on his theory of relativity on 2 February 1915.

In the **Astronauts' Grove** close by, the successes scored by Soviet space exploration are acclaimed. There a bust of the GDR astronaut Sigmund Jähn (*1937) commemorates the first German to fly in space, in a Soviet Soyus Rocket on 26 August 1978.

To the north of the observatory is **Gasthaus Zenner** (Alt-Treptow 14–17, Phone: 030/533 73 70), an inn on the banks of the Spree that looks back on a long tradition. Built in 1821/22 by Carl Friedrich Langhans, a pupil of Schinkel's, in the Neo-Classical style, it was rebuilt after it had been destroyed in the Second World War. Seating 1900 guests, 1500 of them outdoors, Zenner is one of Berlin's biggest garden restaurants. The beer garden is one of the best places to watch *Treptow in Flames*, the spectacular fireworks show put on annually in June from the offshore **Insel der Jugend**. This artificial island in the Spree (once Abbey Island) has been linked to the mainland since 1916 by a 76-m-long steel and concrete bridge flanked by handsome towers topped with half-timbered gables. The little oval island, consisting of a green surrounded by a belt of trees, is, as its name indicates, a popular place for young people to hang out.

If you get out of the suburban train at S-Bahnhof Treptower Park and look north, the first things you notice are the **Treptowers** on the Elsenbrücke. With thirty floors and 125 m high, the structure is the tallest Berlin office high-rise. The service-sector complex, built in 1995–98, is based on a design by Gerhard Spangenberg, who also integrated the brick buildings that once belonged to the electricity concern AEG into the concept. In front of the Elsenbrücke, the **Molecule Men** (1999), an installation 30 m high and weighing 45 tonnes by the American sculptor Jonathan Borofsky, rises out of the Spree. Three men facing each other and made of perforated aluminium, they symbolize the point at which the old districts of Kreuzberg, Friedrichshain and Treptow converge.

Right next to the S-Bahnhof is **Spreehafen Treptow**, the river port from which excursion boats depart for Charlottenburg, Köpenick and cross Großer Müggelsee to the Woltersdorfer Lock. From here you can take an eight-hour cruise around Berlin.

To the west, towards Kreuzberg, one of four Wall watch-towers left in Berlin stands in a little park known as *Schlesischer Busch*. During the cold war, 17 kilometres of the Wall ran through Treptow. The square **Watch-tower**, 9 m high and of the BT 9 type, has been restored and re-

Romance glimmers on the old district boundary – the Molecule Men in the evening

opened in 2005 as an exhibition venue by the **Kunstfabrik am Flutgraben** (Phone: 030/53 01 32 80, www.kunstfabrik.org, Th–Su 2 pm–7 pm) under the motto 'one last check'. The works shown here deal with the theme of borders.

The old 1916 bridge is a fittingly vibrant link with the Island of Youth

Around Potsdamer Platz – the city's new centre

The seat of government and an amusement quarter until the Second World War, Potsdamer Platz spent several years as a gigantic construction site after reunifaction. Now, thanks to its ambitious urban architecture, it is one of Berlin's most popular places with sightseers. Set at the heart of the metropolis, it was once home to Europe's heaviest traffic. Before the war it was criss-crossed by six hundred trams an hour and hotels and restaurants lured visitors and Berliners alike. The square has long since been reawakened to new life and there are still some historic buildings recalling the glamour of the Empire as well as the cosmopolitan urbanity of the Weimar era amid all the ultra-modern architecture.

63 Potsdamer Platz

The famous square at the centre of Berlin is emerging as an oasis for sightseers and shoppers.

S1, S2, S26 and U2 Potsdamer Platz
Bus M41, 123, 148, 200

In the mid-1990s still one of the world's biggest construction sites, Potsdamer Platz is a new quarter of the city covering roughly 100 000 m² in area. It is home to office buildings, dwellings, hotels, shopping malls, cultural facilities and attracts 100 000 visitors a day.

After four years of building activity, the first new building project was opened for business in October 1998. Covering 70 000m², **DaimlerChrysler City** (architects: Renzo Pinao, Christoph Kohlbecker et al) is a shopping passage with more than a hundred shops as well as a musical theatre stage, a casino and a cinema centre. In June 2000 the **Sony-Center** (surface area roughly 25 000m²) followed. Helmut Jahn designed an ensemble of seven glass-and-steel buildings for cinemas, restaurants, the Berlin Filmmuseum and Sony's European headquarters around a spectacular forum with a tent roof.

A city in the city has grown up around Potsdamer Platz – DaimlerChrysler-City and Marlene-Dietrich-Platz

The crowning touch on the north side of the square is the **Beisheim Center** (2004), a retro tribute to the Chicago School style comprising office blocks and flats, two hotels and five town houses with a view of the Tiergarten, all financed by Otto Beisheim, founder of the Metro chain.

But back to the beginnings: in the late 18th century Potsdamer Platz was still a crossroads with inns frequented by excursionists, it did not come into its own until the age of industrialisation. By the 1920s, however, this had become Europe's most heavily travelled urban traffic junction, with five streets leading into it and crossed by forty public tram lines as well as subway and urban rail trains arriving and departing under ground. From 1924 Germany's first traffic lights ensured that traffic flowed smoothly here.

At the same time Potsdamer Platz was growing into an *amusement quarter* and *shopping district*. The first venue here was **Haus Vaterland**, with about three thousand guests frequenting its numerous halls. One met for five-o'clock tea at hotels such as the Esplanade and the Fürstenhof, went to Weinhaus Huth to drink a glass of good wine and the **Vox-Haus** made headlines with the first experiments in radio. However, the bombs that rained down on Potsdamer Platz during the Second World War and the subsequent partition of the city turned it into a dreary, burnt-out area. After the Wall was built, visitors from all over the world climbed a wooden observation tower to be informed about the border and where the Wall ran. Only a few buildings have survived the bombs and the

building of the Wall, including **Weinhaus Huth** (1912), established in 1871 where Potsdamer Straße fed into Potsdamer Platz. The tavern was once frequented by such celebrated intellectuals as Theodor Fontane und Adolph von Menzel. At one time, incidentally, Alois Hitler – a half-brother of the dictator – was a waiter here. Now the Weinhaus is integrated into the DaimlerChrysler-City complex.

Hotel Esplanade (1907/08) in Bellevuestraße used to be one of the capital's most elegant hotels. The luxurious furnishings of its roughly six hundred rooms were not just popular with the landed aristocracy: when Kaiser Wilhelm II wanted a night out with the boys, he would check into the *Kaisersaal*, which was designed to his specifications for the purpose. The actresses Asta Nielsen and Greta Garbo stayed at the Esplanade when they were in Berlin and so did Charlie Chaplin at a later date. The celebrated film director *Billy Wilder* began his career here – as a dancer hired by the management to start the ball rolling at the popular Esplanade tea dances. A part of what had once been a complex with a floor area of 1600m^2 survived the wartime bombing. For a long time afterwards the ruins were used as a film set, where 'Steiner II' starring Curd Jürgens and Wim Wenders' film 'Himmel über Berlin' were

A dark past

The west side of **Wilhelmstraße** was lined in the 18th century with the palaces of the nobility. During the imperial era, the Weimar Republic and the Third Reich, Germany was governed from this street. Reich Chancellor Bismarck lived here and the presidents of the Weimar Republic, Ebert and Hindenburg, had their offices in Wilhelmstraße.

During the NS era many buildings were remodelled. No. 61 a, extended to incorporate the buildings at Nos. 8 and 9 Wilhelmplatz, housed Goebbels' **Ministry for Enlightenment and Propaganda**. It is the only building in Wilhelmstraße besides the former Ministry of Culture and the Ministry of Justice to have survived from that era. The former Reich Chancellery at the corner of Voßstraße/Wilhelmstraße was remodelled by Albert Speer into the **New Reich Chancellery**, 430 m long and finished by 1939. Behind it sprawled a vast bunker complex with a hospital ward, workshops and Adolf Hitler's **Führer Bunker**. This is where Hitler, his wife Eva Braun and the Goebbels family committed suicide in the last days of the war. The bunker was blown up in 1950 and the ground above it smoothed over. Early in the 1990s members of the State Archaeological Office found the entrance to the bunker that belonged to Hitler's bodyguard. Now a protected historic monument, it is not open to the public.

made. The Esplanade looked back on such a rich tradition that it continued to play a leading role when Potsdamer Platz was given a makeover: it was integrated into the Sony-Center and is now part of the **Filmmuseum Berlin** (Phone: 030/300 90 30, www.filmmuseum-berlin.de, Tu–Su 10 am–6 pm, Th 10 am–8 pm). This repository of historic films takes visitors time-travelling through German cinematic history and the legacies of such famous actresses and actors as Asta Nielsen and Heinz Rühmann.

The location of the **Kaisersaal** in the hotel was shifted by 75 m to reopen in 2002 as a restaurant [see p. 167] featuring German and French cuisine with a large wine cellar.

64 Leipziger Straße

Memories of a glorious past.

S1, S2, S26 and U2 Potsdamer Platz, U2 Mohrenstraße
Bus M41, 123, 148, 200

In the reign of Friedrich II, Leipziger Straße and **Leipziger Platz** were an elegant residential area. By 1900 this was Berlin's leading shopping district. After the Second World War, the area declined. Only the octagonal layout of Leipziger Platz was marked by cobble-stones. Meanwhile new buildings have gone up and the square has been replanted.

At 3 Leipziger Straße stands the former *Preußisches Herrenhaus* (1899–1904), the upper chamber of the Prussian parliament. The **Bundesrat**, the upper house of the Federal German parliament, now convenes here. In 1848 Prussia's first constitution provided for a bicameral legislature: the Preußisches Herrenhaus, reserved for the house of Hohenzollern and representatives of the court, and the Preußischer Landtag. In the GDR era, the *Academy of Sciences* was housed at No. 3.

Next door, No. 4, was the address of the *Königliche Porzellan Manufaktur* (KPM, Royal Porcelain Factory) from 1761 to 1873. *Wertheim* used to be across the street. Designed by Alfred Messel (from 1853) and enlarged until 1900, it was Germany's first department store selling a wide range of goods under one roof. Hit by bombs in the Second World War, the building was demolished in 1955.

65 Museum für Kommunikation

World's oldest post office museum, now Museum for Communications.

Leipziger Straße 16
Phone: 030/20 29 40
www.museumsstiftung.de
Tu–Fr 9 am–5 pm,
Sa/Su/hols. 11 am–7 pm
U2 Mohrenstraße, U2, U6 Stadtmitte
Bus 148, 200

This impressive Wilhelmine Neo-Baroque building at the corner of Leipziger Straße and Mauerstraße houses the Museum for Communications, founded back in 1872 as a post office museum. Its interactive displays deal with all areas of modern communication as well as a collection of antique telegraph equipment, unique early telephones, Berlin's first telephone call-box (1929), historic postal and traffic maps and a rich collection of postage stamps. A must for philatelists, the collection boasts such rare items as the Red and Blue Mauritius and the 'Cosmos Stamp' that accompanied the astronauts into space.

66 Berliner Abgeordnetenhaus & Detlev-Rohwedder-Haus

Two buildings steeped in history.

Niederkirchnerstraße and Wilhelmstraße
S1, S2, S26 and U2 Potsdamer Platz
Bus M41, 123, 148, 200

Restored as the **Berlin Abgeordnetenhaus** where parliamentarians meet, the former *Preußischer Landtag* (1892–97, Friedrich Schulze) looks back on a turbulent history. In 1918 the revolutionary workers' and soldiers' councils met here. Göring turned it into the House of the Aviator in 1936. During the GDR era it was the seat of the Minister President.

The former *Reich Aviation Ministry* (1935/36, Ernst Sagebiel) nearby was the first Third Reich building on a grand scale. On 7 October 1949 the GDR People's Chamber met here to draft a constitution as the cornerstone of a second German state. Later it was the GDR House of Ministries. After reunification, the *Treuhandanstalt* moved in, renaming it in 1992 after its president, **Detlev Rohwedder**, murdered in 1991. Since 1999 the building has housed the *Federal Ministry of Finance*.

67 Topographie des Terrors

Documentation of the Nazi reign of terror in the Third Reich.

Niederkirchnerstraße 8
Phone: 030/25 48 67 03
www.topographie.de
May–Sept. daily 10 am–8 pm,
Oct.–April daily 10 am–6 pm or sunset
S1, S2, S26 Anhalter Bahnhof
Bus M29, M41, 123

The Topography of Terror Memorial in an open area between Martin-Gropius-Bau, Niederkirchnerstraße and Wilhelmstraße is to recall the atrocities committed by

Paying lip service: East Side Gallery with the famous brotherly kiss between Erich Honecker and Brezhnev

Tracking down the stones

No one knows whether they are genuine: stones of all sizes are still sold, either framed or loose, that are 'guaranteed' to be from the **Berliner Mauer**. Even years ago the price of a genuine piece of the Berlin Wall – once a bad omen, now a coveted **souvenir** – supposedly ran to 25 000 €!

The Wall, which ran for 41.5 km around West-Berlin, lost no time in vanishing after 3 October 1990. Large sections, which are now protected historic monuments, still stand at the following sites: about 70 m in Bernauer Straße between Ackerstraße and Bergstraße (Wall Memorial, U8 Bernauer Straße), 200 m in Niederkirchnerstraße (U2 Potsdamer Platz) and 200 m along Scharnhorststraße in the Invalidenfriedhof (U6 Zinnowitzer Straße). The **East Side Gallery**, also known as the Wall Gallery, is right on the Spree, not far from Ostbahnhof (Mühlenstraße; S5, S7, S75, S9 and U1 Warschauer Straße). This part of the Wall is 1.3 km long and was decorated after the turnaround by artists from East and West. The most photographed motif on it is undoubtedly the **Kiss of Brotherhood between Honecker and Brezhnev**. An ironic, decoratively colourful, allusion to the Wall's history lining the motorway but, unfortunately, crumbling fast.

A lot of talking goes on here – where the Berlin parliamentarians meet at Niederkirchner-strasse was once the seat of the Prussian Landtag

the Nazis. While Prussia was a kingdom and during the Wilhelmine Empire, the Prinz Albrecht Palais, the Prinz Albrecht Hotel and a school for the applied and decorative arts occupied the site. The Nazis had their *Command Headquarters of Death* here. This was where Hitler's minions planned the concentration camps, co-ordinated SS and police deployment, interrogated and tortured opponents of the regime. Heinrich Himmler's **Reich Security Main Office** was housed in the hotel, the **SS Security Service** under Reinhard Heydrich occupied the Prinz-Albrecht Palais and the **Gestapo** (Geheime Staatspolizei, Secret Police) was lodged in the school. The war-damaged buildings were demolished in the mid-1950s. The area was converted into an open-air exhibition in 1987. Building began in 1995 on a new **Documentation Centre**. It was supposed to incorporate remaining historic structures and pieces of the Berlin Wall. Because costs had 'exploded' by 2004, architect Peter Zumthor was asked to leave. Three towers already standing were torn down. In 2005 architects were again asked to compete in submitting plans for the Centre project; construction work is to begin in 2006.

Never to be forgotten: the permanent exhibition 'The Topography of Terror' in the Prinz Albrecht grounds recalls the Nazi atrocities

Unconditional: the place in Berlin-Karlshorst where the surrender of the German Wehrmacht was signed in 1945 is now a memorial

In remembrance

Berlin-Reinickendorf: Hundreds of political prisoners and resistance fighters from across Europe died in a brick shed at Plötzensee Prison between 1933 and 1945, executed by the National Socialists. Since 1952 the **Gedenkstätte Plötzensee** (Hüttigpfad, daily 9 am–5 pm) has commemorated the murdered prisoners.

Berlin-Karlshorst: A barracks which housed the Soviet Command Headquarters at the end of the Second World War. On 8 May 1945 the unconditional surrender of the German Wehrmacht was signed here. At the **Deutsch-Russisches Museum Berlin-Karlshorst** (Tu–Su 10 am–6 pm) more than fifteen thousand documents on the Second World War are on display. Since this is a joint German and Russian museum, there are also exhibits on the Red Army, everyday army life and the internment of prisoners of war.

Berlin-Treptow: If you go to Treptower Park, you can't miss it – the monumental **Sowjetisches Ehrenmal** [see p.79]. The monument was built in 1947–49 as the chief memorial to the Red Army soldiers who fell in the battles for Berlin. At the centre of the memorial an 11.6-m-high figure of a soldier stands holding a child in his left arm and in his right a sword that has smashed a swastika.

Berlin-Tempelhof: The Second World War was over but Soviet troops completely blockaded Berlin between June 1948 and May 1949. The *Berlin Airlift* organised by General Lucius D. Clay (1897–1978) to provision the beleaguered city made Tempelhof the pivot of the metropolis. The **Airlift Monument** (1951) in the square in front of the airport, due to its appearance popularly dubbed the 'hunger rake', symbolizes the three air corridors taken to West Berlin by the 'Raisin Bombers' with three arcs rising towards the west.

Berlin-Schöneberg: A summer day in Berlin. On 26 July 1963 the memorable sentence 'I am a Berliner' resounded in New England-accented German from the balcony of the **Rathaus Schöneberg** (John-F.-Kennedy-Platz). A plaque to the left of the entrance recalls the celebrated speech given by US president *John F. Kennedy* (1917–1963). Inside the Rathaus the exhibition **'Struggle for Freedom'** now honours *Willy Brandt* (1913–1992), who for many years was mayor of Berlin and later Federal chancellor. For his efforts to bring about the reunification of Germany and to promote peace both domestically and internationally, he was awarded the Nobel Peace Prize in 1971. Brandt is regarded as one of the most important 20th-century statesmen.

The **Freiheitsglocke** hanging in the 70-m-high tower of the Schöneberg Town Hall is another important symbol of Berlin history. A replica of the Philadelphia Liberty Bell, it was given by the Americans to the people of Berlin in 1950. When it rings daily at 12 noon, it recalls the Berliners' old yearning for a united city.

The sumptuosly decorated façade of the Martin Gropius Building draws liberally on the classical canon of forms

68 Martin-Gropius-Bau

An elegant venue for important international exhibitions.

Niederkirchner Straße 7
Phone: 030/25 48 60
Only opened for rotating exhibitions:
We–Mo 10 am–8 pm
S1, S2, S26 Anhalter Bahnhof,
Bus M29, M41, 123

This handsomely proportioned building in the Neo-Renaissance style (1877–81) was designed by Heino Schmieden and Martin Gropius, a relative of Walter Gropius, the architect who founded the Bauhaus. The building replaced Schinkel's (destroyed) Architecture Academy. Until 1920 it housed the *Royal Museum for the Decorative and Applied Arts*, to inspire Prussian craftsmen by documenting historic products from all over the world. Destroyed in the war, the building was reconstructed in 1979–81. The lightwell, surrounded by two gallery-like mezzanines, is particularly striking. Since the late 1980s and early 1990s, this impressive building has been the venue for international **touring exhibitions**.

The **Werkbund Archives** (Phone: 030/ 25 48 69 00, www.werkbundarchiv-berlin. de), in which historic documents on everyday life in the 20th century are collected, returned in 1999 to the second floor of the Gropius Building, although without exhibition space of their own (access to the archives and library by appointment Mo–Th 9 am–2 pm). In 2006 the archives and the museum are to move to Kreuzberg, 25 Oranienstraße.

The *Berlinische Galerie* [see No. 94] which used to be here has found an attractive new home in Kreuzberg near the Jewish Museum.

69 Ehem. Anhalter Bahnhof

Only a ruin recalls Berlin's most celebrated train station, which always made a splendid backdrop.

Askanischer Platz
S1, S2, S26 Anhalter Bahnhof
Bus M29, M41, 123

As long ago as 1 July 1841 a train drawn by the first locomotive from August Borsig's machine factory left Anhalter Bahnhof for Jüterborg. The station building itself was not completed until 1880. Designed by Heinrich Seidel as a Neo-Renaissance structure with arcades, it had a roof 62.5 m across made of glass and steel, designed by Franz Schwechten, a leading architect of the Wilhelmine era. The Anhalter Station soon became Berlin's number one main-line station: a terminus for trains departing for southern destinations – Dresden, Munich, Rome and Athens. By the mid-1920s trains were arriving and departing from here every few minutes.

The Anhalter Station also has its place in history: in 1889 *Kaiser Wilhelm II* laid on a lot of pomp and circumstance to receive King Umberto of Italy here. The monarchs met in the *Kaiserzimmer*, which was specially decorated and furnished for the purpose. In 1919 thousands welcomed the communist leader *Karl Liebknecht* here on his release from Luckau prison. And an even bigger crowd was on hand in 1938 to welcome Adolf Hitler on his return to Berlin from annexing his native Austria. The Red Army troops reached Anhalter Station on 30 April 1945. The SS tried to stop their advance by blowing up the locks of the nearby Landwehr Canal and the water poured into the S-Bahnhof tunnel in which many people had sought shelter from the bombing. The station building sustained severe damage in the war but it fulfilled its original function until 1952. It was blown up in 1961. All that is left standing is part of the façade.

For strong nerves: the **Berliner Gruselkabinett** (Phone: 030/26 55 55 46, www.gruselkabinett.de, Su–Tu, Th 10 am–7 pm, Fr 10 am–8 pm, Sa 12 noon–8 pm) invites aficionados of horror scenarios to a gruesome visit in the old bunker beneath the Anhalter Station at 23 a Schöneberger Straße.

The station premises are also home to the **Tempodrom** (Möckernstraße 10, Phone: 030/69 53 38 85, www.tempodrom.de), a music and cultural centre that started out near the House of World Cultures but had to relocate when the new government precincts were built.

Bypassed by the traffic now: ruins are all that recall the former Anhalter Bahnhof at Askanischer Platz

Tiergarten, the government precincts and Kulturforum – nature, culture and politics in perfect harmony

The Reichstag and the new government precincts, Schloss Bellevue and the Victory Column – packed with important sights to see, this tour also takes you through the Tiergarten, one of Berlin's most popular recreation parks. A day trip destination in the 19th century, the Tiergarten quarter south of the park went upmarket to become Berlin's most elegant residential section and, by the end of the Second World War, the embassies and consulates were located here. The ambassadors have returned and this section of the capital, with museums and concert halls at the Kulturforum, is also one of the city's most important cultural locales.

70 Reichstag

A building heavily symbolic of German history and the seat of the Deutscher Bundestag, the Federal parliament.

Platz der Republik
Phone: 030/22 73 21 52, 030/22 73 59 08
www.deutscher-reichstag.de
daily 8 am–12 pm, last admission
10 pm. Phone to arrange guided tours by appointment.
S1, S2 Unter den Linden, Bus 100, TXL

When Germany was proclaimed an empire on 18 January 1871, Berlin became the capital of the Reich. The Reichstag, or parliament, temporarily lodged at 74 Leipziger Straße, needed a bigger building more suitable to its function. So a splendid complex, designed by Paul Wallot and measuring 137 m by 97 m, was erected north of the Brandenburg Gate between 1884 and 1894.

Even before it was dedicated on 5 December 1894, the Reichstag made the headlines. Kaiser Wilhelm II, who, incidentally, dubbed this important symbol of the fledgling German parliamentary democracy the 'Reich Monkey House', insisted on the Reichstag dome being lower than the dome on the Berliner Stadtschloss. The planned inscription 'To the German People' was too democratic for the Kaiser. It wasn't added until 1916.

It was from a window of the Reichstag that the Social Democrat Philipp Scheidemann proclaimed the *Weimar Republic* on 9 November 1918. Fifteen years later, in February 1933, the building burnt down. After this assault – imputed to the Communists – Hitler was able to push his *Enabling Act* through the legislature, thus removing all obstacles to the establishment of a Nazi dictatorship. To the Soviet Russians, the Reichstag symbolised Germany so this was where they flew the USSR flag on 30 April 1945 to demonstrate to the world that Hitler's Germany had been defeated.

Between 1957 and 1972 the Reichstag, which had sustained bomb damage, was restored: it provided an assembly hall for party working conferences and committees of the German Bundestag, thirty rooms for special sessions and roughly two hundred offices. The building was often used as a grand backdrop for state occasions or concerts. The **reunification celebration** was held here on 3 October 1990.

However, no event has made the public so aware of the historic significance of the building as the spectacular **Wrapped Reichstag Action** by Christo and Jeanne-Claude in 1995. After the rolls of material were removed, the building was reclad – in scaffolding. Between 1996 and 1999 the Reichstag was converted after plans by the British architect *Sir Norman Foster* in-

The list of sights to see in Berlin is headed by the Reichstag, modernised throughout by Sir Norman Foster and crowned by a 'miracle' of modern architecture – a glass dome affording an insider's view of parliament

to the seat of the **Deutscher Bundestag**, the lower house of the Federal German parliament. It was given a new **glass dome** – where visitors can walk around and observe the Bundestag in session. The Federal government moved from Bonn to Berlin in autumn 1999. Since then hundreds of thousands of visitors have climbed the 50 m up the spiral ramp inside the dome to the observation platform to peer down into the Plenary Session Hall of the Bundestag.

A further highlight is a visit to the *Roof-Garden Restaurant* [see p. 167], where you can enjoy superlative views and excellent food.

71 Regierungsviertel

The new government precincts, the 'Bond of Federation', add a monumental touch to the bend in the Spree.

Spreebogen, Dorotheenstraße, Konrad-Adenauer-Straße, Schiffbauerdamm, Willy-Brandt-Straße
S1, S2, S5, S7, S75, S9 and U6 Friedrichstraße, S1, S2 Unter den Linden
Bus 100, 147, TXL

The most important government buildings stand on the bend in the Spree near the Reichstag and are linked with it by a

system of tunnels. Historic buildings – the Reich President's Palace, the Chamber of Technology and the old Dorotheenstadt bank building – were integrated into the most extensive part of the complex, the **Jakob-Kaiser-Haus** (1997–2000, five teams of architects), lining Dorotheenstraße to the south-east. The complex now comprises eight buildings housing parliamentary committee rooms and offices for members of parliament, the parties and the vice-president of the Bundestag.

Here, as in the gigantic ultra-modern architectural complexes spanning the bend in the Spree like bars north of the Reichstag, the planners have made full use of glass façades and galleries as well as glass-walled rooms to symbolize in architecture the democratic principles of transparency and openness. This was done in the **Paul-Löbe-Haus** (1997–2001, Stephan Braunfels) on the inner bend of the Spree. Berliners say it 'runs on eight cylinders' because of its double comb structure and eight rotundas in the outer courtyards. It houses the offices of members of parliament, twenty-one committee rooms and the great *Europasaal* which figures prominently in the east rotunda. A double-decker bridge across the Spree, which is designed to continue the bar form eastwards, connects the Löbe House with the **Marie-Elisabeth-Lüders-**

Clad all in white – Gerhard Schröder presided over the inauguration ceremony for the new chancellery complex from the Ehrenhof court in front of its main building in May 2001

Haus (1998–2002, Braunfels), which contains the academic services. The separate west rotunda is home to the German Bundestag *Parlamentsbibliothek* (after Washington and Tokyo the third largest legislature library worldwide). Another notable architectural achievement is the neighbouring cubic *Anhörungssaal* for parliamentary hearings. Public space is provided by Spreeplatz at the centre of the complex and a stepped terrace affording a view of the Reichstag.

The **Bundeskanzleramt** (1997–2001, Axel Schultes and Charlotte Franke) is another government building with a view of the Reichstag. The central, 36-m-high *Leitungsgebäude* housing the chancellor's offices and rooms for the cabinet

Openness and transparency – the bold arc of a bridge links the Paul-Löbe-Haus (left) with the Marie-Elisabeth-Lüders-Haus (right) on the opposite bank of the Spree

and executive conferences is flanked by two office wings 18 m high and up to 335 m in length. The lobby of the main Chancellery building opens on to the Ehrenhof, used for important state receptions. At the back are the *Chancellor's Garden* and the *Chancellor's Park*, which can be reached by the Spree bridge at Moabiter Werder. Often criticised as pompous and box-like, the Chancellery complex has been evocatively christened the 'Washing Machine' by Berliners.

72 Haus der Kulturen der Welt

A venue dubbed the 'Pregnant Oyster'.

John-Foster-Dulles-Allee
Phone: 030/39 78 70
www.hkw.de
Tu–Su 10 am–9 pm
Bus 100

The House of World Cultures on the north-eastern fringe of the Tiergarten was the American contribution to the 1957 International Architecture Exhibition and initially featured as a *Congress Hall*. It was designed by Hugh Stubbins, once assistant to Walter Gropius, in collaboration with Werner Düttmann and Franz Mocken. Its location on an artificial lake and its curvilinear roof gave rise to the name 'Pregnant Oyster'. The 1000 steel beams supporting the cantilevered part of the roof rusted through, causing it to collapse in 1980. The hall was reopened in time for the citywide festival in 1987. Now the House of Cultures is the venue for international **touring exhibitions** and **cultural events**. To the left of the hall, the Henry Moore *bronze sculpture* 'Two Forms' (1956) stands in the large artificial pond.

The surroundings of the old Congress Hall are of historical interest: back in the 18th century two Huguenots set up tents here to sell refreshments. In 1844 the *Krollsche Etablissement*, named after its builder, Joseph Kroll, went up on the site, providing amusement for nearly five thousand guests at a time. The building was later taken over by the New Royal Opera House – as the legendary **Kroll Opera**, it was a focal point of Weimar Republic social life. After the Reichstag fire in 1933, the legislators moved into it. Hitler announced the *invasion* of Poland from the building, which was destroyed by bombs in the Second World War. The ruins were demolished in 1956.

Since 1987 the Berlin **Carillon** has been next to the House of World Cultures: a tower clad in black granite, whose *Glockenspiel* rings out daily from a height of 42 m at 12 noon and 6 pm. Weighing 47.7 t, the sixty-eight bells with a tonal range of 5.5 octaves can be played by hand or from a computer-controlled console. This is the biggest and heaviest instrument of its kind in Europe.

The House of World Cultures has long been known as 'The Pregnant Oyster' in the Berlin vernacular. A Henry Moore bronze sculpture (1956) adorns the water basin

Frederick the Great's younger brother lived in this fine building, where the president of the republic now has his office – Schloss Bellevue, set in a lovely park by Spreeweg

73 Tiergarten

 Berlin's favourite park, the city's biggest recreation area at 200 ha.

Straße des 17. Juni
S3, S5, S7, S75, S9 Tiergarten or Bellevue, U9 Hansaplatz, Bus 265, 343

Idyllic stretches of water, ponds and meadows, the many arms of the *Neuer See* with a café and boats for hire as well as many footpaths past monuments to important German poets and composers – the Tiergarten again looks as it used to. After the war the starving Berliners had cut down the trees to plant potatoes and turnips. By 1949, however, governing Mayor Ernst Reuter had given the all-clear for reafforestation of the grounds by planting a symbolic lime (linden) tree.

The history of the Tiergarten goes back to 1527, when the electoral Crown Prince Joachim the Younger had a **zoo** and *pleasure grounds* laid out here for court use as a game reserve. Frederick the Great had the green oasis redesigned as a Baroque garden open to the public. In the 19th century it underwent a further transformation when Peter Joseph Lenné converted it into a landscaped park in the English style.

Straße des 17. Juni, which bisects the Tiergarten, was laid out under the Prince Elector Friedrich III as a link between the Berliner Stadtschloss and Schloss Char-

Architecture triumphant: a view of the Moabiter Ufer with the Sorat Hotel Spree-Bogen (left) and the Federal Ministry of the Interior ▷

lottenburg in 1695. Hitler's pet architect Albert Speer had it widened in 1938 to form an avenue for parades 40 m wide. Renamed after the popular revolt in the GDR in 1953, today the street is still as wide as it was when it was part of 'Germania', Hitler's foray into urban planning on a monumental scale. Where the boulevard meets the Brandenburg Gate stands the **Sowjetisches Ehrenmal** (1946), a 6-m-high figure of a Red Army soldier shouldering his rifle. It is made of marble taken from Hitler's new Reich Chancellery.

74 Schloss Bellevue

The first early Neo-Classical palace from the era of Frederick the Great.

Spreeweg 1
S3, S5, S7, S75, S9 Bellevue and
U9 Hansaplatz, Bus 265, 343

Schloss Bellevue, official residence of the **President of the Federal Republic**, looks back on a long history. In 1710 mulberry trees were still growing here to feed the royal silkworms. A few decades later, Knobelsdorff, Frederick the Great's architect, built himself a house in the park. In 1785 Philip Daniel Boumann erected a country house in the French Baroque style with formal gardens for Augustus Ferdinand of Prussia, youngest brother of Frederick the Great. The Hohenzollerns owned the palace and its park until 1918. Bellevue was reconstructed after the Second World War as the president's Berlin residence. Only the furnishings of the oval *Banquet Hall* (1791) by Carl Gotthard Langhans are original.

Covering 20 ha, the **Schlosspark** was once one of the city's finest parks. The English Garden in the west was reafforested in 1952. The ellipsoid administration building with the **President's Office** (1996–98, Gruber and Kleine-Kraneburg) stands here.

75 Hansa-Viertel

The Hansa Quarter to the north of the Tiergarten is an ageing 'city of the future'.

Straße des 17. Juni, Altonaer Straße, Bachstraße
U9 Hansaplatz, Bus 343

The settlement structure of the Hansa Quarter is mixed, boasting detached mansions set back from the street and urban housing surrounded by green belts –

a casual blend of flat-roofed dwellings, blocks of flats with four to six storeys and high-rises incorporating social and cultural facilities. No fewer than forty-eight architects from thirteen countries – including Alvar Aalto, Walter Gropius, Bruno Taut and Pierre Vago – collaborated on building the quarter, which was the focal point of the 1957 International Architecture Exhibition.

At 22 Altonaer Straße is the **Grips-Theater** (Phone: 030/39 74 74 77, www.grips-theater.de), which became the best-known German theatre for children and adolescents under Volker Ludwig's management.

The building belonging to the **Akademie der Künste** (Hanseatenweg 10) was erected in 1960 after plans by Werner Düttmann. The Art Academy goes back much further, however: in 1696 the Elector Friedrich III founded an Art Academy – Europe's third after the Paris and Rome academies. First housed in the Marstall on Unter den Linden boulevard, it was then moved to Pariser Platz and became world-famous as the Prussian Academy. In 1933 numerous celebrated artists connected with the academy, including Max Liebermann, were forced to leave. An independent *Deutsche Akademie der Künste* was founded in East Berlin in 1950. The two academies were united in 1993. The new Academy building on Pariser Platz was inaugurated in autumn 2005. The old academy rooms here are the setting for *exhibitions* and other cultural events. There are notable pieces of modern sculpture, including a Henry Moore 'Recumbent Figure' (1956), in front of the building.

76 Siegessäule

The Victory Column symbolizes Prussian victory in wars against Denmark (1864), Austria (1866) and France (1870/71).

Großer Stern
Bus 100, 187, 343

Disrespectful Berliners dub their **Victoria** 'Gold Else'. She surmounts the Victory Column at the centre of Großer Stern.

◁ *Sure to be radiantly happy – golden girl Victoria looks down from the Victory Column at Grosser Stern with pride in her new city*

Scandinavian lightness – the complex comprising the embassies of Norway, Finland, Denmark and Sweden boasts intriguingly airy wood façades

The goddess of Victory replete with laurel wreath and lance may be elegant but she is certainly not of slight build: she weighs 35 t and is 8 m tall. If you want to keep her company on the **observation platform** at 48 m, you have to climb all 285 steps of the spiral staircase inside the column.

In 1864 Kaiser Wilhelm I commissioned a monument adorned with historic battle trophies from Johann Friedrich Strack. The architect had the original idea of articulating the fluted column shaft with gilded enemy *cannon barrels*. *Bronze reliefs* on the square red granite base show scenes from the wars of liberation from Napoleon. A *glass mosaic* by Anton von Werner decorates the interior of the column: it tells the story of German unification after the victory over France in the Franco-Prussian War (1870/71).

Statues of military heroes Otto von Bismarck, Field-Marshal General Helmuth, Count Moltke, and Minister of War Albrecht von Roon stand at **Großer Stern**, with five busy thoroughfares and some pedestrian paths radiating out from it. Like the Victory Column, Bismarck and Moltke stood in front of the Reichstag until 1938, when the Nazis moved them to their present location.

77 Botschaftsviertel

Diplomats have returned to be showcased by contemporary architecture.

Stauffenbergstraße, Tiergartenstraße, Rauchstraße, Klinghöferstraße
S1, S2, S26 and U2 Potsdamer Platz
Bus M41, 123, 148, 200, 343

After the Second World War the Embassy Quarter south of the Tiergarten was abandoned to decay. In recent years, however, life has returned to the old diplomats' residences and some spectacular new buildings have joined them presenting a small but spectacular review of early 21st-century architecture.

Hans Hollein designed the new **Austrian Embassy** (Stauffenbergstraße 1) with a sweeping show façade. The stringently austere cube that is the new **Indian Embassy** (Tiergartenstraße 16/17) seems to owe more to the Bauhaus. The **Japanese**

In the courtyard of the former Bendler Block: the memorial commemorates resistance against the National Socialists

Embassy (Tiergartenstraße 24/25) is older, built between 1938 and 1942 after plans by Ludwig Moshammer and faithfully reconstructed in 1987. Until the diplomats moved in again, this was a Japanese-German Centre. Next door (Nos. 21–23) is the **Italian Embassy** (1938–42) designed by Friedrich Hetzel in a 1930s take on Neo-Classical style and fully restored by 2002. The **Scandinavian countries** have treated themselves to an ultramodern diplomatic complex at 1 Rauchstraße. The Norwegian section, for example, is an airy building of aspen wood. Across from it the lamella façade of the **Mexican Embassy** (Klinghöferstraße 3–11) is reminiscent of Corbusier and the cynosure of all eyes.

The scene is further enlivened by the quirky new buildings designed to house the representatives of the *German federal states*. Particularly notable is the representatives of **North Rhine-Westphalia building** (Hiroshimastraße 12–16, Petzinka and Pink) with a parabola-shaped wooden diamond façade. Other federal states buildings are located in the Minister Gardens north of Leipziger Platz.

78 Bauhaus-Archiv

A late work by Bauhaus co-founder Walter Gropius. Overview of one of the most important art schools of the 20th century.

Klingelhöferstraße 14
Phone: 030/254 00 20
www.bauhaus.de
We–Mo 10 am–5 pm
U1, U4 Nollendorfplatz
Bus 100, M29, 187, 343 Lützowplatz

The dream Bauhaus co-founder *Walter Gropius* cherished did not come true until ten years after his death: in 1979 the project he had designed in 1964 for a museum building in which the Bauhaus Archives could be kept was finally realised in his native Berlin. The main feature of the building housing the archives is its clearly articulated white *concrete façade* with small windows that face north.

The archives, officially called the *Museum für Gestaltung*, contain a collection of architectural models, plans, paintings and drawings as well as furniture by Bauhaus artists Ludwig Mies van der Rohe, Oskar Schlemmer, Marcel Breuer, László Moholy-Nagy, et al. There are also crafts and industrial products demonstrating the influence exerted by the Bauhaus movement on modern design.

79 Gedenkstätte Deutscher Widerstand

Memorial and documentation of the history of German resistance at a historic site.

Stauffenbergstraße 13–14, entrance via the Ehrenhof
Phone: 030/26 99 50 00
www.gdw-berlin.de
Mo–We, Fr 9 am–6 pm, Th 9 am–8 pm, Sa/Su/hols. 10 am–6 pm
S1, S2, S26 and U2 Potsdamer Platz
Bus M29, M41, 123, 148, 200

In the courtyard of the old *Imperial Naval Office* (1911–14), a plaque commemorates the resistance heroes of 20 July 1944. Where the memorial plaque now hangs Wehrmacht officers von Stauffenberg, von Quirnheim, von Haeften and Olbricht faced a firing squad after failing to assassinate Hitler. As the **Bendlerblock**, the building was Wehrmacht Command Headquarters between 1935 and 1945. An

Top: *Superlative: one of the world's biggest prints collections is open to the public in the Kupferstichkabinett at the Kulturforum*
Bottom: *Even this church has a nickname: The St.-Matthäus-Kirche was known as the 'Polka Church' because there were so many pubs nearby*

exhibition on the 2nd floor is devoted to the theme of 'Resistance against National Socialism'.

80 St.-Matthäus-Kirche

St Matthew's in Neo-Byzantine style – surrounded by great cultural institutions.

Matthäikirchplatz 4
S1, S2, S26 and U2 Potsdamer Platz
Bus M29, M41, 123, 148, 200

In the mid-19th century, one of the city's most elegant sections centred on St Matthew's: affluent Berliners first built summer houses here, later suburban villas and by 1900 these dwellings were followed by embassies and palatial mansions. **Villa Parey** at 4a Sigismundstraße exemplifies the trend. Built in the late 19th century, it belonged to the publisher Paul Parey. Now it has been integrated into the new Gemäldegalerie complex.

Built in 1846, St Matthew's was designed by Friedrich August Stüler as a three-aisled hall church in the Neo-Byzantine style. By 1960 extensive postwar renovation had been completed – the *interior* is now modern. The church used to be called the 'polka church', an allusion to the neighbouring inns and taverns that catered for day trippers.

The nearby **Kulturforum** was part of an urban planning concept advanced by *Hans Scharoun* (1893–1972). The architect built the Philharmonie (1960–63) be-

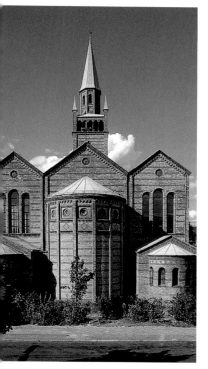

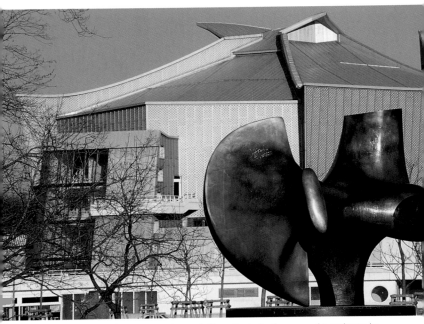

The Philharmonie with its spectacular roof silhouette. In the foreground a sculpture by Henry Moore

tween the Landwehr Canal and the Tiergarten on a site that was ravaged during the Second World War and it was followed by other concert halls and museums. The cultural centre on the southern fringes of the Tiergarten, amalgamating the New National Gallery, the Museum of Decorative Arts, the Museum of Prints and Drawings, the Art Library and the Paintings Gallery is *the* counterpart of the Museum Island.

81 Gemäldegalerie

Old Master paintings from East and West have been permanently reunited in this gallery after fifty years of separation.

Matthäikirchplatz 8
Phone: 030/266 29 51
www.smb.museum
Tu/We, Fr–Su 10 am–6 pm,
Th 10 am–10 pm
S1, S2, S26 and U2 Potsdamer Platz
Bus M29, M41, 123, 148, 200

The opening of the new Paintings Gallery in the Kulturforum in June 1998 represented an important step towards *restructuring* Berlin's museums. The Paint-

ings Gallery grew out of the superlative collections amassed by the Great Elector and Frederick the Great. The collections were separated after the Second World War. For decades some of these art treasures were in the West Berlin *Dahlem Museum Complex* and others in the East Berlin *Bodemuseum*. Eight years after the turnaround, the collections, which are among the most important in Europe, were reunited.

The museum presents Old Masters in seventy-two rooms and cabinets with natural daylight illumination. The main gallery contains about a thousand masterpieces and the study gallery boasts four hundred more. German, Netherlandish and Italian paintings from the 13th to the 16th centuries, French and English paintings of the 17th and 18th centuries and Flemish and Dutch Baroque paintings are hung here.

Highlights include masterpieces by Albrecht Dürer, Lucas Cranach the Elder, Frans Hals, Peter Paul Rubens, Raphael, Titian, Sandro Botticelli and Jean-Antoine Watteau. The **Rembrandt Collection**, comprising twenty paintings, is one of the world's most important groups of works by the Dutch master.

82 Kupferstichkabinett und Kunstbibliothek

A world-class collection of prints and drawings and a prestigious art library.

Phone: 030/266 20 29
www.smb.museum
Tu–Fr 10 am–6 pm, Sa/Su 11 am–
6 pm; Studiensaal in the Kupfer-
stichkabinett: Tu–Fr 9 am–4 pm,
Phone: 030/266 29 51
S1, S2, S26 and U2 Potsdamer Platz,
Bus M29, M41, 123, 148, 200

The Kupferstichkabinett and the Art Library, completed in 1994, represent one of the world's largest prints and drawings collections, with about 100 000 drawings and 550 000 prints from the Middle Ages to the present, more than 100 illuminated manuscripts, over 400 miniatures from the 11th to the 16th centuries, nearly 250 incunabula (very early prints) and about 1500 illustrated books from the 17th to the 20th centuries.

The *Museum für Fotografie* [see No. 105] near Bahnhof Zoologischer Garten is affiliated with the Kunstbibliothek. It shows the collections of contemporary photography.

83 Kunstgewerbemuseum

Arts and Crafts from the Middle Ages to the present.

Phone: 030/266 29 51
www.smb.museum
Tu–Fr 10 am–6 pm, Sa/Su 11 am–6 pm
S1, S2, S26 and U2 Potsdamer Platz;
Bus M29, M41, 123, 148, 200

Designed by Rolf Gutbrod and finished in May 1985, the Museum of Decorative Arts building has a steel skeleton with a brick curtain-wall façade. The collections shown here (the rest is at Schloss Köpenick, see No. 58) in 7000 m² of exhibition space is drawn from all fields of European craftsmanship dating from the Middle Ages to the present. Particularly noteworthy is the exquisite **Guelph Treasure** (11th–15th centuries): reliquaries and the richly ornate 11th-century Guelph Cross. Other remarkable exhibits include the *Lüneburg Council Silver* (15th/16th centuries) and an Abraham Roentgen *convertible table* (18th century). In the basement is an exhibition of contemporary product design.

84 Musikinstrumenten-Museum

Four centuries of music history are reflected in a selection of original instruments.

Tiergartenstraße 1
Phone: 030/25 48 11 78
www.smb.museum
Tu–Fr 9 am–5 pm, Sa/Su 10 am–5 pm
S1, S2, S26 and U2 Potsdamer Platz,
Bus M29, M41, 123, 148, 200

Near the Philharmonie is the Museum for Musical Instruments, planned by Hans Scharoun and inaugurated in 1984. The collection comprising about 2500 instruments from the 16th to the 20th centuries contains one-of-a-kind Renaissance and Baroque instruments as well as the 1929 *Mighty Wurlitzer Organ* (played Sa 12 noon after the guided tour 11 am). The *musicological library* at the museum contains over 40 000 volumes and picture archives with 55 000 documents. A *concert hall* and restoration workshops are a fitting coda to this unique ensemble.

85 Philharmonie

Concert halls notable for aesthetic and acoustic brilliance.

Matthäikirchstraße 1
S1, S2, S26 and U2 Potsdamer Platz
Bus M29, M41, 123, 148, 200

Designed in an exuberantly spacious style, the Philharmonie [see p. 173] was conceived by Hans Scharoun along acoustic lines: the orchestra pit is almost at the centre of the concert hall so that it is surrounded by the rows of seats. The *roof silhouette*, visualised by Scharoun as a celestial tent, is remarkable. The building was inaugurated in 1963 and covered in shimmering *golden plastic cladding* in 1979. The extravagant appearance of the building and the mercurial personality of **Herbert von Karajan** (1908–1989), who conducted the Berlin Philharmonic for so many years, have given rise to the name 'Circus Karajani'. The Philharmonic concerts are high points of Berlin cultural life. Since 2002 *Sir Simon Rattle* has added a quirky note of his own to the orchestra as its chief conductor.

The adjacent **Kammermusiksaal** (1984 –87), known as the Little Philharmonic, seats 1100.

Tours de force: the Neue Nationalgalerie was designed by Mies van der Rohe. In front an Alexander Calder sculpture (1965), in the background St Matthew's

86 Staatsbibliothek zu Berlin – Preußischer Kulturbesitz II

The State Library, united again – yet still so far apart.

Potsdamer Straße 33
Phone: 030/26 60
www.staatsbibliothek-berlin.de
Mo–Fr 9 am–9 pm, Sa 9 am–7 pm
S1, S2, S26 and U2 Potsdamer Platz,
Bus M29, M41, 123, 148, 200

Like so many other institutions, the State Library Unter den Linden suffered from the partition of the city. West Berlin contributed a new building for the Staatsbibliothek Preußischer Kulturbesitz. Even after reunification, the two libraries remain apart, united in 1991 in name only as the Staatsbibliothek zu Berlin – Preußischer Kulturbesitz [see p. 25].

The library building (1967–78) in Potsdamer Straße – one of the biggest modern buildings of its kind in Europe – was also designed by the prolific *Hans Scharoun*. Measuring 229 m in length and 152 m in width, the total surface area including all floors amounts to 81 300 m². It contains about 7 million volumes, periodicals and other printed matter from all over the world (focus: literature after 1956). The **literary legacies** of 430 great German men of letters – the works of Fichte, Herder, Hegel and Schopenhauer, Baedecker, Hauptmann, Mendelssohn and Sauerbruch – are included in the collection.

87 Neue Nationalgalerie

A Greek temple in the modern style houses 20th-century art.

Phone: 030/266 29 51
www.smb.museum
Tu/We, Fr 10 am–6 pm,
Th 10 am–10 pm, Sa/Su 11 am–6 pm
temporary exhibitions:
Mo–Fr Phone: 030/20 90 55 01,
Sa/Su Phone: 030/20 90 55 66
S1, S2, S26 and U2 Potsdamer Platz,
Bus M29, M41, 123, 148, 200

Ludwig Mies van der Rohe designed this cubic structure in glass and steel (1965–68), the realisation of the 'hall as such' envisaged by the Bauhaus architect. The New National Gallery presents important 20th-century works of art. The collection focuses on Cubism (Picasso, Léger), Expressionism (Kirchner, Schmidt-Rottluff, Heckel), the Bauhaus (Klee, Kandinsky) and Surrealism (Dalí, Miró). *Highlights* are Edvard Munch's 'Frieze of Life', George Grosz's 'Pillars of the Establishment', Max Ernst's 'Capricorn' and eleven paintings by Max Beckmann, including 'Birth' and 'Death'. Abstract 1960s/'70s paintings by Frank Stella and Elsworth Kelly round off the collection. *Rotating exhibitions* are mounted on a large scale in the basement and in the glass hall on the ground floor. While they are in preparation, the gallery is closed (look in the daily papers). Important pieces of sculpture stand in front of the National Gallery, including a *steel sculpture* (1965) by the American Neo-Constructivist Alexander Calder.

Kreuzberg – between Istanbul and the scene

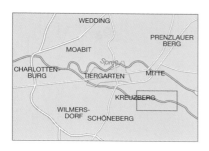

It's the heady Kreuzberg blend: Turkish bazaar ambience, Old Berlin, Punks and counterculture, creative people and, of all things, white collar workers have been spotted as inhabitants of this quirky section. When the Wall was still in place, Kreuzberg was marked out as being on the fringe, a unique cultural biotope with cheap housing. Since reunification this part of the city has, however, been in the limelight because it is so close to Berlin-Mitte. Investors appreciate its conveniently central location. And many streets display outsize signs saying 'Office space for rent'. If you want to go on a typical Berlin pub crawl, Kreuzberg is just the place for it – after all 'Kreuzberg nights are long' as a popular song goes!

88 Viktoria-Park

Between waterfall and vineyard.

S1, S2 Yorckstraße, U6 Platz der Luftbrücke, Bus M19, 104, 140, 184

Berlin has no natural hills to boast of. **Kreuzberg**, the highest hill the inner city has to offer, rises to an elevation of 66 m. Berliners, counting in centimetres, refer to it as their 'six-thousand-peak'. From its 'summit' you can look down on the 20-m-high **Nationaldenkmal**, a monument commemorating the wars leading to German liberation from Napoleon (1813–15). Surmounted by a Neo-Gothic spire and designed by the Prussian state architect Karl Friedrich Schinkel, it was dedicated in 1821. Alcoves on the monument display twelve *statues* of field commanders and members of the Prussian royal family, the work of sculptors Christian Daniel Rauch, Christian Friedrich Tieck and Ludwig Wichmann. Inscriptions on the cruciform base of the monument commemorate the most important battles of the wars of liberation. The hill and, in 1920, the district were named after the iron cross that tops the spire, donated by Friedrich Wilhelm III.

Viktoria Park surrounding the hill was not laid out until the 1990s. A star attraction is the artificial *waterfall* flowing towards Kreuzbergstraße, a miniature replica of the Zackenfall cataract in the Riesengebirge range. Thirteen thousand litres of water gush down the Kreuzberg waterfall every minute. At its end a fountain called *'The catch of a lifetime'* features a bronze fisherman who has caught a mermaid in his net.

The **Tivoli Brewery** in Methfesselstraße abutting the Kreuzberg recalls the 1870s boom era. The *Victoria Quarter* is nearing completion (2006) on the brewery premises. Covering 5.5 ha of land, they were bought by Schultheiss in 1891 and not sold until 1993. Besides chic penthouses and lofts in the old stables and workshops belonging to the smithy, there are new condominiums and town houses. The historicizing Tivoli Brewery brick buildings are also to be converted for use. To the west of Methfesselstraße is the Kreuzberg **vineyard** area. Since 1435 grapes have been harvested in the Cöllnischer or Götzscher vineyard, which is Europe's northernmost site. As the wine yield amounts to only a few hectolitres, the Berlin vintage is only served at official occasions in Kreuzberg Town Hall.

Further north, above the Bergmannstraße intersection, two centuries of homosexual history and destiny are documented at the **Schwules Museum** (Mehringdamm 61, Phone: 030/69 59 90 50, www.schwulesmuseum.de, We–Fr, Su/Mo 2 pm–6 pm, Sa 2 pm–7 pm) in biographies, photos, works of art, etc. Rotating exhibitions supplement the permanent display.

A 'Raisin Bomber' hovers over the new building on the Landwehr Canal – this celebrated Deutsches Technikmuseum exhibit can also be visited by boat

89 Bergmannstraße

Kreuzberg puts its best foot forward.

U6, U7 Mehringdamm and
U6 Platz der Luftbrücke
Bus M19, 104, 140, 184, 341

A stroll across Bergmannstraße with occasional forays into side streets – better than leafing through the history books. What you encounter is a well-preserved old residential area, in fact Berlin or Kreuzberg as they were in 1900.

The façades lining **Chamissoplatz** are still decorated with stuccowork. Cobblestone paving, gas-lit streets and water pumps take you back to the 1870s boom era. Entrepreneurs, physicians and lawyers lived here – usually ensconced in the coveted *Bel étage*, the first floor of the front building. Many houses that survived the Second World War have been restored to pristine condition.

In Bergmannstraße the buzzword *multicultural* reflects reality. There are junk shops, stylish boutiques, eateries offering international fast-food specialities, pubs and cafés. If shopping is what you're after, head for **Marheinekeplatz**. Only four of the original fourteen covered markets built in Berlin in 1900 have survived and one of them is in this square. The **Passionskirche**, a striking structure built in the Neo-Romanesque manner in 1904–07, is notable for its massive, stepped tower while the interior is dominated by a powerful dome. Music events are held in this church, which was restored in the 1990s.

The rest of Bergmannstraße is – in the literal sense of the word – almost without a living soul: no fewer than five **cemeteries** line the street as far as the Südstern and the former Garrison Church (1896).

There is not much human habitation beyond Südstern either since the **Hasenheide** adjoins the cemeteries. Jahn, the father of gymnastics, had a playing-field laid out here back in 1810. The Hasenheide is inviting in summer as a place for rest and recreation, with meadows, cycle paths, an open-air stage for concerts and cinema nights under the stars.

90 Riehmers Hofgarten

A magnificent court garden surrounded by patrician town houses from the 1870s boom era.

Yorckstraße 83–86
U6, U7 Mehringdamm, Bus M19, 341

Riehmers was a pioneering urban planner. In 1900, while Berlin was sprawling into a sea of monotonous tenements, the city fathers were squabbling over every square metre of ground and building speculators were in their heyday, Riehmers managed to realize an ambitious project: between 1881 and 1892 he built an attractive garden suburb settlement comprising about twenty houses with flats and Neo-Renaissance façades that were not just sumptuously decorated on the street side. He also made good use of green belts and sunny courtyards linked by inner streets. Two *statues* on the portal in Yorckstraße invite visitors to tour the best of 1900s Berlin replete with cobble-stone paving and gas lamps into the bargain. The front buildings have been put to modern use as shops and cafés.

Friedhöfe Hallesches Tor

Cultural history immortalised beneath ivy-covered cast iron and in marble – funerary monuments from Rococo to Jugendstil.

Mehringdamm/Zossener Straße
U1, U6 Hallesches Tor, Bus M41, 265

Five small cemeteries comprise the Friedhöfe vor dem Halleschen Tor. The oldest burial grounds in Berlin, they are the last resting place of 80 000 people. The necropolis was laid out in 1735, as Friedrich Wilhelm I decreed, outside the confines of Berlin. The first cemetery, *Jerusalemskirchhof*, was intended for the poor from Friedrichsstadt and residents of the Bohemian community. Other graveyards were added with time, each demarcated by walls and handsomely decorated with marble statuary. The poor were soon joined by celebrated figures from public life, who left their stamp on Berlin and Prussia in the 18th and 19th centuries. To name just a few of the distinguished residents of this city of the dead: the architect Georg Wenzeslaus von Knobelsdorff († 1753), the poets Adalbert von Chamisso († 1838) and E. T. A. Hoffmann († 1822), the composer Felix Mendelssohn-Bartholdy († 1847), the actor August Wilhelm Iffland († 1814) and Carl Ferdinand Langhans († 1869), who designed theatres.

92 Deutsches Technikmuseum Berlin

TOP TIPP

Technology in its cultural and historical context and new technologies are presented interactively in this museum.

Trebbiner Straße 9
Phone: 030/90 25 40
www.dtmb.de,
Tu–Fr 9 am–5.30 pm,
Sa/Su 10 am–6 pm
U1, U7 Möckernbrücke
U1, U2 Gleisdreieck

A junction formed by railway, underground and suburban rail lines as well as canal shipping and street traffic, this triangular area was once very important for

Like a Star of David shattered by lightning – the fascinating Berlin Jewish Museum with the Garden of Exile

providing Berlin with vital goods. The *Anhalter Goods Station* used to be located here as well as a marshalling yard with two locomotive sheds and the goods shed of the Society for Covered Markets and Cold Storage.

The historic buildings located on the site have been home to the Deutsches Technikmuseum Berlin since 1982. Completed in 2005, it boasts an exhibition space of 50 000 m², making it the world's largest technology museum, where **17 sections** present a wealth of treasures and rare objects.

The old goods station is now an old-timer depot; the locomotive sheds show historic stations, a S10 steam locomotive, which is in perfect running order for demonstrations, and a V200 diesel locomotive. The textile technology section where suitcases are made was opened in April 2003 in the railway officials' goods office between the two locomotive

Memories of the 1948/49 Berlin Airlift – the Douglas C-47 on the roof of the Deutsches Technikmuseum Berlin

sheds. The shipping section of the museum opened on the ground floor and the first floor of a spectacular new building on the Landwehrkanal in December 2003. Exhibits include a canal barge 33 m long and numerous navigation instruments. The Aeronautics and Space Division has occupied the two upper floors since April 2005. Flying machines ranging from the hot-air balloon through Lilienthal's gliders to the Stuka bombers and the V2 rocket from the Second World War bring alive the turbulent history of flight. On the roof of the new building a 'Raisin Bomber' is perched, a Douglas C-47 of the kind used by the Allied Airlift during the Berlin blockade in 1948/49.

Interactive **demonstrations** take place throughout the museum to get visitors involved: an antique workshop, a processing centre, a diesel motor and a power loom are demonstrated in the lobby area. Visitors can weave in the textiles section and mill paper when they move on to the paper-making section. Demonstration dates and times are shown on a board in the lobby and also announced over loudspeakers.

A highlight of the museum is the **Science Centre Spectrum**, in which more than two hundred and fifty experiments

in acoustics, optics, electricity and radioactivity explain scientific and technological phenomena.

The buildings are surrounded by a **museum park**, which is earmarked for enlargement into a district park. It features rare flora and fauna, a fully functional German post windmill and a Dutch smock windmill. Blacksmiths clatter away in a forge near the Mühlenteich pond and in a brewery you can learn everything you ever wanted to know about early 20th-century brewing techniques.

93 Jüdisches Museum Berlin

A spectacular building dedicated to the history of the Jews in Germany.

Lindenstraße 9–14
Phone: 030/25 99 33 00
www.juedisches-museum-berlin.de
Mo 10 am–10 pm, Tu–Su 10 am–8 pm
(closed 24 Dec., Rosh Hashana and
Yom Kippur, details see website)
U1, U6 Hallesches Tor; Bus M41, 265

The cornerstone for the Jewish Museum (1993–99) was laid on 9 November 1992, the 54th anniversary of the pogrom committed by Germans against their Jewish fellow citizens. The US architect *Daniel Libeskind* created this metal-clad building, shaped like a flash of lightning with jagged fenestration, which drew crowds even before it was inaugurated in 2001.

Visitors enter via the Baroque **Kollegienhaus** (formerly seat of the Berlin Museum). Three 'avenues' lead from its basement to three points in the Libeskind building: the *Garden of Exile*, the *Holocaust Tower* and the exhibition *'Two Thousand Years of German-Jewish History'*. A wealth of documents, works of art, utilitarian artefacts and multimedia exhibits sheds light on numerous facets of Jewish culture in Germany from its earliest testimonies through the Middle Ages and down to the present. One of many interesting facts highlighted here: the first Jews reached what is now Germany as traders with the Roman legions. The earliest known evidence for their presence is a decree issued to the Cologne municipal authorities by the Emperor Constantine in 321.

Background information on the exhibition is available in the library, the archives and the multimedia *Rafael Roth Learning Centre*.

Long live the seventies – Edward Kienholz's eccentric sculptural group 'The Art Show' (1963–77) gets on well with Helmut Middendorf's 'Born in the Big City' (1979, left) and Rainer Fetting's runners (1979, centre)

94 Berlinische Galerie

A memorably vivid collection dealing with modern urban art and architecture.

Alte Jakobstraße 124–128
Phone: 030/78 90 26 00
www.berlinischegalerie.de
Mo-Sa 12 noon–8 pm, Su 10 am–6 pm
U6 Kochstraße, U1, U6 Hallesches Tor,
Bus M29, M41, 265

Near the Jewish Museum, the Berlinische Galerie, also called the *State Museum for Modern Art, Photography and Architecture*, formerly in the Martin Gropius Building [see No. 68], has found a permanent home. Since 2004 the light and airy new building, a converted glass warehouse, has shown art of all kinds from 1870 to the present, including paintings by Dix and Baselitz, Grosz and Kirchner prints, photos by Zille and Hannah Höch. The architecture collection presents 20th and 21st-centuries Berlin construction projects. There are also topical rotating exhibitions as well as an archive of artists, rooms for studying prints, a café and a studio for children.

Between the Jewish Museum and the Berlinische Galerie large sculpture and installations owned by the gallery are set up as signposts, as it were, under the motto 'art – city – space'.

95 Zeitungsviertel

Berlin's 'Fleet Street'.

Kochstraße, Lindenstraße, Axel-Springer-Straße, Schützenstraße
U6 Kochstraße, Bus M29

In 1900 Berlin was Germany's leading newspaper metropolis. Pioneering newspaper publishers were **Mosse**, **Scherl** and **Ullstein**. A broad range of dailies and weeklies catered for the entire political spectrum: for a conservative readership there was the 'Kreuz-Zeitung', for left-wing liberals the 'Vossische Zeitung' and the 'Berliner Tagblatt', for Social Democrats 'Vorwärts'. One tabloid was the 'BZ am Mittag' (from 1904: now 'BZ' on Sundays and 'Bild' daily) to have survived to the present day and another is the 'Berliner Morgenpost', which by 1930 had attained a circulation of 400 000 and on Sundays 630 000.

The Berlin 'Fleet Street' used to be located in Kochstraße, Lindenstraße, Axel-Springer-Straße and Schützenstraße. Sixty-four of one hundred and twenty Berlin printing houses had settled here by 1925. In the midst of all the publishing houses, in Alte Jakobstraße, was the Reich Printing Press (1889–93, Carl Busse), now the **Bundesdruckerei**. The Federal Printing Office prints stamps, banknotes and citizens' identity cards and passports. In 1959 the publishing mogul Axel Springer acquired a majority of the Ullstein shares and built a press house on the premises of what had been the Scherl publishing house. The editorial staffs of 'Bild', 'BZ', 'Berliner Morgenpost' and 'Die Welt' work from here. In 1993 a 20-storey high-rise with a bronze, mirrored façade, the **Springer-Hochhaus**, went up on the site. The editorial staff of the left-wing 'taz' is close by at 18 Kochstraße.

Mosse was at the corner of Jerusalemer Straße and Schützenstraße from 1874. In the early 1990s the **Druckhaus Berlin-Mitte** was built to replace the venerable publishing house. Part of the old building was integrated into the new complex, which houses publishers, printers and advertising agencies.

96   Checkpoint Charlie

Recollections of a partitioned city and the cold war.

Zimmerstraße/Friedrichstraße
U6 Kochstraße, U2, U6 Stadtmitte
Bus M29

During the cold war, Checkpoint Charlie, the border-crossing point between West and East Berlin often made the headlines. Tanks from the US and the USSR confronted each other here on 27 October 1961 only 200 metres apart. The Wall had been built two months before, turning bustling Friedrichstraße into a dead end. Only non-Germans, diplomats and mem-

bers of the victorious Allied armed forces were permitted to go through this heavily guarded border checkpoint between East and West until the Wall fell in 1989. The checkpoint was dismantled on 22 June 1990. Only pieces of the Wall, a watchtower and one last sign warning 'Attention! You are leaving the American Sector' recall the partition of the city. As everywhere in Berlin, building went on at a frantic pace here; modern blocks of flats and office buildings have mushroomed around the checkpoint.

At 43–45 Friedrichstraße, the **Mauermuseum Haus am Checkpoint Charlie** (Phone: 030/253 72 50, daily 9 am–10 pm) tells the story of how the Wall was built and what it was like to live in the partitioned city between 1961 and 1989. An overriding theme is the worldwide non-violent struggle for human rights.

97   Künstlerhaus Bethanien

From hospital to internationally renowned artists' studio and exhibition centre.

Mariannenplatz 2
Phone: 030/616 90 30
www.bethanien.de
exhibitions: We–Su 2 pm–7 pm
U1 Görlitzer Bahnhof, Bus M29

Bethanien, the old diaconate hospital complex on the north-west side of Mari-

Last stop desire

Built in 1901, **Bahnhof Schlesisches Tor** was the last stop on the U1-line between 1961 and 1995. This link between Kreuzberg and Friedrichshain remained severed for decades. Only old-age pensioners from the East and their Western counterparts going in the opposite direction were allowed to walk through the *border checkpoint* here. Now the train again crosses **Oberbaumbrücke**, the longest bridge spanning the Spree, to continue on as far as S-Bahnhof Warschauer Straße in Friedrichshain. Reunification has made the Oberbaum Bridge into an architectural synthesis of traditional and modern. Built in Brandenburg brick Neo-Gothic by Otto Stahn in

Stopped here: Bahnhof Schlesisches Tor was the last stop on the U1 for many years

1894–96, the bridge was given a modern makeover by Spanish architect *Santiago Calatrava* (design 1992).

From hospital to artists' hostel – Bethanien provides studios and exhibition rooms for artists from around the world

annenplatz, has been converted into an art centre. It has housed the Künstlerhaus Bethanien since 1976. King Friedrich Wilhelm IV financed the hospital and adjoining buildings, which were completed in 1847. The novelist *Theodor Fontane* lived and worked here as an apothecary in 1848/49 until he defied his father to devote himself entirely to writing. The *Fontane Apothecary* is still open to visitors.

Bethanien was closed down in 1970 and grabbed the domestic headlines in 1971 when hundreds of demonstrators occupied the complex to protest against its planned demolition. Although the police were out in full force, the demonstration was successful and the buildings was left standing. As an artists' house, it has progressed to the cultural centre of the quarter. Now there are twenty-five studios, three exhibition studios and a media laboratory in Bethanien. Artists from all over the world work here and catalogues as well as an art magazine are published.

Nearby Lutheran **St-Thomas-Kirche** (1864–69), built by Friedrich Adler, a pupil of Schinkel's, in the Historicizing style, can seat a congregation of 1500, making it one of Berlin's biggest churches.

The elongated green, which is **Mariannenplatz** was designed by Peter Joseph Lenné in 1853. Most neighbourhood summer festivals take place here and are exuberantly multicultural: music and ethnic soul food, crafts and political commitment forge bonds between the various social and ethnic groups.

98 Paul-Lincke-Ufer

Istanbul on the Landwehr Canal.

U1, U8 Kottbusser Tor and
U8 Schönleinstraße, Bus 140

The Paul-Lincke-Ufer and Maybachufer across from it are the idyllic banks of the Landwehrkanal. When the canal was laid out between 1845 and 1850 after plans by landscape architect *Peter Joseph Lenné*, its economic importance outweighed its charms as a feature of urban planning. Tonnes of building material were transported along its 10.3 kilometres since mid-19th-century Berlin was in the throes of rapid expansion. Now the only vessels puttering down the canal are *excursion boats* (quay stops include Kottbusser Bridge).

On the Paul-Lincke-Ufer restaurants do a flourishing trade and little garden inns and cafés provide sit-down refreshment with delightful canal-side views.

The Maybach side of the Landwehrkanal has an Oriental feeling on Tuesdays and Fridays when the **Türkenmarkt** is in full swing, an open-air bazaar overflowing with fruit and vegetables as well as stalls selling organic products, cheeses, household wares and textiles.

All around the Ku'damm – long live the shopping frenzy!

The commercial and cultural centre of West Berlin still is one of the city's best addresses. All 3.5 kilometres of the Kurfürstendamm, fondly abbreviated to Ku'damm, constitute the number one sightseeing and shopping boulevard although it now has stiff competition from both Friedrichstraße and Unter den Linden boulevard. A host of hotels, restaurants, cafés, cinemas, boutiques and department stores dominate the Ku'damm area, which boasts some remarkable modern architecture. Culture also looms large: galleries, museums and auction houses lure culture vultures.

99 Kurfürstendamm

From bridle-path to boulevard.

U1, U9 Kurfürstendamm and U1 Uhlandstraße, Bus X10, M19, M29, M46, 100, 109, 110, 200

The Kurfürstendamm started out in the 16th century as a bridle-path leading to the Grunewald royal hunting lodge. As the name 'Kurfürstendamm' indicates, it was long reserved for the use of the Kurfürst (prince elector in the Holy Roman Empire) and members of his family.

The Kurfürstendamm owes its boulevard status to plans laid by Reich Chancellor Otto von Bismarck in 1883: western Berlin was to have an elegant, upmarket **high street** conveying 'pleasure traffic' to Grunewald. Running through Charlottenburg and Wilmersdorf districts, the Kurfürstendamm is 3.5 km long. Affluent middle-class Berliners, merchants, speculators and artists soon settled on and near the boulevard whereas the aristocracy and the government preferred Unter den Linden.

The Kurfürstendamm was in its **heyday** during the 1920s when entertainment establishments – cabarets, revues, variety shows and cinemas – mushroomed along it. Unfortunately, only a very few of the magnificent buildings that lined it in 1900 survived the bombing during the Second World War. Some buildings have, however, been faithfully reconstructed.

In recent years the ambience of this Berlin boulevard has gone upmarket: elegant boutiques, exclusive jewellers and shopping arcades with luxury shops have opened. And the Ku'damm, like the rest of Berlin, has been gripped by a spate of building activity. Property speculation is rife. Buildings were torn down in 1995 across from the Gedächtniskirche but the site where they once stood still remains empty since the planned *Zoofenster Berlin* high-rise building project intended to fill it has not yet materialised.

The Kurfürstendamm has traditionally boasted large hotels, cinemas and two theatres for light comedy: **Theater am Kurfürstendamm** and the **Komödie** (No. 206, see p. 174). One of the best-known hotels is the **Kempinski Hotel Bristol** (No. 27, see p. 181), built in 1952 by Paul Schwebes. This is where international celebrities like to stay when in Berlin – and, with only a little bit of luck, you'll spot VIPs at the Bristol Bar in the hotel.

The fabled **Café Kranzler** moved in 1944 from Unter den Linden [see p. 23] to the Ku'damm (at the corner of Joachimsthaler Straße). Now the café and its rotunda are part of the **Neues Kranzler Eck**, a complex comprising both old and new buildings, over which looms an eccentric high-rise designed by Helmut Jahn (1998–

2000). In 1900 the *Café des Westens* (also called Café Größenwahn, meaning 'swelled head') was at this intersection, a place where Berlin bohemians, writers and actors could spend hours at a time discussing the world over a cup of coffee.

Right across from the Kranzler, at the old **Ku'damm Eck**, a round building (2001) 44 m tall is the luxurious *Swissôtel* (Phone: 030/22 01 00, http://berlin.swissotel.com).

Interesting stories are also linked with the Charlottenburg section of the Kurfürstendamm (running between Breitscheidplatz and Adenauerplatz): **No. 234**, long a café, was frequented before the First World War by officers' wives out husband-hunting for their nubile daughters.

The building at **No. 218** was acquired in 1902 by imperial China. Until 1979 it belonged to the People's Republic of China and, as embassy premises, was extraterritorial, with all that that legally implies. House **No. 217** was a revue theatre in the 1920s, where Josephine Baker appeared on stage in her banana costume. Until 2002 it was the Astor Cinema but now Tommy Hilfiger is the leading man here. The complex at **No. 193** was supposed to open its doors in 1912 as a grand apartment building on American lines but went bankrupt immediately. Now it appropriately houses the Berlin *Oberfinanzdirektion*, the Main Revenue Office.

A stroll through the side-streets off the Ku'damm between Joachimstaler Straße and Leibnizstraße is well worth your while. Here and around **Savignyplatz** there are even more boutiques, specialist shops, cafés and (scene) eateries. No wonder that these streets are the insider's choice for anyone interested in a good Berlin residential address.

Top: *Tracking the denizens of the big city – panorama with Breitscheidplatz, the Gedächtniskirche and the Europa-Center*
Left: *Generation conflict? Not a sign of it where the Neues Kranzler Eck with the chubby Café Kranzler and a brash glass house designed by Helmut Jahn bring young and old together*

100 Kaiser-Wilhelm-Gedächtniskirche

The ruined tower of the Kaiser-Wilhelm-Gedächtniskirche is a Berlin landmark.

Breitscheidplatz
S5, S7, S75, S9 and U2, U9
Zoologischer Garten
Bus X9, X10, X34, M46, 100, 109, 145, 149, 200, 204, 245, 249

On ascending the throne, Kaiser Wilhelm II wanted to commission an impressive official church which – in the interior especially – would demonstrate the unity of throne and church in Prussia and at the same time commemorate Kaiser Wilhelm I. Franz Heinrich Schwechten designed it in the Neo-Romanesque style with a high **west tower** and four corner towers. The Kaiser Wilhelm Memorial Church did not, however, play much of a role in ecclesiastical circles in the decades that followed its consecration although Henny Porten, the leading lady of German silent film, was married here all in white in 1921. Allied bombers destroyed the church on a Sunday in November 1943. All that remained was the west tower.

Monarch and spouse immortalised in mosaics – Kaiser Wilhelm II and his wife in the Gedächtniskirche at Breitscheidplatz

tower (53 m high) were added. Consecrated on 17 December 1961, the new church is colloquially known in Berlin as the 'lipstick and compact'.

A *memorial hall* in the tower is a reminder that we should live in peace and reconciliation. The *Frieze of Princes* is a parade of Hohenzollern portraits from the Elector Friedrich I (1415–40) to the last crown prince, Friedrich Wilhelm. A *Glockenspiel* marks the hours in the old tower – with a melody composed by Prince Louis Ferdinand, a great-grandson of the last Kaiser.

In 1957 plans were mooted for demolishing the tower but the Berliners voiced vehement protest against the idea. A compromise was reached: the tower, by now dubbed 'the hollow tooth', was left standing. Egon Eiermann designed a flat-roofed octagon of concrete slabs with glazed apertures to surround it. A sacristy, a lobby with a library and a second

101 Europa-Center

Vom Künstlertreffpunkt zum Touristenzentrum.

Breitscheidplatz
S5, S7, S75, S9 and U2, U9 Zoologischer Garten
U1, U2, U3 Wittenberplatz
Bus X9, X10, X34, M19, M29, M46, 100, 109, 145, 149, 200, 204, 245, 249, 343

The Europa-Center is on the site of the legendary 1920s *Romanische Café* – the Berlin scene venue of its day. Celebrities

The legendary Loveparade

Every year the big question had everybody worried: was it going to take place or not? The event is the Love Parade, which lured hundreds of thousands of young people to Berlin every year. And it was a Berlin scene institution until 2003. The whole thing started as a joke. In 1989 DJ Dr. Motte wanted to bring the **Techno Scene** out of the dark cellar clubs and into the light of day. And it came forth from the cellar to spill out into the street. In 1989 a band of 150 venturous young souls drove down the **Ku'damm** on a colourful float throbbing to the beat of Techno. No one could have dreamt then that the Love Parade would become a growth industry. In 2003 about 750 000 'Techno-freaks' were in Berlin to celebrate their mass love-in.

Unregenerate spoil-sports shook their heads over the Love Parade. Why all the fuss about music? Why all the woofers and the **garish outfits** (some of them skimpy)? To shake off inhibi-

tions that no longer exist? Whatever, the Love Parade meant 48 hours of dancing and reeling from one club to another, the scene celebrating itself. Then funding petered out. After the Love Parade was downgraded from 'demonstration status', there were enormous expenses to be met yet not enough sponsor money was raised in 2004 and 2005. Now the big question is: will 2006 see a Love Parade revival?

Berlin, a cosmopolitan metropolis – similarities with London, for example, are quite obvious in details such as this scene captured on Kurfürstendamm

such as Max Reinhardt, Alfred Döblin, Gustaf Gründgens, Richard Tauber and Egon Erwin Kisch sat in a room called the 'Pool for Swimmers' reserved just for them. Wannabes sipped their coffee in the 'Pool for Non-Swimmers'. But it was curtains for the Kaffeeklatsch in November 1943. British bombs destroyed the building. In 1963–65 a 22-storey Europa-Center, 86 m high, went up on the site (Hentrich/Petschnigg, Düttmann/Eiermann) to house shops, eateries, the tourist information office *Berlin Tourismus*, the 'Stachelschwein' ('Porcupine') cabaret and a casino.

Breitscheidplatz in front of the Europa-Center is a favourite with tourists, Berliners, street artists and skateboarders. Designated a pedestrian precinct in 1983, it was named after the Social Democrat Rudolf Breitscheid (1874–1944), who died in Buchenwald concentration camp. At the centre of the square is the **Weltkugelbrunnen**, a fountain designed by sculptor Joachim Schmettau and referred to as the 'Water Dumpling' because of its shape.

102 Käthe-Kollwitz-Museum

Expressionism and memories.

Fasanenstraße 24
Phone: 030/882 52 10
www.kaethe-kollwitz.de
We–Mo 11 am–6 pm
U1 Uhlandstraße
Bus M19, M29, 109, 110

Fasanenstraße, which boasts handsome 19th-century mansions and fine early 20th-century dwellings, is one of the most beautiful and elegant side-streets off the Kurfürstendam from the architectural standpoint.

The Käthe-Kollwitz-Museum at 24 Fasanenstraße is housed in a palace that was remodelled in the late Neo-Classical style in 1897. It contains most of the work done by the Expressionist artist Käthe Kollwitz (1867–1945). The Berlin painter and art dealer Professor Hans Pels-Leusden endowed the museum with his collection of 100 prints, 70 drawings and original posters by Kollwitz, who was noted for her social commitment.

The auction house owned by Professor Pels-Leudsden was next door, at No. 25, **Villa Grisebach** (1891–95). **No. 26** (ca 1900) was owned by the entrepreneur Salomon Wertheim, who founded the department

Memories: the portal of Berlin's first synagogue has been incorporated in the Jewish Community Building

store chain Wertheim. His home was an early 20th-century salon.

The 1870s boom-era mansion built by a high-ranking officer in the Imperial Navy (No. 23) is now a **Literaturhaus** and its gardens and conservatory are a café. The House of Letters also incorporates a bookshop and a *Kurt Tucholsky Room* with furniture from the satirist's home in Hindas, Sweden. Incidentally, in 1912 Tu-

cholsky opened a book bar at *No. 12 Ku'-damm*, where literature and strong liquor made for a heady cocktail.

In Fasanenstraße, as in other side-streets off the Kurfürstendamm, there are still numerous old Berlin **pensions**. Women left widows after the First World War who had to eke out a living from a meagre pension used to rent out their flats, which were often huge, with up to 600 m². The boarding houses were highly popular in the 1920s and 1930s with actresses, artists and other celebrities. Silent film star Asta Nielsen, aviator ace Erich Udet and the great Franz Kafka were more than delighted to stay here.

103 Jüdische Gemeinde

The cultural centre of Germany's largest Jewish congregation.

Fasanenstraße 79–80
Phone: 030/88 02 80
S5, S7, S75, S9 and U2, U9 Zoologischer Garten, U1, U9 Kurfürstendamm, U1 Uhlandstraße
Bus X9, X10, X34, M19, M29, M46, 100, 109, 110, 145, 149, 200, 204, 245, 249

The first synagogue in the western part of Berlin opened its doors at Fasanenstraße on 26 August 1912. This magnificent building, designed in the Neo-Byzantine style by Ehrenfried Hessel, could accommodate a congregation of 1700. The synagogue was almost destroyed in the

Ideals and idylls: the exchange of ideas goes on over hot chocolate and cakes in the bibliophile Café Wintergarten run by the Literaturhaus in Fasanenstraße

The domain of the operetta and the musical: entertainment is writ large at the Theater des Westens in Kantstraße

104 Theater des Westens

Modern entertainment behind old walls: Berlin's operetta and musical theatre.

Kantstraße 12
Phone: 0 18 05/44 44
www.stage-entertainment.de
S5, S7, S75, S9 and U2, U9 Zoologischer Garten
Bus X9, X10, X34, M46, 100, 109, 145, 149, 200, 204, 245, 249

November pogrom night of 1938 and the ruins were blown up in 1958. Architects Dieter Knoblauch and Heinz Heise, who designed the new Jewish Community House (1957–59), were able to integrate the old portal as its main entrance. Two columns rescued from the façade of the demolished ruin are now a *memorial*. A wall in the colonnaded court at the rear commemorates the Berlin Jews murdered by the Nazis. Inside the community house there is also a kosher restaurant: *Gabriel's* (Phone: 030/882 61 38).

Nearby is the **Kantdreieck** (1994), a high-rise office building by Josef Paul Kleihues, with a gigantic silver weather-vane on its roof. Across from it is the **Ludwig-Erhard-Haus** (1998) designed by the London architect Nicholas Grimshaw. The complex dubbed 'the Armadillo' houses the Board of Trade and Commerce and the Berlin Stock Exchange.

Designed by Bernhard Sehring (1895/96) in the bombastic Wilhelmine historicizing style, the Theater des Westens was the perfect setting for staging classical *operettas*. The *Deutsche Oper* was lodged here after the war until a new building could be made ready for it in Bismarckstraße. The Theater des Westens building was remodelled and restored in 1978. With Helmut Baumann as artistic director, succeeded in 1999 by Elmar Ottenthal, the theatre earned a deserved reputation as the place in Berlin to see modern **musicals**. Since 2003 run by Stage Entertainment of Hamburg, it now mounts

21st-century stage hits such as the adventure musical 'The Three Musketeers'.

Next door is the **Delphi-Filmpalast** (Phone: 030/312 10 26), once Berlin's biggest cinema, where films had their first showings. This is where Martin Scorcese's 'Aviator' premièred in 2005. There is an attractive terrace café and the venerable *Club Quasimodo* (Phone 030/312 80 86) in the vaulted cellar provides live jazz.

105 Museum für Fotografie – Helmut Newton Stiftung

Contemporary photography and a bevy of Newton lovelies against a romantic setting.

Jebensstraße 2
Phone: 030/266 36 66
www.smb.museum
Tu/We, Fr–Su 10 am–6 pm,
Th 10 am–10 pm
S5, S7, S75, S9 and U2, U9 Zoologischer Garten
Bus X9, X10, X34, M46, 100, 109, 145, 149, 200, 204, 245, 249

The **Bahnhof Zoologischer Garten** station, immortalised in the 1994 film 'Wir Kinder von Bahnhof Zoo', has changed its image in recent years, not least thanks to modernisation. A concourse with shops and snack-bars now lend the station a bit more cosmopolitan flair. But it is not a railway junction worthy of a metropolis.

Designed by Fritz Hane and built in 1934–36, the station is currently only for trains departing for westward destinations. All trains going east and south leave from Ostbahnhof or Bahnhof Lichtenberg.

Just across from Bahnhof Zoo the Museum für Fotografie – Helmut Newton Stiftung opened in June 2004. The Photography Museum is part of the Kunstbibliothek [see No. 82] and its collections are shown in special exhibitions. Added to the museum collections are those of *Helmut Newton* (1920–2004), photographer of the stars. A Berliner who emigrated to the US in 1938, he gave the collection to his native city to be on permanent loan during his lifetime. His photographs are presented in exhibitions that change every few months. Since June 2005 spectacular fashion photos shot for magazines such as Vogue and designers including Chanel, Yves Saint Laurent and Versace have been drawing crowds in a show entitled 'A Gun for Hire'.

The Neo-Classical museum building was built in 1908/09 after plans by Heino Schmieden and Julius Boethke as the officer's mess of the Landwehr-Inspektion Berlin. The halls and suites of rooms were sumptuously decorated and furnished: most of them colourful and opulent to suit the Wilhelmine taste yet also incorporating Jugendstil decorative elements and, even then, indirect lighting.

The barrel-vaulted *Kaisersaal* on the second floor, with a floor space of 665 m^2 and a ceiling 11 m high, was a gem. A

A stairwell with nudes – where officers paraded about in uniform a century ago, Helmut Newton's perfect nudes now strutt their stuff

picturesque ruin it awaits restoration while providing a backdrop for exhibitions of contemporary works from the Photography Museum collections. Now that the museum has moved into the building, a circle is complete because its parent collection, the Kunstbibliothek, was housed here once before, in 1954, before moving to the Kulturforum in 1993.

106 Zoologischer Garten

Germany's oldest and by far most popular zoo.

Entrances: Hardenbergplatz 8 (Löwentor), Budapester Straße 34 (Elefantentor)
Phone: 030/25 40 10
www.zoo-berlin.de
15 March–14 Oct. daily 9 am–6.30 pm, 15 Oct.–14 March daily 9 am–5 pm
S5, S7, S75, S9 and U2, U9 Zoologischer Garten
Bus X9, X10, X34, M46, 100, 109, 145, 149, 200, 204, 245, 249

The magnificent entrance gate at Budapester Straße with its seated stone ele-

Patient pachyderms – the Elefantentor gate at Budapester Straße puts visitors in just the right mood for visiting the Zoo

phants supporting a pagoda roof prepares visitors for a treat. This imposing portal is a copy of the original (1899) that was destroyed in the war. The zoo opened back in 1844. The founders of Germany's first zoo were Martin Lichtenstein, a scientist, the polymath explorer Alexander von Humboldt and the landscape architect Peter Joseph Lenné. The first animals were part of the *Royal Fauna Collection* given to the people of Berlin by Friedrich Wilhelm IV. In 1943 most of the buildings were destroyed in just 15 minutes and only 91 of the 10 000 animals survived.

The zoo covers 35 ha. It is now home to 14 249 animals representing more than 1500 different species. The Avian House, covering an area of over 3300 m², is one of the world's largest.

Close to the Elephant Gate, at 32 Budapester Straße, is the **Zoo Aquarium** (Phone: 030/25 40 10, www.aquarium-berlin.de, daily 9 am–6 pm), founded in

A spread presented by Confiserie Gaston Lenôtre of France – just looking at these delectable pastries in the KaDeWe gourmet foods department makes your mouth water

the mid-19th century by the pioneering zoologist Alfred Brehm. The first building was on the site by 1913. Thousands of creatures are housed on three floors, classified according to the elements they inhabit: water (aquarium), earth (terrarium) and air (insectarium) – including reptiles, amphibians, fish and insects. The *Crocodile Hall* is a stellar attraction.

107 KaDeWe

Shop 'til you drop at the biggest department store in Europe.

Tauentzienstraße 21–24/
Wittenbergplatz
U1, U2, U3 Wittenbergplatz
Bus M19, M29, M46, 100, 200

The **Kaufhaus des Westens** at Wittenbergplatz, abbreviated to KaDeWe, is shopper's heaven, the biggest department store of its kind on the continent (approx 60 000 m² sales area).

The entrepreneur Adolf Jandorf commissioned Johann Emil Schaudt to design the shopping complex. Built in 1906/07 in the quarter growing up around the Gedächtniskirche, the department store was intended to cater for discriminating tastes. The takeover by Hermann Tietz (the Hertie chain) in 1927 marked a first substantial upswing in growth. You name it, you can find it at KaDeWe: from eve-

ning dresses to toothbrushes this department store has an incredible range of wares in stock. In the spectacular KaDeWe **food department** on the 6th floor you are spoilt for choice: just take your pick of 1300 cheeses, 400 types of bread and 2400 wines from all over the world. Of course souvenirs such as the *Berlin Bear*, in marzipan, plush or porcelain, are also on sale. All the culinary treats you can possibly imagine and superlative views of the city are in store for you at the KaDeWe **Restaurant** (7th floor), which has an impressive glass dome of its own!

Tauentzienstraße off Wittenbergplatz lures visitors with more department stores, boutiques, booksellers and shoe shops. South-east of Wittenbergplatz is **Nollendorfplatz**, once celebrated for the *Neues Schauspielhaus*. Built in 1906, the theatre was made famous by Erwin Piscator, who opened the 'Piscator stage' chapter in the annals of German theatre on 3 September 1927 with the Ernst Toller play 'Hoppla, wir leben!' More recently the theatre housed a disco called the Metropol. Since November 2005, however, the **Goya** (www.goya-berlin.de), an upmarket night-club, has occupied these elegantly decorated rooms. By acquiring shares as club members and thus becoming 'Goyans', guests can enjoy a stylish blend of restaurant, cocktail bar and dance floor.

Around Schloss Charlottenburg – heaven for art lovers

The section of the city surrounding Schloss Charlottenburg is a must for anyone interested in art. The palace, the exhibitions in it and the superlative museums nearby provide a survey of cultural history from ancient Egypt through Jugendstil to Modernism. The palace and its grand park are in Charlottenburg District (formerly Lietzow). Before it was incorporated in Greater Berlin in the early 20th century, Charlottenburg was Prussia's second richest city, which is still evident in the splendour of its historic buildings and elegant private dwellings, especially the houses between Kaiserdamm and Neuer Kantstraße on the Lietzensee.

108 Schloss Charlottenburg

The biggest and most glamorous Hohenzollern palace in Berlin.

Spandauer Damm/Luisenplatz
Phone: 03 31/969 42 00
www.spsg.de
Altes Schloss: Tu–Su 9 am–5 pm
Neuer Flügel: Tu–Su 10 am–5 pm
Be sure to telephone in advance for current opening hours
U7 Richard-Wagner-Platz, U2 Sophie-Charlotte-Platz, Bus 145, 309

Johann Arnold Nering, chief architect to the Elector of Brandenburg, started to build Schloss Lietzenburg, named after the nearby village of Lietzow, in 1695 in a wooded rural setting. Friedrich III gave it to his wife Sophie Charlotte as a **summer residence** and she lost no time in turning it into the intellectual centre of Berlin. One of her closest friends was the great philosopher Johann Gottfried Leibniz, who founded the Berlin Academy of Sciences.

After the Elector Friedrich III crowned himself 'King in Prussia' in 1701 and in this

Wrought iron curlicues and glittering gold – these graceful ornaments are perfectly attuned to the magnificent rooms of Schloss Charlottenburg

Versailles was the model: Schloss Charlotten-burg, named after Queen Sophie Charlotte, is generally regarded as Hohenzollern Baroque at its opulent zenith

capacity styled himself Friedrich I, the summer residence was not big enough for state receptions and other official affairs. Consequently it was enlarged until it superlatively exemplified Baroque architecture under the Hohenzollerns.

It took almost a century for the magnificent palace, which is known as the **Altes Schloss**, to attain its present size and appearance. The first to embark on this ambitious project was the Swedish architect Johann Friedrich Eosander von Göthe, who extended both sides of the building. After Queen Sophie Charlotte died, Schloss Lietzenburg was renamed Schloss Charlottenburg after her. The 48-m-high *domed tower* over the central section was added in 1713. The finishing touch was a gilded Fortuna, who tops the tower as a weather-vane. The **Orangerie** abutting the west wing, where important art exhibitions are now mounted, was also erected in the early 18th century. The architecture of the Schloss is clearly modelled on Versailles.

Not to be outdone, Frederick the Great, an inveterate builder, commissioned Georg Wenzeslaus von Knobelsdorff to add the **Neuer Flügel** (1740–47) in the east as a counterpart to the Orangery. In the reign of Friedrich Wilhelm II the **Schlosstheater** (1788–91) was built by Langhans, which lengthened the palace to 505 m.

After the revolution of 1918/19, the palace became the property of the state and during the Weimar Republic was used as a museum. It was gutted by fire during the Second World War. Decades of patient reconstruction have restored it almost to its former splendour.

Monument to the Great Elector

The *Ehrenhof*, the court in front of the central section of the palace, has been honoured since 1952 by the presence of a bronze equestrian statue of the Great Elector, cast in one piece in 1700 from the model that *Andreas Schlüter* had made in 1696/97. Portraying the monarch as victorious in battle, it is the most important German Baroque equestrian statue in existence. From 1703 it stood near the Berliner Stadtschloss. During the Second World War it was shipwrecked in Tegel harbour

on its way to storage and not salvaged until 1950.

Historic rooms

The historic rooms in the central tract and the right-hand wing of Charlottenburg were reconstructed in the 1950s and almost all of them are open to the public. The Eichengalerie and the world-famous **Porzellankabinett** are on the ground floor. The Porcelain Cabinet contains Chinese and Japanese porcelain from the 17th and 18th centuries. To enhance the dazzling effect created by his magnificent collection of china, Friedrich I had large mirrors set into the walls to multiply its glories.

Frederick the Great had his magnificent bedchamber and apartments on the upper floor of the **New Wing** as well as the *Weiße Saal*, which doubled as the enlightened monarch's banquet hall and throne room. The 42-m-long *Golden Gallery*, lavishly decorated throughout with gilded stuccowork over delicate green, is 'eye candy' from a golden age.

We are indebted to Frederick's exquisite taste and his passion for French Rococo painting for the eight important paintings by *Jean-Antoine Watteau* hanging in his apartments. A personal touch is his celebrated collection of snuff-boxes.

The former Schlosstheater houses the **Museum für Vor- und Frühgeschichte**

So much gold brings happiness: a major attraction is the 42-metre-long Golden Gallery in the New Wing – a superlatively imaginative German Rococo interior

Precious exhibits at the Museum für Vor- und Frühgeschichte in Schloss Charlottenburg:

Fantastic – the Berlin gold orb came from southern Germany

Ornamental even in the Dark Age migrations (5th/6th centuries)

(Museum for Prehistory and Early History, Phone: 030/32 67 48 40, www.smb.muse um, Tu–Fr 9 am–5 pm, Sa/Su 10 am–5 pm), based on the art and antiquities collections amassed by the Hohenzol-lerns. For a long time it was one of the three largest collections of its kind in the world but was decimated in the Second World War. Still the museum provides ex-tensive documentation of the prehistoric cultures of Europe and the Near East. Ex-hibits from ancient Rome and the Middle Ages round out the display. The *Heinrich Schliemann collection* with some of the treasures Schliemann (1822–1890) exca-vated in ancient Troy is a must.

A replica of a statue of the Elector Fried-rich III by Andreas Schlüter stands in front of the New Wing. The original has been missing since the Second World War.

 ## 109 Schlosspark Charlottenburg

TOP TIPP *A gem of European landscape architecture.*

Spandauer Damm/Luisenplatz
U7 Richard-Wagner-Platz,
U2 Sophie-Charlotte-Platz
Bus 145, 309

The Schloss Charlottenburg park is one of Berlin's most popular public parks. Ger-many's first Baroque garden in the grand

French manner, it was laid out by Simeon Godeau in 1687. Peter Joseph Lenné en-larged it by adding an English-style land-scaped garden in the 18th century. It still exemplifies European landscape archi-tecture at its best.

None of this grandeur is visible from the street as the gardens extend behind the palace. The *Baroque Garden*, bound-ed on the east by the Spree, is symmetri-cal in layout: large borders, so richly and intricately patterned that they are like embroidery, stretch as far as a *carp pond*. The central section is enclosed by av-enues of trees in rows of four across. At the centre is an octagonal basin with a jet of water spouting from its centre.

In the northern part of the park, the *En-glish Landscaped Garden*, stands a three-storeyed teahouse in the Baroque style, the **Belvedere** (April–Oct. Tu–Su 10 am–5 pm, Nov.–March Tu–Fr 12–4 pm, Sa/Su 12–5 pm) designed by Carl Gotthard Langhans in 1788. It is the perfect setting for displaying pieces of 18th and 19th-cen-turies porcelain made at the *Königliche Porzellan Manufaktur* (KPM).

At the end of a conifer avenue in the western part of the park stands a small

Pleasures all around you – Schloss and Park Charlottenburg. On the left the garden is bounded by the Spree; the fishpond abuts on the parterre

Doric temple, the **Mausoleum** (Phone: 030/32 09 14 46, www.spsg.de, 25 March –Oct. Tu–Su 10 am–5 pm) commissioned by King Friedrich Wilhelm III from Heinrich Gentz in 1812 as the last resting place of his wife, *Queen Luise* (1776–1810). The queen's marble sarcophagus, a splendid example of 19th-century German sculpture, was made in Italy by Christian Daniel Rauch in 1811–14. Rauch, in the queen's personal employ, was given time off by his royal mistress to study sculpture. Still beloved today, the queen receives tributes of flowers laid at the foot of her sarcophagus by Berliners commemorating the anniversary of her death.

Other important members of the royal family are also buried here: Luise's spouse Friedrich Wilhelm III († 1840), his second wife, Princess Liegnitz († 1873) and Prinz Albrecht († 1872). The heart of King Friedrich Wilhelm IV († 1861), is buried in a stone capsule between his parent's graves. The marble sarcophagi of Kaiser Wilhelm I († 1888) and the Empress Augusta († 1890) are the work of Erdmann Encke.

At the eastern entrance to the park, the **New Pavilion** (Phone: 030/32 09 14 43, www.spsg.de, Tu–Su 10 am–5 pm, Tu–Fr guided tours only) fits harmoniously into the landscape design. A summer house, it was planned by Schinkel at the suggestion of Friedrich Wilhelm III but built by Albert Dietrich Schadow in 1824/25. It was modelled on the *Villa Chiatamone* in Naples, where the king had lived in 1822. The monarch and his second wife spent the summers here. The *interior* of the pavilion was also planned by the great Schinkel. Despite uniformity in shape and layout, the rooms are individualised by being based on different colour schemes. Furniture, painting and sculpture from the Schinkel era are on display.

110 Museum Berggruen

Important private collection of classic modern art.

Schlossstraße 1/Spandauer Damm
Phone: 030/32 69 58 15
www. smb.museum
Tu–Su 10 am–6 pm
U7 Richard-Wagner-Platz
U2, U12 Sophie-Charlotte-Platz
Bus 145, 309

In October 2004 Heinz Berggruen, an art collector and patron of the arts, was made an honorary citizen of Berlin. One of his many services is to have bequeathed his important art collection to the city. It has been exhibited in the western tract of the Stüler building opposite Charlottenburg Palace since 1997.

Immersed in the local scene: the bronze monument to Heinrich Zille (1965, Heinrich Drake) in Koellnischer Park

Milieu painter

Schlossstraße is surrounded by a quarter typical of Berlin recalling the era of the vernacular painter **Heinrich Zille** (1858–1929). He lived and worked at *No. 88 Sophie-Charlotten-Straße* for thirty-seven years. Painting from the 'kerb', Zille became famous for his drawings of proletarian Berlin, his humorous captions and the many photographs he took and published in satirical magazines such as 'Lustige Blätter' and the sophisticated 'Simplicissimus'. A memorial plaque was put on the wall of his house in 1931 but the Nazis later removed it. Thanks to the efforts of a working man who hid the plaque, it could be restored to commemorate the 20th anniversary of Zille's death and put on the entrance to the *Zille Eck* in Zillestraße. So the memory of the man who so skilfully captured the **'Berlin milieu'** in his drawings lives on.

In 'Matador and Nude' (1970, Museum Berggruen) Picasso is rehearsing his big theme: painter and model – in the bullfighting arena and as a mischievous self-portrait

The focus of the collection is on Pablo Picasso, who is represented by one hundred works, including paintings, sculptures and prints. The Picassos include 'Fernande', which is a bronze sculpture, a portrait of the poet Jaime Sabarté and 'Seated Harlequin'. There are sixty exquisitely poetic works (1917–40) by Paul Klee. Among the over twenty works by Henri Matisse are six of his celebrated silhouettes. Sculptures by Alberto Giacometti and African sculpture round off the collection.

Heinz Berggruen with his loved ones – a loving couple and a Matisse tightrope walker

111 Bröhan-Museum

Jugendstil in an old barracks.

Schlossstraße 1 a/Spandauer Damm
Phone: 030/32 69 06 00
www.broehan-museum.de
Tu–Su 10 am–6 pm
U7 Richard-Wagner-Platz
U2 Sophie-Charlotte-Platz
Bus 145, 309

The Bröhan-Musuem, also called *Landesmuseum für Jugendstil, Art Déco und Funktionalismus* (1899–1939), is housed in an infantry barracks built in 1893. Since this comprehensive collection of Jugendstil, Art Déco and Functionalist applied and decorative arts was given by Professor Karl H. Bröhan (1921–2000) to the Federal state of Berlin, the museum is named after him. Bröhan had assembled this top-quality collection of porcelain, paintings, furniture, glass and industrial design between 1966 and 1975. The paintings, drawings and prints accompanying the collection are by the artists of the *Berlin Secession* (founded 1899).

The upper floor is devoted to documenting the contribution made to the decorative and applied arts by the prolific and versatile Belgian Art Nouveau artist, designer and architect *Henry van de Velde* (1863–1957).

127

112 Rathaus Charlottenburg

A successful blend of Baroque, Neo-Classicism and Jugendstil.

Otto-Suhr-Allee 96–102
U7 Richard-Wagner-Platz
Bus 145

In 1900 Charlottenburg was one of the richest communities in the German Empire. This is shown by its Town Hall, the work of architects Heinrich Reinhardt and Georg Süßenguth. The monumental building was enlarged by Heinrich Seeling not long afterwards (1911–15). The 88-m-high copper-clad tower of the Town Hall is still visible from a great distance.

The front façade is decorated with figures illustrating the various crafts guilds. The interior, the stairwell and the rather gloomy banquet halls are as impressive as the showy exterior.

Across from the Town Hall, at 89 Otto-Suhr-Allee, is the street's oldest house, built about 1820. The inscription on it, which translates as *'Privileged Court Apothecary 1799'* recalls the old court chemist's, which used to be next to the Town Hall.

If you head north-west, you reach the former parish church **Luisenkirche** (1716) at Gierkeplatz, altered by Schinkel 1823–26. After sustaining severe damage in the war, it was rebuilt and the tower was given a low, pyramidal roof.

When Charlottenburg Rathaus was built, the Neo-Gothic style was in full swing. This stately and formal Town Hall building exemplifies modified Jugendstil with reticent borrowings from earlier period styles.

The Westend –
great vistas guaranteed

In the late 19th and early 20th centuries, the Westend was the new elegant address just outside the city. Visitors today tend to be more familiar with the Messegelände, where all the great Berlin trade fairs take place. A walk through the Westend District is also interesting for anyone intent on seeing the Olympiagelände with the modernised Olympic Stadium and the Waldbühne or who is fascinated by 20th-century art and architecture. And then there's the Funkturm, dubbed 'Long Shanks' by Berliners for obvious reasons. It provides wonderful views of the city!

113 Internationales Congress Centrum (ICC)

A world-class conference venue hosting 400 conferences and meetings annually.

Messegelände
S5, S75 Messe Süd, S41, S42, S45, S46, S47 and U2 Messe Nord, U2 Kaiserdamm, Bus X34, X49, 139, 149

Laughed at for years as teratogenic architecture, the aluminium-clad Internationales Congress Centrum (ICC) is today widely accepted by Berliners. Designed by Ralf Schuler, it was built in 1973–79. Its elongated (320 m long, 80 m wide and 40 m high) form, recalling a ship, was necessitated by the circumstance that the Stadtautobahn runs right past it. The unconventional ICC design is echoed symbolically by the Jean Ipoustéguy *sculpture* 'A Person Building His City' (1980) at the main entrance.

Once inside the building, visitors are guided to the conference room they want by an electronic system. A mechanism for deadening sounds and vibrations was developed specially for the ICC building so that numerous events can go on at any one time without interfering with each other. Conferences, congresses and press conferences are not the only events hosted here. There are also cultural events, banquets and festivals. What is more, the ICC is used for big internation-al trade fairs such as the International Tourism Exchange, the International Radio Fair and International Green Week. The biggest room in the building (Saal 1) seats about 5000 and boasts Europe's second biggest stage equipped with state-of-the-art technology.

A three-storey bridge links the ICC building with the trade fair exhibition halls of the Messegelände.

114 Messegelände

International trade fairs with record-breaking attendance.

Hammarskjöldplatz
S5, S75 Messe Süd, S41, S42, S45, S46, S47 and U2 Messe Nord, U2 Kaiserdamm, Bus X34, X49, 139, 149

The figures are not to be sneezed at: nearly half a million visitors annually attend *International Green Week*, Europe's biggest food, agricultural and landscape architecture trade fair. And just as many converge on the biennial *International Radio and Television Fair* in August – a superlative media show.

Trade fair halls were on the site even before the First World War. After a fire in 1935, Richard Ermisch gave the fair grounds their present-day appearance although the buildings sustained severe damage in the Second World War. After 1950 new halls were added and, by the

close of the 20th century, the exhibition capacity had been enlarged again. The fair grounds cover a surface area of 188 887 m², of which 160 000 m² are taken up by roofed-over exhibition space.

The **Summer Garden** (40 000m²) goes back to 1930 and was designed by Hans Poelzig as a big flower-bed and pleasure gound at the centre of the fair grounds.

115 Funkturm

Superb panoramic views of the city are to be had from 'Long Shanks'.

Messedamm 11
S5, S75 Messe Süd, S41, S42, S45, S46, S47 and U2 Messe Nord, U2 Kaiserdamm, Bus X34, X49, 139, 149

'Long Shanks', the name given by Berliners to their radio and TV tower, which is 150 m high – including the aerial – was designed by Heinrich Straumer and built in 1924–26 for the Third German Radio Fair on the north-eastern fringes of the trade-fair grounds as an aerial, a signal tower for air traffic and an observation tower with a restaurant.

In 1945 a grenade destroyed one of the main supports of the tower but screws weighing 800 kg kept it balancing on three legs. One for the record books: its corner posts rest on porcelain supplied by the venerable KPM (Royal Porcelain Factory) and can carry an overall weight of 600 t. The *world's first television image* was transmitted from the tower in 1929. Until 1962 'Long Shanks' was also the relay station of the Berlin radio and TV channels. The panoramic views of the city from the double-decker **restaurant** (Phone: 030/30 38 29 96, closed Mo) at 55 m and the observation platform at 125 m are unsurpassed.

Berlin was the cradle of German radio. The first announcement ever made by a German radio channel was committed to the air waves from Berlin on 29 October 1923. The *Deutsches Rundfunkmuseum* (www.drm-berlin.de) at the foot of the tower was inaugurated in 1967. The Radio and TV Museum, which traces the development of the broadcasting media, closed late in 1997. It moved to the *Deutsches Rundfunkarchiv Babelsberg* (Phone: 030/581 20, www.dra.de) but is not open to the public.

116 Haus des Rundfunks

Germany's first radio building.

Masurenallee 8–14
U2 Theodor-Heuss-Platz,
Bus X34, X49, 104, 149

Built by Hans Poelzig in 1929–31, the Radio Building was the most modern in Europe because of its state-of-the-art technology. Built of clinker, it is shaped like a satellite screen. The writers Erich Kästner and Alfred Döblin appeared in radio plays here. This is where Brecht staged Shakespeare's 'Hamlet' for radio. Between 1945 and 1956 the Soviet military administration occupied the building and established their 'Radio Berlin'. Since 1957 the radio divisions of Sender Freies Berlin (SFB) have been housed here. On 1 May 2003 Radio Free Berlin merged with Radio Brandenburg (ORB) to form *Radio Berlin-Brandenburg (RBB)*.

117 Friedhof Heerstraße

One of Berlin's most beautiful cemeteries is the last resting place of famous artists.

Trakehner Allee 1
S5, S75, S9 and U2 Olympiastadion

The graves rise in terraces round a lake: **Sausuhlensee**. The celebrities buried here include the art dealer Paul Cassirer († 1926), the comic poet Joachim Ringelnatz († 1934), the actresses and actor Tilla

Top: *Long decried as a monstrous architecture in aluminium – the stirling qualities of the International Congress Centrum (ICC) are now appreciated as they deserve to be* **Bottom:** *Bodies in harmony: 200 bronzes as well as plaster models and sketches by the artist are on display in the Georg-Kolbe-Museum near the Heerstraße Cemetery*

A façade decked out in bright colours: the world-famous architect Le Corbusier designed this handsome building in Reichssportfeldstraße in the late 1950s

Durieux († 1971), Grete Weiser († 1970) and Victor de Kowa († 1973), the playwright Curt Goetz († 1960), the painter George Grosz († 1959) and the sculptor Georg Kolbe († 1947).

To the south of the cemetery, at 25 Sensburger Allee, the **Georg-Kolbe Museum** (Phone: 030/304 21 44, www. georg-kolbe-museum.de, Tu–Su 10 am–5 pm, S75 Heerstraße, Bus X34, X49, 149), which was the sculptor's dwelling and studio, provides extensive documentation on his life and work. Five larger than life-size sculptures are exhibited in the park, *Georg-Kolbe-Hain*: 'Large Kneeling Woman' (1942/43), 'Resting Woman' (1939–41), 'Dionysos' (1932), 'Large Falling Man' (1939–45) and 'Mars and Venus I' (1940).

er Dreieck. The 17-storey building of reinforced concrete was commissioned in 1956–58 for the Interbau Exhibition. The 557 flats of varying size and arrangement are intended to house 1500 people. They are in a little city of their own, with a power station, a post office and a shopping street. Today lodgings are also available in Le Corbusier House.

Characteristic of Le Corbusier's 'sculptural' style are the articulation of the *façade*: the vibrant colour of the abstract friezes formed by the recessed flat walls and the parapets of the balconies. Once the housing unit was finished, the architect repudiated it because his plans had been altered without his approval.

118 Le-Corbusier-Haus

Modern block of flats designed by one of the most influential and important 20th-century architects.

Flatowallee 16
www.berliner-corbusierhaus.de
S5, S75, Bus X34, X49, 149, 218

After building two versions of his modular 'Unité d'Habitation' housing in Marseilles and Nantes, the great architect *Le Corbusier* (1887–1965) was invited to execute a third version in Berlin at Heilsberg-

119 Olympiastadion

Germany's biggest sports stadium.

Olympischer Platz
Phone: 030/25 00 23 22
www.olympiastadion-berlin.de
daily 10 am–7 pm, Nov.–March until 4 pm, guided tours available.
Call in advance for current opening hours
S5, S75, S9 and U2 Olympiastadion

The Olympic Stadium built for the 1936 Olympic Games in Berlin was designed as the focal point of the *Reich Sports Field* by

Werner March (worked over by Albert Speer). It took 15 million Reich marks and 2600 construction workers, engineers and auxiliaries to complete the building from scratch in two years. On 1 August 1936 Adolf Hitler opened the 11th Olympic Games here before a crowd of 120 000 spectators. The Nazis were still pretending to be cosmopolitan so all anti-semitic language was banned from the city and a Jewish woman was even permitted to be a member of the German Olympic team. In the years after the Games, the NS authorities used the stadium for mass festivals such as May Day and Summer Solstice. Enthusiastic crowds welcomed Benito Mussolini here.

Since the 1960s the stadium has again been used regularly for sports such as track and field events and football matches. For four years, 2000–2004, the stadium was remodelled at a cost of approx 240 million euros. Now it is roofed over and the seating capacity has been enlarged from 75 000 to 76 000.

What is impressive about the stadium is that it is only 16.5 m high on the outside. To achieve this appearance, the field inside had to be lowered by 12 m below the ground level. Now that the stadium has been remodelled, the field is 14.65 m lower. Two high pillars mark the **Olympic Gate** in the east. The **Marathon Gate** with the chalice for the Olympic Flame is in the west. The names of the 1936 Olympic victors are on plaques covering the gate walls.

The **May Field** is behind the West Gate. This was the Nazi-era name for it because the 'German Labour Front' mustered here on 1 May. Badly damaged during the war, the 77-m-high **Bell Tower** – the Führer Tower under the Nazis – was blown up in 1962 but later rebuilt. It affords superb panoramic views. After the war the British occupation authorities held annual parades to celebrate the Queen's birthday here. Now the field is used for the 'Youth Trains for the Olympics' project.

Abutting the Olympic Stadium to the north is the **Schwimmstadion** (seats 7600), which was remodelled for the 1978 world championships. Another relic of the 1936 Olympics is the **Waldbühne** [see p. 173] in a hollow in the Murellen Hills. Seating 20 000, it is one of Europe's biggest open-air theatres, designed by Werner March like a Greek theatre for Nazi cult celebrations. Now classical music, jazz and pop concerts as well as open-air movie nights are held here.

A chic combination of old and new – the Olympic Stadium has flaunted a cool outfit since 2004, definitely appropriate for 2006 World Cup matches

Grunewald and Wannsee – woodland, meadows, water

Berliners have always used the Grunewald with the Havelseen (32 km^2) – Wannsee, Grunewaldsee, Schlachtensee and Krumme Lanke – as an area for relaxation and recreation. Here there are fine bathing beaches and enjoyable inns as well as beautiful forest footpaths, elegant residential areas and romantc little palaces. Until the 19th century this wooded and marshy area east of the Havel was known as Spandauer Forst. A natural mixed forest, Spandau Forest was the Prussian royal game preserve.

120 Villenkolonie Grunewald

Beautiful mansions with lake views.
S7, S9 Grunewald, Bus M19, 186

An elegant colony of villas was built in 1877 on the lovely lakes Hundekehlesee, Dianasee and Königssee: entrepreneurs, artists and Jewish industrialists moved to this residential area. From 1890 the S-Bahn ensured good connections with the city. The suburban rail station was built in the English country-house style.

During the Third Reich the villas owned by Jews were confiscated. Nazi bigwigs such as Hermann Göring and Joseph Goebbels moved into them (Königsallee 68 and 70) while from Grunewald goods station Berlin Jews were deported to the concentration camps.

Ship ahoy! Fun sailing on the Havel – and looking up at the Grunewaldturm

121 Teufelsberg

A mountain made of rubble.
On the northern edge of Grunewald
S7, S9 Grunewald (approx 20-minute walk)

The Teufelsberg, all 115 metres of it, rises on the northern fringe of the Grunewald. Greater Berlin's highest elevation, it doesn't look as if it was made of 25 million cubic metres of rubble from buildings destroyed in the war. Berliners don't care if it is manmade. They take advantage of every free minute to enjoy it. During the cold months you see people sledging and skiing and in autumn it's a great place for flying kites. In winter 1986 a world slalom championship was held on the Teufelsberg. Walkers appreciate the enchanting **views** from here: looking south-west you can see far across the green Grunewald all the way to the Havel. The *Teufelssee*, Berlin's deepest lake, is at the foot of the Teufelsberg.

A hunting we will go! Enjoying the Grunewaldsee scenery and Grunewald Hunting Lodge in its idyllic setting

122 Jagdschloss Grunewald

Berlin's oldest castle on the south-eastern shore of Grunewaldsee.

Hüttenweg 100
Phone: 030/813 35 97
www.spsg.de
15 May–15 Oct. Tu–Su 10 am–5 pm, rest of the year Su guided tours only at 11 am, 1 pm and 3 pm
Bus X83, 115, 183 (approx 20-minute walk)

Grunewald royal hunting lodge is one of Berlin's oldest surviving secular buildings. In a truly idyllic setting, this gem of a cas-tle, built by Caspar Theyss in 1542, belonged to the Elector Joachim II in the 16th century. Called 'Zum grünen Wald' because it was located in a green wood, it gave its name to the woodland. A simple Renaissance building, it underwent Baroque renovation in the 18th century and outbuildings were added. Only the lobby and the stairwell tower retained their original appearance.

The Jagdschloss Grunewald houses an important **collection of paintings** comprising roughly 200 German and Dutch masterpieces from the 15th to the 19th centuries by Bloemaert, Bruyn, Jordaens, Cranach, Rubens, etc.

Who is more fair, Nature or Nymph? 'The Water Nymph' (ca 1515) by Lucas Cranach the Elder in the Grunewald Hunting Lodge gallery

123 Großer Wannsee

For almost one hundred years the lake and its bathing beach have been a favourite with Berliners

S1, S7 Nikolassee or Wannsee
Bus 112, 114, 118, 218, 316, 318, 620

Older Berliners fleeing the summer heat of the city for Wannsee beach still hum the old popular song 'Pack your bathing suit and…' The **Strandbad**, a bathing beach with facilities, was laid out in 1907 but remodelled by Richard Ermisch (1929–30) in the New Objectivity style. Even today it is Berlin's most popular place for swimming and recreation. The spacious grounds with terraces and a sandy beach 80 m wide and stretching 1.3 km is Europe's biggest lakeside day resort. Four hundred old-fashioned basket sun chairs and 1800 canvas-covered deck-chairs are available for hire.

If you want more than just lazing by the lake then you can walk north to the **Schwanenwerder** peninsula, which covers 25 ha. In the late 19th century a **villa settlement** was built here. The 1930s saw

Summer fun at Grosser Wannsee, with the basket-chair colony and ladies' beach volleyball

Making a splash at Grosser Wannsee beach – many a sun worshipper promenades beachwear fashions with elegance and poise

Nazi VIPs move in. After the war General Dwight Eisenhower resided here as military governor. Later the Aspen Institute, a think-tank, was set up on what was once the Goebbels property at 10–14 Inselstraße. Publishing mogul Axel Springer had a mansion built at Nos. 24–26.

124 Villenviertel Alsen

High society summer colony and the Wannsee Conference memorial house.

S1, S7 Wannsee, Bus 114

The woodland area surrounding Wannsee is only thinly populated. For centuries it was the Prussian *royal game preserve*, unsettled except for a scattering of farmsteads and fishermen's cottages as well as inns such as Stimmings Krug at the present-day Wannsee Bridge (Königstraße 4). The playwright *Heinrich von Kleist* spent his last night there before shooting his mistress Henriette Vogel and committing suicide on 21 November 1811. His ivy-covered grave is at 3 Bismarckstraße.

The banker Wilhelm Conrad had the Stimmings Krug inn demolished in 1863 so he could build a villa on the site. An influential businessman, he planned a villa colony on his 70 ha property along the south-eastern shore of Großer Wannsee and succeeded in persuading friends of his to build there too. After Conrad ensured planning permission for the **Wannseebahn** rail connection (now the S1) in 1874, Berlin's high society built **summer mansions** here. Gustav Meyer, a pupil of Lenné's, landscaped this woodland and marsh area. Wilhelm Conrad called the villa colony, the first of its kind near Berlin, Alsen after the island Germany snatched from Denmark in the war of 1864.

The **Villa Minoux** (Am Großen Wannsee 56–58) attained historic notoriety: on 20 January 1942 SS Obergruppenführer Reinhard Heydrich, SS Obersturmbannführer Adolf Eichmann and other top-echelon officials from the Reich Ministry of the Interior and the Foreign Ministry met here to decide the murder of eleven million Jews. Their meeting made history as the Wannsee Conference. On the 50th anniversary of this fateful violation of human rights, the villa was declared the **Gedenkstätte Haus der Wannseekonferenz** (Phone: 030/805 00 10, www.ghwk.de, exhibition: daily 10 am–6 pm, library and media collection: Mo–Fr 10 am–6 pm), a memorial warning against racism.

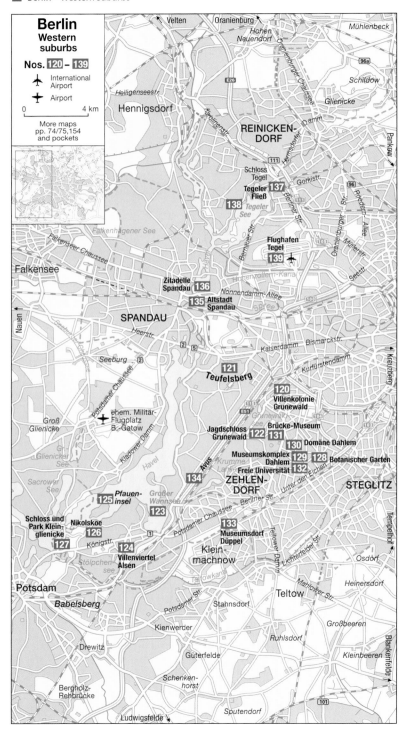

Berlin
Western suburbs

Nos. 120 – 139

✈ International Airport
✈ Airport

0   4 km

More maps
pp. 74/75,154
and pockets

Velten

Oranienburg

Mühlenbeck

Hohen Neuendorf

Schildow

Glienicke

Heiligenseestr.

Hennigsdorf

Karolinenstr.

Oranienburger Chaussee

96a

E26

Pankow

REINICKEN-DORF

Hermsdorfer Damm

111

Schloss Tegel

Gorkistr.

Tegeler Fließ **137**

96

138 Tegeler See

Berliner Str.

Roedern-Allee

Oranienburger Str.

Müllerstr.

Flughafen Tegel

139 ✈

101

Seestr.

Falkenhagener See

Falkensee

Falkenseer Chaussee

Spree

Hohenzollern-Kanal

Zitadelle Spandau **136**

Nonnendamm-Allee

100

135 Altstadt Spandau

SPANDAU

Nauen

Heerstr.

Seeburg

2

2

5

Kaiserdamm

Bismarckstr.

Kreuzberg

Potsdamer Chaussee

121 Teufelsberg

Kurfürstendamm

120 Villenkolonie Grunewald

Groß Glienicke

ehem. Militär-Flugplatz B.-Gatow

Grunewald See

E51

Brücke-Museum

103

Gr. Glienicker See

Kladower Damm

Havel

Jagdschloss Grunewald **122** **131**

130 Domäne Dahlem

Sacrower See

Avus

Krumme Lanke

Museumskomplex Dahlem **129** **128** Botanischer Garten

Freie Universität **132**

Unter den Eichen

STEGLITZ

Pfaueninsel **125**

134

ZEHLEN-DORF

Tempelhof

Großer Wannsee

123

Berliner Str.

Schloss und Park Klein-glienicke **127**

Nikolskoe **126**

Königstr.

1

133 Museumsdorf Düppel

Klein-machnow

Potsdamer Chaussee

Tellower Damm

Lichterfelder Str.

Osdorf

Stölpchen-see

124 Villenviertel Alsen

Teltowkanal

Heinersdorf

Potsdam

Babelsberg

Potsdamer Str.

Stahnsdorf

Teltow

Mahlower Str.

Blankenfelde

Drewitz

Kienwerder

Güterfelde

Schenken-horst

Großbeeren

Ruhlsdorf

Kleinbeeren

Bergholz-Rehbrücke

Sputendorf

101

Ludwigsfelde

125 Pfaueninsel

The Pearl of the Havel is German landscape architecture at its best.

Phone: 030/80 58 68 30
www.spsg.de
Ferry: May–Aug. daily 8 am–9 pm,
March/April, Sep./Oct. daily 8 am–
6 pm, Nov.–Feb. daily 10 am–4 pm
Castle: 25 March–31 Oct. Tu–Su
10 am–5 pm
S1, S7 Wannsee, Bus 218, 316

The idyllic Pfaueninsel tucked away in the southern arm of the Havel can only be reached by ferry. Cars and bicycles must be left at *Nikolskoer Weg* and dogs are also unwelcome. There is no question about it: Peacock Island is rightly called the 'Pearl of the Havelmeer' since it is a prime example of the 'sentimental landscaped park' in the Romantic style, complete with artificial ruins and Neo-Classical architecture. Berliners flocked to the island in their thousands during the 19th century to admire exotic animals in a fairy-tale landscape setting. Now the Pfaueninsel is Berlin's most beautiful nature reserve, boasting magnificent old *trees* and a wide variety of *bird species*.

In the Great Elector's (1640–88) day, hares were bred for hunting on the island, which is about 1.5 km long and 500 m wide. The prince elector had a *glassworks* built on the eastern side of the island, where the chemist Johann Kunckel von Löwenstein made his highly prized ruby glass.

Summer palace

During the 18th century Peacock Island was only used for cattle and sheep until Friedrich Wilhelm II had a bower built here in 1794 to enjoy the company of his mistress, Countess Lichtenau: a Romantic summer castle was built in the ruined style with two towers linked by an airy bridge. But Wilhelm had no joy of his charming love nest. He died in 1797, the year it was finished. The little castle later became the favourite summer residence of his son Friedrich Wilhelm III and his wife Queen Luise.

The original *furnishings* of the castle have all survived, superlatively exemplifying the Neo-Classical style fashionable in the reign of Friedrich Wilhelm II. Rich stuccowork, wall and ceiling paintings and inlaid hardwood floors lend the rooms their elegance.

A love nest without turtle doves: Friedrich Wilhelm II had a castle built for trysts with his mistress on Peacock Island. But poor 'Fat Wilhelm' died a year after it was completed

Landscaped park

The great landscape architect Peter Joseph Lenné was commissioned to landscape the island. In 1822 he laid out a *menagery* which would form the nucleus of the Berlin Zoo in 1842, and converted most of the Pfaueninsel into a landscaped park in the English manner. He also planted exotic trees and shrubs, including palms, for which Albert Dietrich Schadow designed a palm house (1829–31) that burnt down in 1880.

At the centre of the island is the **Kavalierhaus**, designed by Karl Friedrich Schinkel in 1824. The great architect incorporated elements of the late Gothic façade of a 15th-century patrician town house that had burnt down in Danzig in the *South Tower*. Another Schinkel toy is the **Schweizerhaus** for court employees. South of the Kavalierhaus is a relic of the menagery – the *Volière*, built in 1824 to showcase exotic birds. Not far from it is their *Winter Aviary* (1828). The stars of the island are undoubtedly the peacocks freely strutting about in the gardens.

The **Dairy Farm** (ca 1795) at the northern end of the island was, like the palace, built as a ruin and is in the Gothic Revival style. South of it is the **Memorial Temple** to Queen Luise, a little hall structure erected in 1829.

The epitome of vanity: the eponymous peacock, after which this Havelland island is named, unfurls his magnificent tail. The island is still home to these exotic birds

126 Nikolskoe

Little Russia in Grunewald.
Nikolskoer Weg
Bus 218

Across from the Pfaueninsel is a little observation plateau landscaped by Lenné in the early 19th century. On it stands the log cabin Blockhaus Nikolskoe. King Friedrich Wilhelm III commissioned it in 1819 for his daughter Charlotte and her husband, who would become Tsar Nicholas I. Since the cabin looks Russian and was built for a Russian prince, it was called 'Nicholas' own'. The Tsar's personal coachman used to live there and ran a tavern –

illegally. After arsonists set it on fire, **Blockhaus Nikolskoe** (www.blockhaus-nikolskoe.de, Phone: 030/805 29 14) has been restored to its function as a little inn. From its terrace there are superb views of the river Havel and the Pfaueninsel.

To the east of the Russian log cabin is the Church of **St Peter and Paul** (1834–37), designed by Stüler, an aisleless hall church with a semicircular altar room and an onion-domed tower, echoing the Russian theme. The two Roman *mosaic medallions* on the lofty pulpit bearing the names of the patron saints of the church were a gift to Frederick the Great from Pope Clement XIII.

If you take a walk south-west along the Havel, you come to **Moorlake** (Moorlaker Weg, Phone: 030/805 58 09), an attractive inn with a garden.

127 Schloss & Park Kleinglienicke

Architecture and landscaping in perfect harmony.
North of Königstraße
Phone: 03 31/969 42 00
www.spsg.de
15 May–15 Oct. Sa/Su/hols.
10 am–5 pm
S1, S7 Wannsee, then Bus 316

The **Große Neugierde** ('Great Curiosity'), a round temple with Corinthian columns

Na Stroviye! The Blockhaus Nikolskoe is a Russian-style log cabin with a restaurant. Day trippers are overwhelmed by the views

Roar away, golden lions! This pride of lions guards Schloss Kleinglienicke – a total work of art that was once the summer residence of Prince Karl of Prussia

built by Schinkel in 1835, stands at Glienicker Bridge which crosses the Havel to Potsdam. After the Second World War **Glienicker Brücke** attracted attention worldwide. This was the perch from which the international press could observe the *exchange of spies* between East and West. Now that the cold war has been consigned to history, visitors come here to enjoy the natural beauty of the area and Kleinglienicke castle and park. At first there was just a small country house here that Chancellor Prince Karl August von Hardenberg acquired in 1814.

In 1824 Prince Karl of Prussia, third son of King Friedrich Wilhelm III, had the idea of making a summer residence and landscaped park out of it. He commissioned Karl Friedrich Schinkel to convert the existing building into **Schloss Kleinglienicke** and add a host of ancillary buildings. Schinkel's pupils Ludwig Persius und Ferdinand von Arnim also had a hand in the design. Schinkel added a north-east wing (1825–28) to the castle, turning it into a simple structure with three wings, and put a tower on the Kavalierhaus. The interior is elegant and harmonious with rooms decorated in different colour schemes.

Prince Karl of Prussia brought back modern and ancient sculpture and frag-

ments of architecture from his extensive travels – some of them from Pompeii and Carthage – which were incorporated in the decoration of the buildings.

Peter Joseph Lenné, who had laid out the English-style *Pleasure Ground* for Hardenberg in 1816, also designed the 116-ha **Park Kleinglienicke**. The *Löwenfontäne* with its gilded lions ceremoniously introducing the central section of the palace, is modelled on a fountain at the *Villa Medici* in Rome. The *fountain* in the inner garden courtyard is a replica of the ancient *Ildefonso Group* ('Sleep and Death') in the Madrid Prado. Fragments of ancient architecture are set into the rear façade of the palace.

To the west of the Lion Fountain and directly on Königstraße, is Schinkel's **Kleine Neugierde** (1825). The 'Little Curiosity', a tea pavilion, was decorated with ancient sarcophagus reliefs as well as fragments of Pompeiian mosaics and frescoes.

Schinkel also created the **Casino**, with its elongated pergolas, in the street along the Jungfernsee, in 1824 by enlarging a billiards house.

The prolific architect added the **Jägerhof** in the north of the park in 1828. Its crenellations and Tudor arches were borrowed from English Gothic Revival.

Dahlem and Zehlendorf – village life in the big city

Zehlendorf and the incorporated village on the green of Dahlem were once little rural settlements outside the confines of the city. Now they are among Berlin's best residential areas. Rents and property prices are so exorbitant here that only the rich can afford flats and houses in this section of the city. No wonder that the neighbourhood is so attractive: much of Zehlendorf consists of woodland, water, landscaped parks and gardens while 173 ha are still arable land. Dahlem also has a distinctive village core around 'Alter Krug', with its important museums, research facilities and university institutes as well as the elegant residential areas where public figures active in culture, politics and business have their homes.

128 Botanischer Garten

Europe's biggest botanical gardens.
Königin-Luise-Straße 6–8
Phone: 030/83 85 00 27
www.botanischer-garten-berlin.de
May–July daily 9 am–9 pm
April, Aug. daily 9 am–8 pm
Sep. daily 9 am–7 pm
March, Oct. daily 9 am–6 pm
Feb. daily 9 am–5 pm
Nov.–Jan. daily 9 am–4 pm
S1 Botanischer Garten, Bus 385

The Botanical Gardens are Europe's biggest, home to more than 18 000 species of flora. They were laid out under the supervision of Adolf Engler between 1897 and 1903. For centuries before that, rare specimens of flora had been cultivated in the Lustgarten in front of the Berliner Stadtschloss. There were even botanical gardens from 1679 until 1897 in Schöneberg in what is now Kleist Park – its venerable trees are still there. The present botanical gardens cover 42 ha. Plants are arranged according to different scientific criteria: there is a geographical section, an area with useful and medicinal plants, a hands-on garden for sniffing and touching, a tree garden (Arboretum) and an antique garden modelled on those the prince elector of Brandenburg knew with plants popular in the 17th century.

If you enter the botanical gardens by the southern entrance in Unter den Eichen street, you walk through the **Baumgarten**, which harbours about 1800 spe-

cies of trees and shrubs in a setting of meadows and ponds. The **16 Gewächshäuser**, glasshouses for tropical and subtropical flora, are a magnet for the public. The Großes Tropenhaus is 60 m long, 30 m wide and 25 m high. Air temperatures between 24 und 30°C and high humidity ensure that giant bamboos can grow 10–30 cm a day. Rare orchids, carnivorous plants, cactuses and water-lilies also grow magnificently here. The **Botanisches Museum** (daily 10 am–6 pm) at the northern entrance has an interesting collection of prepared plant specimens, models, dioramas and Botanic Channel, an interactive video installation.

129 Museumskomplex Dahlem

Four museums present ethnographic collections that are among the most important and the richest in Europe.

Arnimallee 23–27/Lansstraße 8
www.smb.museum
U3 Dahlem Dorf, Bus X11, X83

The oldest building in the Dahlem Museum Complex was built between 1914 and 1923 at the instigation of Wilhelm von Bode, director-general of Berlin museums. Designed by the versatile Bruno Paul, it originally housed the Asian Museum.

A *bronze centaur group* of statuary by Reinhold Begas (1881) stands in front of the Arnimallee entrance. At the corner of Fabeckstraße is a bronze *sculpture* of 'Heracles with the Nemean Lion' by Max Klein (1897).

The building was enlarged by Wils Ebert and Fritz Bornemann in the 1960s to accommodate collections rendered homeless by the partition of the city. After reunification it was only consistent to reunite the collections concerned with those on the Museum Island. The following collections have already left Dahlem: the Paintings Gallery (now in the Kulturforum, see No. 80), the Sculpture Collection, the Museum of Byzantine Art (both due to be in the Bodemuseum from 2006, see p. 40) and the Museum of Islamic Art (now in the Pergamonmuseum, see p. 41).

Jungle in Berlin – visiting the rare exotic plants in the Tropics House at the Botanical Gardens is a memorable experience

An invitation to the Japanese Tea Ceremony – the Dahlem Museum für Ostasiatische Kunst captures the lifestyle and customs of faraway lands

Ethnologisches Museum

Lansstraße 8
Phone 030/830 14 38
Tu–Fr 10 am–6 pm, Sa/Su 11 am–6 pm

The Ethnological Museum is one of the most interesting and largest of its kind. Established in 1873, it goes back to the famous 17th-century *Cabinet of Art and Rare Curiosities* assembled by the Great Elector. The present collection comprises over 500 000 ethnographica, countless recordings of ethnic music, over 140 000 documentary photos and 1000 ethnological films.

The Museum is arranged thematically and geographically, with sections on Africa, American archaeology, American ethnology, the Islamic Orient, eastern, northern, southern and south-eastern Asia, the South Seas, Australia and ethnology of music. The European Collection was made part of the Museum of European Cultures years ago (see below). In August 2005 the permanent exhibition 'Art from Africa' opened with one hundred and eighty

Magic moments – Wuzhiqi, the tutelary deity of the rivers Huai and Guo (PR China, Song Dynasty, early 12th century), and his shadow

masterpieces spanning eight centuries and representing seventy of the continent's peoples. The thematic focus is on art history, figurative sculpture, performance and design. Further, there is an ethnographic music museum and a junior museum invites interactivity under the heading 'Cross the Desert'.

Museum für Indische Kunst

Lansstraße 8
Phone: 030/830 13 61
Tu–Fr 10 am–6 pm, Sa/Su 11 am–6 pm

Founded in 1963, the Museum for East Indian Art is the most recent museum to have joined the Staatliche Museen Preußischer Kulturbesitz. It was created to take over collections of the Ethnological Museum devoted to India, Indonesia and Central Asia. Although many items have been lost because they were stolen by the Soviet troops in 1945, about 15 000 notable exhibits have remained. Especially interesting are the *Turfan Collections* (2nd–12th centuries) from Buddhist caves and temples in Chinese Turkestan, showcasing wall paintings and textile paintings, statues in clay and wood, etc. Further sights to see: the *Gandhara statues* (1st–5th centuries) and the earliest known bronze *statue* of the god Vishnu from Pakistan (7th century).

Museum für Ostasiatische Kunst

Lansstraße 8
Phone: 030/830 13 82
Tu–Fr 10 am–6 pm, Sa/Su 11 am–6 pm

The Museum of East Asian Art goes back to the *East Asian Art Collection*, which was established in 1907. Most of that collection was, however, removed by Soviet troops in 1945 and is now in the State Hermitage Museum in St Petersburg. The Museum in Dahlem primarily exhibits art from *China*, *Japan* and *Korea* from the Neolithic to the present. Highlights include Chinese and Japanese drawings, prints and paintings, exquisite Japanese pottery used for the tea ceremony and 150 unique bronzes from the Ordos desert region of northern China (5th century BC–3rd century AD).

Museum Europäischer Kulturen

Arnimallee 25
Phone: 030/830 13 87
Tu–Fr 10 am–6 pm, Sa/Su 11 am–6 pm

Rudolf Virchow, physician and anthropologist, is credited with being the founder of the *Museum for Ethnic Costumes and Household Products*, which was inaugurated in 1889 in Palais Creutz at 36 Klosterstraße. The ethnological exhibits assembled for the 1893 Chicago Exhibition were subsequently added to that collection. In 1904 the collections were placed under the jurisdiction of the royal museums as the *Royal Collection of German Ethnology*. However, 80 % of the 45 000 items comprising the collection were lost during the Second World War. The remaining pieces were placed in the rebuilt (1970–76) magazine tract of the Geheimes Staatsarchiv Preußischer Kulturbesitz (Im Winkel 6–8). Founded again in 1999 as the Museum of European Cultures, it then also incorporated the European collection of the Ethnological Museum as well as exhibits from the Pergamonmuseum.

Since May 2005 the Museum Europäischer Kulturen has been in the Museumskomplex Dahlem; its exhibitions deal with European everyday living from the 19th to the 21st centuries. The collections showcase jewellery, devotional images,

The Hindu pantheon – terracotta reliefs in the Museum of Indian Art

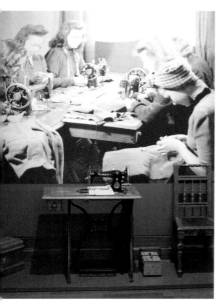

The Pfaff sewing machine and 'Surviving 1945' at the Museum of European Cultures

ceramics (including the 1665 Winterthur tiled stove), textiles, household implements and toys. The programme includes rotating exhibitions as well as themed culture days devoted to particular countries and the European Christmas and Easter market.

Brücke-Museum: 'Otto Mueller with Pipe' by Ernst Ludwig Kirchner (1913)

130 Domäne Dahlem

Open-air museum and peasant life in the raw.

Königin-Luise-Straße 49
Phone: 030/666 30 00
www.domaene-dahlem.de
We–Mo 10 am–6 pm
U3 Dahlem Dorf, Bus X11, X83

The village centre of Dahlem has been preserved and includes The Dahlem Demesne open-air Museum. Dahlem Manor House was built in 1680 on the land of a medieval manor with privileges of court-leet. The demesne was owned by District Commissioner Cuno Hans von Willmerstorff. The Baroque manor now houses a teaching and training section of the Free University *Institute of Veterinary Medicine*. A small Museum is informative on the history of the demesne. Crowd pleasers are the big *Eco Market* (We 12 noon–6 pm, Sa 8 am–1 pm).

At the centre of the village is the *Dahlem Village Church* (ca 1220), also called St Anna's. Built of brick, it was given a Late Gothic sanctuary in the 15th century. The Baroque pulpit and the gallery were added in 1679. The carved altar, consecrated to St Anne, is remarkable.

The centre of Dahlem boasts *U-Bahnhof Dahlem Dorf*, a railway station built in 1913 to resemble a thatch-roofed Lower Saxon half-timbered house, as well as the *Dorfanger*, the village green with a mound concealing an ice house dating from 1709.

131 Brücke-Museum

Excellent selection of Expressionist masterpieces.

Bussardsteig 9
Phone: 030/831 20 29
www.bruecke-museum.de
We–Mo 11 am–5 pm
Bus 115

The Brücke Museum (1967) in Zehlendorf was designed by Werner Düttmann at the suggestion of the Expressionist painter Karl Schmidt-Rottluff (1884–1976): he wanted to commemorate the group of Expressionist artists known as **'Die Brücke'** (until 1913), which he and fellow artists had founded in Dresden in 1905. Schmidt-Rottluff and his colleague Erich Heckel shared the construction costs. A bungalow-like, flat-roofed structure was built at the edge

Daily life in the good old days: A medieval settlement was discovered in the village of Düppel. Now visitors can learn all about the crafts practised there 900 years ago

of Grunewald, a building with lots of glass and béton brut (rough textured concrete) walls at the entrance.

The four exhibition rooms centred about an inner courtyard display a collection of 400 vibrant and expressive oil paintings as well as numerous drawings, watercolours and prints by the Brücke artists Schmidt-Rottluff, Erich Heckel and Ernst Ludwig Kirchner as well as Otto Müller, Emil Nolde and Max Pechstein. Themed rotating exhibitions give deeper insights into the work of these artists.

Behind the museum is a colossal studio where sculptor Arno Breker used to create the monumental hero statues that so delighted the NS regime. Now the studio houses the **Bernhard-Heiliger-Stiftung** (Käuzchensteig 8, Phone: 030/831 20 12, www.bernhard-heiliger-stiftung.de) and a fine sculpture garden dotted about with works by Bernhard Heiliger (1915–1996). A pupil of Breker's, Heiliger subsequently embraced an abstract formal idiom.

132 Freie Universität Berlin

Germany's first new postwar university now boasts a library by Sir Norman Foster.

Boltzmannstraße/Garystraße
U3 Thielplatz, Bus M11, 110

The Free University (FU) was founded in West Berlin in 1948 with the governing Mayor Ernst Reuter as its head – professors and students felt that they were being deprived of their academic freedoms in the Soviet occupation zone and wanted a West Berlin university of their own. Professors lectured in the American Sec-

tor, at first in several Dahlem villas. Funding from the Ford Foundation made it possible to erect the main building the *Henry Ford Building*, in 1952, and, in 1954, the university library. Between 1967 and 1972 the *'Rusty Arbour'*, a complex of pavilion-like institute buildings was added to house the arts and humanities. Designed by Paris architects Candilis, Josic and Woods, it owes its derogatory name to its brown steel façade. Another building was added between 1972 and 1979. Since it was aluminium-clad, it is called the *'Silver Arbour'*. The *Philological Library* designed by Sir Norman Foster was inaugurated in 2005 next to the 'Rusty Arbour', which is undergoing extensive renovation and restoration to be completed by 2007. As the spectacular new building is shaped like a brain, it is called 'The Berlin Brain' and houses about 700 000 volumes. The FU has an enrolment of 35 500 students in twelve departments.

133 Museumsdorf Düppel

Reconstruction of a medieval settlement on the fringes of the big city.

Phone: 030/802 66 71
www.dueppel.de
April–Oct. Th 3 pm–7 pm,
Su 10 am–5 pm
S1 Zehlendorf
Bus X10, 101, 112, 115, 285, 623

Berlin has everything, including a medieval settlement replete with dwellings, granaries and workshops. Museumsdorf

Speed limit included: Germany's first car-racing track – the Avus (top right) runs straight through the Grunewald. Left: the International Congress Centre (ICC)

Düppel is an open-air museum, a reconstruction of the settlement that was excavated in southern Zehlendorf at Machnower Krummes Fenn. Archaeologists unearthed a 12th-century village here in 1967. Its inhabitants are thought to have abandoned the site as early as 1220 to move to Zehlendorf, which had just been founded, because the loamy soil there promised better crop yields.

During the summer months *demonstrations* of traditional medieval crafts take place at Museumsdorf Düppel: blacksmithing at the forge, making pottery, weaving and carving as well as baking bread. Moreover, there are events dealing with agricultural and historical themes.

134 Avus

Germany's first car-racing track.
S3, S5, S7, S75 and U9 Hansaplatz
Bus 343, 265

Grunewald, most of which belongs to Zehlendorf, is bisected by the Avus (Automobil-, Verkehrs- und Übungsstraße) running between Messegelände and Nikolassee. Opened in 1921, the Avus was

Germany's first car-racing track. Exciting speed records were set and broken here. The round-the-track record was set by Bernd Rosemeyer in 1937: 276 km/h. Down the straight stretch Rudolf Caracciola set a speed record of nearly 400 km/h. Now the Avus, which is 8 km long, is part of the city motorway network – and the speed limit has been reduced to a boring 100 km/h!

Heavenly peace

If you're driving, you should take the time to turn off at Zehlendorf and visit the **Südwestfriedhof** of the Berliner City Synod at **Stahnsdorf**. Famous Berliners have been laid to rest in this beautiful cemetery: the industrialist Werner von Siemens († 1892), the publisher Gustav Langenscheidt († 1895), the film director F. W. Murnau († 1931), the painter Lovis Corinth († 1925) and the composer Engelbert Humperdinck († 1921). The popular painter Heinrich Zille is also buried here – more than 2000 mourners accompanied him on his last journey to Stahnsdorf in 1929.

Spandau and Reinickendorf –
on the city's western fringes

Spandau has always been a special place: once a fortified city, it is older than Berlin. It was first settled in the 8th century by Slavs and was also registered as a city in 1232 even before Berlin. However, 1920 meant the end of independence for Spandau: with the neighbouring communities of Gatow, Kladow, Pichelsdorf, Staaken, Tiefwerder, Spandau-Zitadelle and Pichelswerder it was incorporated in Greater Berlin. Not without acerbic comments from the inhabitants of Spandau: 'May the Kaiser's hand keep us safe from Greater Berlin and expedient bond.' Reinickendorf (first mentioned in records in 1375) became known mainly for Flughafen Tegel (the airport was inaugurated in 1974) and the Märkisches Viertel (1963–74), a controversial satellite settlement that provides housing for 50 000. Tegeler See and the hinterland of the lake are particularly scenic.

135 Altstadt Spandau

Medieval small-town ambience on the west bank of the river Havel.

U7 Altstadt Spandau
S5, S75, U7 Rathaus Spandau Bahnhof
Bus X33, M32, M37, 130, 131, 134, 135, 136, 145, 236, 237, 337, 638, 639, 671

Spandau Old Town sustained severe damage from bombing raids during the Second World War. To make matters worse, even more was razed by bulldozers in the 1970s. The Spandau authorities belatedly approved restoration of the Old Town, which began in 1978. As a result, **Reformationsplatz** and nearby **Marktplatz** have been pedestrian precincts since 1982, centres of an historic core, Spandau Old Town, with streets and alleys in which the past still seems very much alive.

St.-Nikolai-Kirche in Reformationsplatz with its steeply pitched roof and massive *west tower* dates from the first half of the 15th century and is an important example of Brandenburg brick Gothic. St Nicholas' was built on the founda-

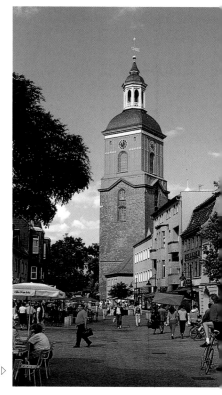

Sensational Spandau: the Old Town with St.-Nikolai-Kirche is older than Berlin ▷

149

Spandau Fortress evokes the days when chivalry flowered

tions of a 13th-century church. Gutted by fire in 1944, St Nicholas' was restored by 1988. A focal point of the three-aisled nave is the 8-m-high *Reniassance altar* of coloured limestone and tufa. It was donated by Rochus, Count zu Lynar, in 1581. His family crypt is beneath the altar. The Baroque pulpit (ca 1700) was donated by Friedrich Wilhelm I to the chapel of the Potsdam Stadtschloss but was moved here in 1904. The *Crucifixion group* at the entrance to the north chapel is dated to the first half of the 16th century.

A **monument to the Elector Joachim II** (1889), the work of Erdmann Encke, stands before the west portal of the church. It was Joachim II who officially inaugurated the Reformation in Brandenburg. In 1816 Schinkel designed the memorial to those who fell in the wars of liberation from Napoleon.

Many of the houses near the church have been restored and are now listed historic buildings. Among them is the early 18th-century inn, **Gasthof zum Stern** (Carl-Schurz-Straße 41), and, at 20 Breite Straße, a house with a Neo-Classical façade (ca 1800) is from the school of the architect David Gilly. The **Heinemann-**

Haus (Behnitz 5, 1795), a half-timbered house with Late Baroque elements, is on the Havel. The **Alte Kolkschänke** (Kolk 3, 1750) and the Catholic **Marienkirche** catch the eye. Built in 1848, St Mary's is a simple three-aisled basilica. Destroyed in the war, the Catholic church was restored in 1964.

If you want to take a excursion boat to Wannsee, the landing-place here is at the *Charlottenbrücke* bridge.

136 Zitadelle Spandau

One of the most important 16th-century fortresses extant in Germany.

Zitadellenbrücke
Phone: 030/354 94 42 00
www.zitadelle-spandau.net
Tu–Fr 9 am–5 pm, Sa/Su/hols.
10 am–5 pm
U7 Zitadelle, Bus X33

Spandau Fortress is one of the earliest examples of monumental secular architecture in Berlin and at the same time one of the most important 16th-century fortresses in Germany.

Strategically situated and surrounded on all sides by water, the fortress was first mentioned in records in 1197. It was probably built as a fortress in 1160 under the Margrave Albrecht the Bear.

The earliest part of the structure to have survived is the early 14th-century keep or donjon, which is named the **Juliusturm**. The crenellated parapet of the tower (with an observation platform) was renewed in 1848 after plans by Schinkel. The **palas**, the living quarters in the fortress, is also medieval in origin. Jewish gravestones dating from the 13th and 14th centuries were found in the base of the building, which was erected in about 1350. The tombstones probably came from the Spandau Jewish cemetery, which was ravaged in about 1510, and used as building materials when the palas was remodelled.

The fortress was reconstructed on the lines of Italian forts from 1560 in the reign of the Elector Joachim II. The fortifications were completed by Rochus, Count zu Lynar, between 1578 and 1594.

The fortress was not just a military base. It was also used both as a *prison* until 1876 and as a *vault*. In 1874 Reich Chancellor Otto von Bismarck had some of the reparations (120 million gold marks) the French were forced to pay after losing the Franco-Prussian War of 1870/71 stored in the dungeon.

In 1935 the National Socialists set up a *laboratory* in the fortress, where chemical weapons were developed and tested. At the end of the war they threw what was left into the ward well – a toxic legacy.

The core of the fortress is a square, 200 m to a side, with a bastion forming a salient angle at each corner. The **bastions** are named König (King: SW), Königin (Queen: SE), Kronprinz (Crown Prince: NW) and Brandenburg (NE) and are linked by a curtain or outer wall. The fortress is entered from the south via a causeway and a bridge through the barbican or **Commandant's House** (16th century). The commandant's living quarters used to be on the upper floor. The barbican façade was reconstructed in 1839.

Now the fortress is a Spandau cultural centre for concerts and exhibitions. The Neues Zeughaus (New Armoury, 1856–58) houses the **Stadtgeschichtliches Museum Spandau**, with local finds ranging from prehistory to the present, including the remains of a mammoth skeleton.

137 Tegeler Fließ

Idyllic scenery at the city gates.
U6 Alt-Tegel, Bus 124, 125, 133, 222

The Tegeler Fließ, which flows through Reinickendorf District from Lübars to Tegeler See, is surrounded by beautiful countryside. The last body of water in Berlin left to flow in its natural bed, it was made a protected area of outstanding natural beauty in 1955. If you want to walk along Tegeler Fließ, you should start at **Lübars**, a Brandenburg village that is now a listed historic monument. First mentioned in records in 1247, Lübars has retained its rural charm, with a village green and cobble-stone paving, a village church (1793), voluntary fire brigade and a village school.

138 Tegeler See

A lovely water landscape with a palace, parks and villas.
U6 Alt-Tegel, Bus 124, 125, 133, 222

The Tegeler Fließ flows into Tegeler See, the biggest and most beautiful of the lakes on the Havel. Here there is yet another Schinkel masterpiece, **Schloss Tegel** (Adelheid-Allee 19–21, Phone: 030/434 31 56, phone for opening hours as currently closed), also known as 'Humboldt Castle'. The Elector Joachim II first used the building in about 1550 as a country residence. After that it changed hands several times until it was bought by the Humboldt family in 1765. The famous brothers *Wilhelm* and *Alexander von Humboldt* grew up here. Wilhelm, the founder of Berlin University, and his wife Karoline had the castle altered by Karl Friedrich Schinkel (1820–24) in the Neo-Classical style: the *show façade* was embellished with Doric pilasters and emphatic cornices to approximate the antique style as closely as possible. Marble copies of famous statues from antiquity were placed in alcoves. The four *corner towers* were designed by Christian Daniel Rauch, who decorated them with reliefs of the eight wind deities. The *interior* is notable for displaying the original furnishings as well as the replicas of ancient *sculpture* collected by Wilhelm von Humboldt as Prussian envoy in Rome. Schinkel's approach to the interior decoration of the castle can be studied in the vestibule, the library, the Blue Salon and the Antikensaal. The atrium is adorned with the 'Fountain of St Calixtus', a Roman original dating from the 3rd century.

The **Schlosspark** features a magnificent lime (linden) avenue laid out in 1792 leading past the 400-year-old Alexander von Humboldt oak to the Humboldt family burial-place. Schinkel designed it on Karoline's death 1829. A granite column stands at the centre of her grave with a copy of the statue 'Hope' by the Danish sculptor Bertel Thorvaldsen.

Well worth seeing at **Tegeler Hafen** are the buildings designed by contemporary architects for the 1987 Interbau (IBA), forming an almost maritime cityscape with villas and terraces of houses painted in different colours. The most striking building complex from that architectural competition is the **Kultur- und Freizeitforum** by Charles Moore.

Other facilities are to be built on the artificial island in the harbour basin.

The landing-place for excursion boats to Spandau and Wannsee is at the northern end of the lake, on *Greenwich Promenade*. The harbour bridge leads from here to **Freizeitpark Tegel**, where Berliners like to grill and take boat trips at weekends. From the harbour bridge you can easily reach the **Tegeler Seeterrassen** (Wilkestraße 1, Phone: 030/433 80 01), a restaurant that looks back on a fine culinary tradition. The view across the water from the inn terrace on the western shore of the lake is magnificent.

Another rewarding excursion is a walk south along the lake shore path to **Villa Borsig** (1911–13), an exuberantly castle-like Neo-Baroque country house built by the industrialists Friedrich-Ernst and Konrad Borsig so they could be near their factories. Now the villa is a training centre and guest-house run by the *Foreign Ministry*.

Berliners also enjoy aquatic sports on Tegeler See, which boasts some of the most beautiful Havel scenery to be found around these lovely lakes

Ready for take-off: Tegel, to the west of the metropolis, is the capital's most important airport. Graf Zeppelin landed his Z3 airship here in 1909

139 Flughafen Tegel

Berlin's most important airport.

www.berlin-airport.de
Phone: 01 80/500 01 86
Bus TXL, X9, 109, 128

Its destiny was sealed by 1909: where Tegel Airport is now, *Graf Zeppelin* landed his legendary Z3 airship in the midst of the Jungfernheide and was treated to an overwhelming reception ceremony by the Kaiser. Later, the grounds were used by the Airship Battalion to practise and as *rocket-testing grounds*: Hermann Oberth and Wernher von Braun conducted their first trials here in 1931. During the Berlin Blockade of 1948/49, Tegel was vital as an airport for landing provisions: its 2400-m-long runway was Europe's longest at the time. After the Berlin Airlift, Tegel was used by the French as a military airport but by 1960 it had been approved for civilian use only.

Between 1969 and 1974 the starting and landing runways were lengthened and a *terminal for short distances*, a prize-winning hexagonal departure terminal building designed by Meinhard von Gerkan, Volkwin Marg and Klaus Nickels, was added. Since 1988 the airport has borne the name of **Otto Lilienthal** – a faithful replica of one of the pioneering aviator's flying machines adorns the main concourse.

Since about 430 planes depart from and arrive at Tegel a day and 11.3 million passengers pass through it per year, it is still Berlin's *main airport* for both domestic and intercontinental flights.

Potsdam und Babelsberg –
glamour, a glorious past and action

It was Friedrich Wilhelm of Brandenburg (1640–1688), the Great Elector, who made Potsdam the second royal seat of the Hohenzollern dynasty. The city today, however, bears the stamp of two other Prussian kings: Friedrich Wilhelm I, the Soldier King, had Potsdam turned into a garrison city in the 18th century. Potsdam did not epitomize Prussian power and its royal wealth until Frederick the Great, the Soldier King's son, ascended the throne. Diametrically the opposite of his practical and austere father, Frederick the Great made the city a centre of court life and Enlightenment culture. Schloss Sanssouci is Frederick's Versailles at the gates of Berlin.

140 Potsdamer Altstadt

On the heels of the Soldier King.

S1, S2, S26 and U2 Potsdam Hauptbahnhof, Bus 148, 200, 248, 348

Potsdam's historic centre was destroyed by bombs in 1945 and the Socialist urge to demolish what would be too costly to reconstruct did for the rest. Now magnificent historic buildings and simple socialist architecture rub shoulders in the city centre. By 1990 large parts of the inner city had been declared a UNESCO World Cultural Heritage Site and fourteen more groups of historic monuments in Potsdam and environs were added in 1999.

The Old Town is in the southern part of Potsdam, with the vast dome of the **Nikolai-Kirche** (Mo 2 pm–5 pm, Tu–Sa 10 am–

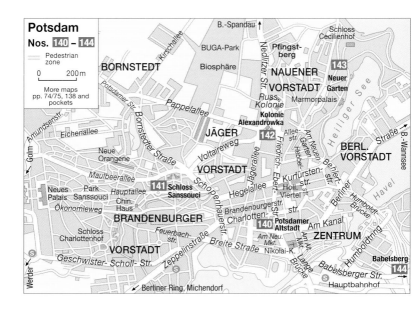

A Potsdam landmark: Neo-Classical Nikolaikirche with its huge dome was designed by none other than the great Karl Friedrich Schinkel

5 pm, Su 11.30 am–5 pm) looming above Alter Markt. Karl Friedrich Schinkel designed St Nicholas' (from 1830) and, because of its size and magnificence, it became the symbol of the city.

Beside the Schinkel church, the **Altes Rathaus**, also at Alter Markt, looks delicate. The gilded *Atlas figure* on the domed roof of the Old Town Hall, which was designed by Johann Boumann, has a story of its own. Not long after the building was finished in 1776, the figure, a lead cast, plummeted from the roof. A year later an identical figure, made of copper, was set in place. That Atlas even survived the bombing in 1945 although the Town Hall was destroyed and was later restored. Now the *Potsdam Forum* here is a venue for events of all kinds; a permanent exhibition is informative on architectural history. The **Knobelsdorff House** (1750) next door, named after its architect and also rebuilt after the war, also belongs to the Forum.

The grandest building at Alten Markt, the **Stadtschloss**, built in 1662 in the reign of Friedrich Wilhelm, the Great Elector, was left a ruin by the war. Although the remains of the palace were torn down in the 1960s, its *Fortuna Portal* has been reconstructed in 2002.

The **Marstall**, built in the 17th century as an orangery, was part of the Stadtschloss and was converted by the Soldier King into stables in 1714. It owes its present appearance to modifications undertaken by Georg Wenzeslaus von Knobelsdorff in 1746. The **Filmmuseum Potsdam** (Breite Straße 1 a, Phone: 03 31/27 18 10, daily 10 am–6 pm) is now housed in the Marstall. It possesses extensive historic collections of UFA and DEFA films and also mounts exhibitions dealing with the cinema.

Miscalculated: To keep skilled Dutch crafts-men at his court, Friedrich Wilhelm I had houses built for them in the Dutch style – but very few chose to stay

Brandenburger Straße, Potsdam's main shopping street, is still lined with historic houses, some of them dating from 1733–39. Its western end is punctuated by the *Brandenburger Tor* (1770). Twenty years older than Berlin's Brandenburg Gate, Potsdam's was designed by Karl von Gontard and Georg Christian Unger.

The **Holländisches Viertel** is the only settlement of its kind in Germany. The Dutch Quarter covers the area between Friedrich-Ebert-Straße, Gutenberg-Stra-ße, Hebbel-Straße and Kurfürstenstraße. To attach Dutch craftsmen to his court, the Soldier King had one hundred and thirty-four charming gabled dwellings built in the Dutch style around four squares under the supervision of Johann Boumann. The royal plan did not bear fruit as only twenty-two Dutch families chose to remain in Potsdam. The Dutch settlement became an artists' colony. One hundred and twenty-eight of the houses have survived.

141 Schloss Sanssouci

A breathtaking German royal palace.

Schopenhauerstraße
www.spsg.de
Phone: 03 31/969 41 90
25 March–31 Oct. Tu–Su 9 am–5 pm,
Nov.–24 March Tu–Su 9 am–4 pm,
guided tours only.
Call in advance for current opening hours.
S1, S2, S26 and U2, Bus 148, 200, 248, 348 Potsdam Hauptbahnhof, then Bus 695 or Tram 96, 98

No question about it: Schloss Sanssouci is what most tourists come to see in Pots-dam. Frederick the Great planned it as his *summer residence* at the gates of the city.

Exemplifying the proverbial Prussian discipline and head and shoulders above the crowd: 'Longshanks' – the Soldier King's guardsmen had to be tall – in Potsdam

Over two centuries it evolved into a unique architectural complex that is unparalleled in Germany or anywhere else for that matter.

On reluctantly ascending the throne in 1740, Frederick II set about redesigning his father's dreary kitchen garden. In 1744 he replaced rows of cabbages and an orchard with a cascade of six **vineyard terraces** as the extraordinary setting for the little summer castle already on the site. A year later construction work on a new palace began. Far from court ceremony and the affairs of state, Frederick the Great wanted to live here *'sans souci'*, without a care in the world. The brilliant frederician court architect Knobelsdorff had a hand in designing the building, which suited Frederick so well that he chose to live in it as his **main residence**. The choice to reside here is not surprising. Even though Sanssouci may look simple and only has twelve rooms, the interior is stunningly sophisticated. The most distinguished guest to stay there was the French philosopher *Voltaire*, who spent three years from 1750 at Sanssouci.

Frederick the Great gradually had Sanssouci enlarged and its surroundings transformed into a **park** modelled on Versailles. There was even a *Ruins Hill* (1748): the ancient-looking ruins were to guide the eye to the water reservoir for the *fountains* in front of the palace. During Frederick's lifetime, all attempts at making the fountains work failed miserably. A century later, Friedrich Wilhelm IV finally succeeded in making them spout by building a steam-driven pumphouse, the **Dampfmaschinenhaus** (Breite Straße 28, Sa/Su 10 am–5 pm), on the Havel that looks like a mosque.

Since his airy palace did not provide enough wall space for hanging his vast collection of paintings, Frederick the Great had a *picture gallery* (Tu–Su 10 am–5 pm) built on the east side in 1753. Germany's first royal museum still boasts important Caravaggios, Rubens, van Dycks and Tintorettos.

The craze for China and all things Chinese was sweeping Europe so the king had Johann Gottfried Büring design a **Chinesisches Haus** (Tu–Su 10 am–5 pm) for his park in 1754. Now Meißen and East Asian porcelain is displayed there. The **Drachenhaus** (1770), also architectural chinoiserie, was designed by Karl von Gontard as a vintner's cottage and is now a café.

Pilgrimage to Potsdam or pomp and circumstance: Schloss Sanssouci attracts tourists from all over the world

Following the Seven Years War (1756–63), Frederick launched his biggest project: building the **Neues Palais** (Sa–Thu 9 am–5 pm, winter until 4 pm) in the western part of the spacious garden, a 'fanfaronnade', just a bit of swagger, as Frederick, who spoke the idiomatic French of his day, put it. It was intended as a demonstration that Prussia, despite the hardships of war, was still flourishing. This vast but elegantly articulated structure has 400 rooms and galleries as well as a *theatre*.

Frederick's last wish († 1786), to be buried at Sanssouci, was not fulfilled until 1991 when his mortal remains were brought from Burg Hohenzollern to the **crypt** on the east side of Sanssouci. Now the most versatile and gifted monarch of the Enlightenment rests under a simple slab next to his beloved whippets.

Prussia shows off: Frederick the Great had the vast Neues Palais built to demonstrate (the appearance of) wealth and power

The commitment to Sanssouci shown by Friedrich Wilhelm IV, grand-nephew of Frederick the Great, gave rise to the next spate of building. While still crown prince, he had commissioned the Neo-Classical **Schloss Charlottenhof** (1826–29, Tu–Su 10 am–5 pm) from Karl Friederich Schin-kel and Ludwig Persius and had the land-scape architect Peter Joseph Lenné de-sign a park to match. Hidden away as it was in the south-western corner of the garden, Charlottenhof escaped renova-tion so that its *interior* is still largely origi-nal. Friedrich Wilhelm IV's predilection for

Royal chamber music: Frederick the Great, a gifted musician and all-round aesthete, used to play the flute here, accompanied by his ensemble

a romantic, dream-like ambience is evident throughout – here he could get away from it all.

Sporting arbours, a pergola and statuary from antiquity, the nearby **Römische Bäder** (1829–40, Tu–Su 10 am–5 pm) owe more to the Italian country-house style than to ancient Roman baths.

The Orangery (1748) was converted into the **Neue Kammern** (1771–74, Tu–Su 10 am–5 pm) a guest house with sumptuous rooms in the Mediterranean manner.

Persius' **Neue Orangerie** (1851–60, Tu–Su 10 am–5 pm) represents a return to the Renaissance in the historicizing mode. It affords superb views of the palace and the city. Copies of famous Raphael paintings are hung in the Raffaelsaal.

The **Friedenskirche** (1845–54), designed by Ludwig Persius and Friedrich August Stüler, has a campanile and 12th-century mosaics in the chancel, a tribute to Early Christian churches in Rome.

The **Historische Mühle** (Maulbergallee 5, daily 10 am–6 pm, winter Sa/Su 10 am–4 pm) outside the palace gardens dates from 1787–91 and was modelled on Dutch windmills. Reconstructed in 1993, the mill affords lovely views and houses an art gallery and a technical exhibition dealing with mills.

142 Kolonie Alexandrowka

A piece of Russia in the Brandenburg sand.

Puschkinallee, Am Schragen, Nedlitzer Straße, Kapellenberg
Bus 148, 200, 248, 348, then Tram 92

The Alexandrowka Russian Colony in the north of Potsdam is a curiosity. Friedrich Wilhelm III had this settlement built in 1826 as a gift for twelve singers in the Russian Soldiers' Chorus who had remained in Potsdam after having been interned there as prisoners of war. The settlement consists of thirteen little **log cabins**, decorated in the Russian dacha style with plenty of gingerbread in the form of *wood carvings* on the barge boards and balconies. The central building was allocated to the overseer. But singers in the chorus were not automatically eligible for residence: they could only occupy the houses on condition that they were in good health and were married, preferably to Prussian women. Inheritance law was regulated on strictly Prussian lines.

Only a family with a son could bequeath one of these houses to descendants. To prevent babies being exchanged, an official was always present at births. Nameplates on the buildings reveal the families' genealogies. Descendants of the Russian singers still live in the houses, which have remained virtually unchanged.

The Russian Orthodox Church of *St Alexander Newsky* stands on the Kapellenberg to the north of the settlement.

Enormous efforts revealing extraordinary civic commitment have been made since 1988 to restore the historic buildings on the adjacent **Pfingstberg**. They include Schinkel's first work, the *Pomona Temple* (1801). In April 2001 the **Belvedere** (Phone: 03 31/270 19 72, June–Aug. daily 10 am–8 pm, Sept., April/May daily 10 am–6 pm, Oct. daily 10 am–4 pm, Nov./March Sa/Su 10 am–4 pm) by Persius, Hesse and Stüler, a magnificent structure (1847–63) boasting Neo-Renaissance colonnades and towers, was reopened to the public. The views from the West Tower, which has a fine Roman gallery, are magnificent.

If you look west, you see the **Volkspark**, laid out for the 2001 Federal Garden Show BUGA. The entrance is near the Pfingstberg. In September 2003 **Biosphäre Potsdam** (Georg-Hermann-Allee 99, Phone: 03 31/55 07 40, www.biosphaere-potsdam.de, Mo–Fr 9 am–6 pm, Sa/Su/hols. 10 am–7 pm) opened on the grounds,

A bit of home: A log cabin in the Alexandrowka Colony. Friedrich Wilhelm III had this settlement built for Russian singers

a glasshouse biotope with a tropical garden covering a surface area of 5500 m² in which about 20 000 plants are kept. The facility can be explored by land, by water or from the air. There is a jungle path, an underwater station and a mountain trail.

143 Neuer Garten

An idyllic park and palace, where the Potsdam Conference was held.

Am Neuen Garten
S1, S2, S26 and U2, Bus 148, 200, 248, 348 Potsdam Hauptbahnhof, then Bus 692 or Tram 92

From the Pfingstberg you can also reach the Neuer Garten. Not only was this garden designed by Lenné, it is in an extraordinarily romantic setting on the **Heiliger See**. Friedrich Wilhelm II had his pleasant summer residence built directly by the lake. The **Marmorpalais** (Phone: 03 31/969 42 46, Tu–Su 10 am–5 pm, Nov.–March Sa/Su 10 am–4 pm) was designed by Karl von Gontard (1787) in the early Neo-Classical style. During the GDR era, it housed an army museum. The *kitchen building* (1788, Gontard) belonging to it was designed to look like a ruin, the height of fashion then. To the south is the pavilion of the **Gotische Bibliothek** (1792–94, restored in 1997), the Gothic Revival library for the king's collection of books.

Yet another architectural curiosity looms up to the north: the **Pyramid** was an ice house, the predecessor of the refrigerator. Supplies were kept chilled here on ice cut from the lake in winter.

At the northern end of the lovely park is **Schloss Cecilienhof** (Phone 03 31/969 42 44, Tu–Su 9 am–5 pm, Nov.–March until 4 pm). The last palace built by the Hohenzollerns, it was designed during the First World War in the English country-house style (1913–17, Schultze-Naumburg) for Crown Prince Wilhelm. He only stayed a year until the 1918 revolution made him flee to Holland, leaving his wife Cecilie and the children behind.

Cecilienhof became famous because the **Potsdam Conference** was held here in August 1945. Stalin, Truman and Churchill as well as his successor Attlee met here to agree on the further conduct of the occupation powers in Germany. The rooms in which the conference took place are now a museum dealing with the historic meeting.

144 Babelsberg

Imperial summer residence and film capital in the Babelsberg section of Potsdam.

S7 Babelsberg or Griebnitzsee, Tram 94, 95, Bus 601, 602, 603, 618, 619, 690, 693, 694, 696, 699, 750

The Babelsberg section of Potsdam is inseparably linked with the history of German cinema: from 1912 films were made at the **Studiogelände** in August-Bebel-

Walk into a celluloid dream world! Once Europe's greatest cinecity, Babelsberg is fast linking up with its glorious past. Shooting the film 'Sonnenallée' (1999)

The owners are absent now but catching a glimpse of the past is always rewarding: The private apartments of Wilhelm I are open to the public in Schloss Babelsberg

Straße. Bioscop Film was followed by the UFA and, in the GDR era, the DEFA on the studio grounds. Now they belong to the French concern Vivendi, with Gerhard Bergfried as managing director.

If you want to soak up studio ambience and cinematic history, a studio tour in **Filmpark Babelsberg** (August-Bebel-Straße 26–53, entrance: Großbeerenstraße, Phone: 03 31/721 27 55, www.filmpark. de, guided tours April–Oct. daily 10 am–6 pm, closed in winter) would be just what you're looking for. Further attractions are the Metropolis 4 D Action Cinema, the Adventure Simulation, the film animals and stunt shows. The food is satisfyingly hearty at the *Prinz Eisenherz* restaurant, decorated with props from this 1996 film.

The *UFA Film Studios*, where such milestones of cinematic history as 'Metropolis' and 'The Blue Angel' were made as well as comedies such as 'Die Drei von der Tankstelle', were Europe's biggest tinsel town before the Second World War. Stars lived near the studios: Heinrich George in Kohlhasenbrück, Johannes Heesters at Stölpchensee and other luminaries in the **Villenviertel Neu-Babelsberg** on the shores of Griebnitzsee. Many of the villas – some belonged to Jewish industrialists before the Nazis came to power – where UFA stars lived have been restored.

Near the villa section is an attraction that once starred royalty. **Schloss Babelsberg** (Phone: 03 31/969 42 50, currently closed for restoration) was built for Prince Wilhelm, later Kaiser Wilhelm I, in 1833 as a *summer residence* on the heights of the Babelsberg. Princess Augusta dabbled in architecture and Schinkel followed her suggestions in drawing up the plans for a palace in the English Neo-Gothic style. Persius and Strack kept enlarging it until 1859. The first Kaiser († 1888) loved this palace and often stayed here. Otto von Bismarck was a frequent guest.

Some rooms, such as the Kaiser's private apartments, the library and the *ballroom*, designed by Persius as an octagonal tower all in white and gold, will again be open to the public after restoration.

Lenné started out designing the **park**, followed from 1843 by the eccentric Prince Pückler-Muskau. The imaginatively laid out grounds boast a **Kleines Schloss** (1841/42, Persius), where the heir to the throne and his tutors lived. Now it is a delightful restaurant. Then there are the Seamen's House (1842), the Flatow Tower (1853–56, views), the Marstall and the Steam-Powered Engine Room (1843). A 13th-century **Gerichtslaube**, until 1871 part of the Berlin Red Town Hall as its court summer house, is hidden away in the park.

Berlin – Travel Information

Before setting off

ADAC Information Service, Phone: 018 05/10 11 12, Fax 018 05/30 29 28 (0,12 €/min.).

ADAC, the German Automobile Club, is associated internationally with other Clubs like AA, AAA, CAA etc

ADAC on the internet:
www.adac.de
www.adac.de/reisefuehrer

ADAC Traffic News:
Mobile Phone: 224 99 (0,51 €/call plus connection fee)

ADAC Traffic Information Service:
T-Mobile, Vodafone, O$_2$: 224 11 (€ 1.10/ min. plus connection fee), E-Plus: 114 11 (€ 1.10/min. plus connection fee). Indi-vidual traffic advice while on the road, informative on congestion risks, alternative routes, snow depth, water quality, service stations in the vicinity and much more.

Berlin on the internet:
www.berlin.de
www.berlinonline.de

BTM, Berlin Tourismus Marketing GmbH, Phone: 030/25 00 25, Fax 030/ 25 00 24 24, www.berlin-tourist-information.de, from outside Germany: Phone: 00 49/30/25 00 23 55. General information, hotels, tickets etc (not open to the public).

Berlin WelcomeCard and **City TourCard**, see p. 183

General Information

Tourist offices

BTM, Brandenburger Tor, south wing, Pariser Platz (Mitte), daily 10–6 pm

BTM, Europa-Center (next to Kaiser-Wilhelm- Gedächtniskirche), Budapester Straße 45 (Charlottenburg), Mo–Sa 10 am–7 pm, Su 10 am–6 pm

BTM, Fernsehturm, Alexanderplatz/ Panoramastr. 1 a (Mitte), May–Sept. Mo–Sa 9 am–8 pm, Su 10 am–6 pm, Oct.–April daily 10 am–6 pm

For what is on currently also check daily papers and the **city magazines** 'Zitty', 'Tip', 'Prinz' and '030'.

www.zitty.de
www.berlinonline.de/tip
www.berlin030.de
www.prinz.de

Emergency numbers

Police: Phone: 110

Fire Brigade and Medical Emergencies: Phone: 112

Glimpses of Berlin: a pulsing, vibrant city featuring grand architectural gestures

ADAC Roadside Assistance:
Phone: 018 02/22 22 22 (0.06 €/call), Mobile phone: 22 22 22 (connection fee)

ADAC Rescue Helicopter:
Phone: 110 or 112

Österreichischer Automobil Motorrad und Touring Club
ÖAMTC Emergency Helpline:
Phone: 00 43/(0)1/251 20 00

Touring Club Switzerland
TCS Central Emergency Helpline:
Phone: 00 41/(0)224 17 22 20

Medical emergencies

Medical Emergency Service:
Phone: 030/31 00 31

Dental Emergency Service:
Phone: 030/89 00 43 33

Poison Emergency Centre:
Phone: 030/192 40

Lost and Found

Zentrales Fundbüro, Platz der Luftbrücke 6 (Tempelhof), Phone: 030/756 00

Fundbüro der Deutschen Bahn, Phone: 018 05/99 05 99

BVG Fundbüro, Potsdamer Str. 182 (Schöneberg), Phone: 030/25 62 30 40

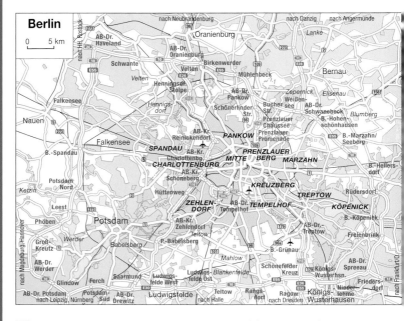

Arrival

Car

Berlin is reached from the *west* via the **A 2**, from the *south* from Hof via the **A 9** or from Dresden/Cottbus via the **A 13**, from the *east* from Frankfurt/Oder via the **A 12**, from the *north* from Szczecin (Stettin) via the **A 11**, from Hamburg via the **A 24**.

Information and maps are available free to **ADAC** (German Automobile Club) members: Phone: 018 05/10 11 12 (0,12 €/Min.). Also available from ADAC Publishing: ADAC Reisemagazin *Berlin*, city map of *Berlin* (1:25 000), CityPlan *Berlin* (1:20 000), City Atlas *Berlin/Potsdam* (1:15 000), Leisure Activities Atlas *Brandenburg/Berlin*, federal state map *Berlin/Brandenburg* (1:300 000), Leisure Activities Map *Berlin, Märkische Schweiz, Spreewald* (1:100 000) as well as the ADAC travel guide *Brandenburg* (www.adac.de/karten and www.adac/reisemagazin).

Train

For long-distance arrivals: **Bahnhof Zoologischer Garten** (from W, NW and SW), **Ostbahnhof** and **Berlin-Lichtenberg** (both directions N, E, S). A central station, the **Hauptbahnhof**, for long-distance travel on four subterranean levels is scheduled to be in operation by 2006 on the premises of the former *Lehrter Bahnhof*.

Timetable & Ticket information

Germany

Deutsche Bahn, Phone: 118 61 (charge), Phone: 08 00/150 70 90 (recorded message), www.bahn.de

DB Autoreisezug, Phone: 018 05/24 12 24, www.dbautozug.de

DB Nachtzug, Phone: 018 05/14 15 14, www.dbnachtzug.de

City Night Line, Phone: 018 05/21 34 21, www.citynightline.ch

Austria

Österreichische Bundesbahn, Phone: 05 17 17, www.oebb.at

Switzerland

Schweizerische Bundesbahnen, Phone: 09 00 30 03 00, www.sbb.ch

Bus

Buses leave for Berlin from more than 300 German cities. The main bus terminal in Berlin:

ZOB, Zentraler Omnibusbahnhof am Funkturm, Masurenallee 4–6, Phone: 030/302 53 61. From there to the inner city take U2 at Kaiserdamm Station or Bus X34, X49, 139, 149.

BerlinLinienBus, Mannheimer Str. 33/34, Phone: 030/86 09 60, www.berlinlinienbus.de. Central reservations.

Plane

Berlin has three airports: Tegel (approx 8 km from the centre), Tempelhof (central) and Berlin-Schönefeld (approx 22 km from the centre).

Central flight information: Phone: 01 80/500 01 86, www.berlin-airport.de

Ground transport

Tegel: Bus TXL, X9, 109, 128

Tempelhof: U6 Platz der Luftbrücke

Schönefeld: S S9, S45, Bus 162, 171

Bank, Post Office, Telephone

Bank

Opening hours: as a rule Mo–Fr 9 am–1 pm and 2.30 pm–4 pm, Th until 6 pm

Post Office

Opening hours: as a rule Mo–Fr 8 am–6 pm, Sa 8 am–12 noon or 8 pm

Telephone

Berlin area code: (0)30
Germany country code: 00 49

Shopping

Antiquarian booksellers

Antiquariat Düwal, Schlüterstr. 17 (Charlottenburg), Phone: 030/313 30 30. Wide range of rare books.

Antiquariatsbuchhandlung Knut Ahnert, Sybelstr. 58 (Charlottenburg), Phone: 030/324 09 07. Wide selection of books on Berlin and illustrated books.

Antiques

Art 1900, Kurfürstendamm 53 (Charlottenburg), Phone: 030/881 56 27. Jugendstil and Art Déco.

Radio Art, Zossener Str. 2 (Kreuzberg), Phone: 030/693 94 35. Historical radio technology, sales and repairs.

Auction houses

Auktionshaus Altus, Kalckreuthstr. 4–5 (Schöneberg), Phone: 030/218 18 18. Old Masters and modern art.

Auktionshaus – Kunsthandel Prinz-Dunst, Schlüterstr. 16 (Charlottenburg), Phone: 030/313 59 65. Antiques, furniture, porcelain. Seven auctions a year.

Christie's, Giesebrechtstr. 10 (Charlottenburg), Phone: 030/885 69 50. Berlin branch of the famous London auction house.

Kunsthaus Lempertz, Poststr. 22 (Mitte), Phone: 030/208 42 44. Old Masters and contemporary art.

Villa Grisebach Auktionen, Fasanenstr. 25 (Charlottenburg), Phone: 030/885 91 50. Classical modern art.

Extras and Accessories

Ampelmann Galerie Shop, Hof V Hackesche Höfe (Mitte), DomAquarée at Berliner Dom (Mitte), Potsdamer Platz Arkaden (Tiergarten), Phone: 030/44 04 88 09. Ostalgia (GDR nostalgia) with the little green man 'go' traffic sign and the red 'stop' sign.

Grober Unfug, Zossener Str. 32–33 (Kreuzberg), Phone: 030/69 40 14 90. Wonderland of comics.

HanfHaus, Oranienstr. 192 (Kreuzberg), Phone: 030/614 81 02. All hemp products: face-creams, clothing and more.

Hautnah, Uhlandstr. 170 (near Kurfürstendamm), Phone: 030/882 34 34. Extravagant fashions in leather, lacquer and latex. Evening dress. Wine shop.

KPM Königliche Porzellan-Manufaktur, Kurfürstendamm 27 (Charlottenburg) and Unter den Linden 35 (Mitte), Phone: 030/39 00 90, www.kpm-berlin.de. Exclusive collection of porcelain. For less expensive items: the Porcelain Factory outlet in the Berlin Pavilion, No. 100 Straße des 17. Juni.

Scenario, Else-Ury-Bogen 602 (under the elevated S-Bahn tracks, Charlottenburg), Phone: 030/312 91 99. Nice accessories at affordable prices.

Spielbrett, Körtestr. 27 (Kreuzberg), Phone: 030/692 42 50. Board games of all kinds, also very fine wooden games.

Zauberkönig, Hermannstr. 84 (Neukölln), Phone: 030/621 40 82. Traditional joke articles and magic items.

Delicatessens

Confiserie Mélanie, Goethestr. 4 (Charlottenburg), Phone: 030/313 83 30. Delectable deli. The handmade sweets and chocolate creams are irresistible.

KaDeWe (Kaufhaus des Westens), 6th Floor, Tauentzienstr. 21 (Schöneberg), Phone: 030/212 10. A gourmet shrine, specialities from all over the world.

Department Stores

Department stores are located on Kurfürstendamm and Tauentzienstraße in Charlottenburg, in Schlosssstraße in Steglitz und in Wilmersdorfer Straße in Charlottenburg and:

Dussmann – das Kulturkaufhaus, Friedrichstr. 90 (Mitte), Phone: 030/20 25 11 11. Books, CDs, DVDs on 4 floors. Also poetry readings, theatre performances and concerts.

Galerie Lafayette, Französische Str. 23/Friedrichstraße (Mitte), Phone: 030/20 94 80. Greetings from France: elegant shopping at the Berlin branch of the celebrated Paris department store.

Markets

No section of Berlin is without a weekly market. The best-known are the **'Türkenmarkt'**, Maybachufer (Kreuzberg, see p. 110, Tu and Fr 12 noon–6.30 pm) and the **Winterfeldtmarkt**, Winterfeldtplatz (Schöneberg, We 8 am–2 pm, Sa 8 am–6 pm).

Two flea markets are particularly interesting: **Trödel- und Kunstmarkt in Straße des 17. Juni** (Tiergarten, Sa/Su 10 am–4 pm) and **Berliner Kunst & Nostalgiemarkt** (Mitte, Sa/Su 11 am–5 pm) on the Museum Island including Am Zeughaus and Am Kupfergraben streets. Times and venues of other markets are published in the daily press and city magazines.

Fashion

Kurfürstendamm and **Tauentzienstraße** are still the Berlin addresses for shopping.

You may make a find: junk shops

Here international haute couture fashion design and international fashion chains rub shoulders with a host of boutiques. There are also numerous boutiques in the side-streets off Kurfürstendamm and round Savignyplatz. **Friedrichstraße** has also established itself as a shopping boulevard in Berlin-Mitte. There are interesting shopping malls and department stores, especially along the southern section between Unter den Linden and Leipziger Straße. Arkaden shopping mall on **Potsdamer Platz** has branches of many large fashion labels. Scene shops and designer boutiques are in the **Hackesche Höfen** (Rosenthaler Straße) and environs.

Extraweit, Augsburger Str. 35 (Charlottenburg), Phone: 030/21 96 69 00. Fashionable apparel for the lady over size 44.

Jordan, Hackesche Höfe VIII, Rosenthalerstr. 40 (Mitte), Phone: 030/281 50 43. Attractive clothes, sporty and classic.

Mientus, Wilmersdorfer Str. 73 (Wilmersdorf), Phone: 030/323 90 77. Everything for men on three floors.

Molotow, Gneisenaustr. 112 (Kreuzberg), Phone: 030/693 08 18. Bespoke men's and women's fashions from Berlin designers.

Paltó, Kurfürstendamm 184 (Charlottenburg), Phone: 030/885 40 23. Exclusive, top-quality ladies' apparel.

Patrick Hellmann, Bleibtreustr. 36 (Charlottenburg), Phone: 030/882 69 61. Elegant menswear classics.

Rodan Lederdesign, Kurfürstendamm 29, Phone: 030/885 15 09. Evening attire, show outfits, coats and much, much more in leather.

Versace, Kurfürstendamm 185 (Charlottenburg). Colourful loud fashions from Donatella Versace.

■ Eating Out

Gourmet restaurants

Alt Luxemburg, Windscheidstr. 31 (Charlottenburg), Phone: 030/323 87 30. The creations of chef Karl Wannemacher tickle the tastebuds.

Altes Zollhaus, Carl-Herz-Ufer 30 (Kreuzberg), Phone: 030/692 33 00. Very good German and international cuisine, with a summer garden on the Landwehr Canal.

Borchardt, Französische Str. 47 (Mitte), Phone: 030/81 88 62 62. Traditional gourmet restaurant at Gendarmenmarkt with French cuisine and a distinguished clientele.

Facil, in the Hotel Madison, Potsdamer Str. 3 (Tiergarten), Phone: 030/590 05 12 34. Much vaunted modern cuisine, Mediterranean-inspired, in a bamboo green interior at Potsdamer Platz.

Kaisersaal, Bellevuestr. 1, Potsdamer Platz, Sony-Center (Tiergarten), Phone: 030/25 75 14 54. The old imperial Herren-salon of the Hotel Esplanade serves elegant German and French cuisine and a wide selection of wines.

TOP TIPP REmake, Große Hamburger Str. 32 (Mitte), Phone: 030/20 05 41 02. Experimental cuisine by the enfant terrible of the Berlin gastro scene. Creations served by Venetian chef Cristiano Rienzner in an upmarket setting include licorice-scented scallops with Guinness and cherry sorbet or white chocolate with black olives as a sweet.

Restaurant Schloss Glienicke, Königin-str. 36 (Wannsee), Phone: 030/805 40 00, www.schlossglienicke.de. Fresh regional food in a historic setting with a view of the lovely Schloss park.

New cuisine

Abendmahl, Muskauer Str. 9 (Kreuzberg), Phone: 030/612 51 70. Fish and vegetarian dishes amidst devotional kitsch and reliquaries.

TOP TIPP Bovril, Kurfürstendamm 184 (Charlottenburg), Phone: 030/881 84 61. Classic bistro ambience and VIP venue (Su closed).

Café Orange, Oranienburger Str. 32 (Mitte), Phone: 030/28 38 52 42. Reasonably priced, with cosmopolitan ambience.

TOP TIPP Dachgartenrestaurant im Deutschen Bundestag (Roof-Garden Restaurant in the German Bundestag/Reichstag), Platz der Republik (Tiergarten), Phone: 030/22 62 99 33. Elegant cuisine; good breakfast served with fresh dailies. With reservations separate entrance: West C, otherwise during visits to the Reichstag dome.

TOP TIPP Maxwell, Bergstr. 22 (Mitte), Phone: 030/280 71 21. One of the city's best restaurants. Light modern cuisine and excellent wines are served. Stylish décor in a 19th-century building with beautiful glassed-in atrium.

Bye, bye broiler: An update for those who think there's no gourmet food in Berlin – the Lobster Bar in the Hotel Kempinski

Offenbach-Stuben, Stubbenkammer-str. 8 (Prenzlauer Berg), Phone: 030/445 85 02. Five rooms steeped in ambience, decorated with props salvaged from the Comic Opera and the Metropole Theatre.

Paris-Moskau, Alt-Moabit 141 (Tiergarten), Phone: 030/394 20 81. Regional and international cuisine served in a converted train shed.

Berlin cuisine

Brauhaus Georgbraeu, Spreeufer 4 (Mitte), Phone: 030/242 42 44. Pigs' trotters with sauerkraut, washed down with the house brew.

Großbeerenkeller, Großbeerenstr. 90 (Kreuzberg), Phone: 030/722 49 84. Fried potatoes and Silesian dishes. Actor Hans Albers quaffed his beer here.

TOP TIPP Henne, Leuschnerdamm 25 (Kreuzberg), Phone: 030/614 77 30. Old Berlin tavern with beer garden. Excellent crispy grilled chicken (daily from 7 pm).

Klipper, Bulgarische Str. 1 (Treptow), Phone: 030/53 21 64 90. Trendy eatery on a sailing ship at Plänterwald (near Insel der Jugend). Speciality: rainbow trout from the ship's smoke-house. Reservations recommended.

Kolk, Hoher Steinweg 7 (Spandau), Phone: 030/333 88 79. Besides German cuisine, Silesian and East Prussian specialities, outstanding service and lovely summer garden.

Schrörs am Müggelsee, Josef-Nawrocki-Str. 16 (Köpenick), Phone: 030/64 09 58 80. A spacious beer garden known for hearty grilled specialities. Next door is the Bräustübl (Phone: 030/645 57 16) with a 1920s-style ballroom.

Zur letzten Instanz, Waisenstr. 14 (Mitte), Phone: 030/242 55 28. Oldest surviving inn with Berlin home cooking.

Ethnic food

American

Catherine's, Friedrichstr. 90 (Mitte), Phone: 030/20 25 15 55. Elegant fast food and an excellent bar.

City Diner, Bergstr. 7 (Mitte), Phone: 030/797 39 38. Juicy burgers, wraps and a wide assortment of cocktails.

Asian

Daitokai, Europa-Center (Charlottenburg), Phone: 030/261 80 99. Fine Japanese cuisine; meals are prepared in front of guests.

Mao Thai, Wörther Str. 30 (Prenzlauer Berg), Phone: 030/441 92 61. Varied bill of fare featuring Thai and South Chinese delicacies.

Tuk Tuk, Großgörschenstr. 2 (Schöneberg), Phone: 030/781 15 88. Mouthwatering Indonesian food under bamboo roofs with Balinese ambience.

Italian

Ana e Bruno, Sophie-Charlotten-Str. 101 (Charlottenburg), Phone: 030/325 71 10. Fine Italian cuisine, light interior and light food, expensive (Su/Mo closed).

Aroma, Hochkirchstr. 8 (Schöneberg), Phone: 030/782 58 21. Modern regional delicacies (Mo–Fr from 6 pm, Sa from 2 pm, Su from 11 am).

Candela, Grunewaldstr. 81 (Schöneberg), Phone: 030/782 14 09. Chic young people enjoy classic Italian and French cuisine.

Enoiteca Il Calice, Walter-Benjamin-Platz 4 (Charlottenburg), Phone: 030/324 23 08. A wide selection of wines and fine Italian delicacies.

Luigi, Körnerstr. 12 (Tiergarten), Phone: 030/26 55 47 96. Excellent pasta und pizza in an unpretentious setting.

Osteria No. 1, Kreuzbergstr. 71 (Kreuzberg), Phone: 030/786 91 62. Popular, cosy by candlelight.

Portuguese and Latin American

Lafil, Gormannstr. 22 (Mitte), Phone: 030/28 59 90 26. Spanish and Basque cuisine and wines in an elegant Mediterranean setting with garden in summer.

Casa Portuguêsa, Helmholzstr. 15 (Charlottenburg), Phone: 030/393 55 06. Portuguese food, friendly atmosphere.

Locus, Marheinekeplatz 4 (Kreuzberg), Phone: 030/691 56 37. Mexican food in the evenings; Su buffet brunch. Delightful dining in the garden; afterwork specials.

Russian and Eastern European

Marjellchen, Mommsenstr. 9 (Charlottenburg), Phone: 030/883 26 76. Cosy little eatery serving East Prussian and Silesian food (daily from 5 pm).

Pasternak, Knaackstr. 22–24 (Prenzlauer Berg), Phone: 030/441 33 99. Traditional Russian food with typical Prenzlauer Berg scene clientele.

Tadshikische Teestube, Palais Am Festungsgraben, Am Festungsgraben 1 (Mitte), Phone: 030/204 11 12. Russian cuisine and assorted speciality teas with divan ambience.

South German and Austrian

Austria, Bergmannstr. 30 (Kreuzberg), Phone: 030/694 44 40. Austrian cuisine and Viennese coffee.

Kellerrestaurant im Brecht-Haus, Chausseestr. 125 (Mitte), Phone: 030/282 38 43, www.brechtkeller.de. Viennese cuisine cooked to recipes of Helene Weigel's.

Ottenthal, Kantstr. 153 (Charlottenburg), Phone: 030/313 31 62. Austrian atmosphere, homemade cakes, pancakes and soufflés.

Rosalinde, Knesebeckstr. 16 (Charlottenburg), Phone: 030/313 59 96. Tasty delicacies from Swabia.

Turkish

Bagdad, Schlesische Str. 2 (Kreuzberg), Phone: 030/612 69 62. Good Turkish food and belly-dance shows to match.

Vegetarian

Hakuin, Martin-Luther-Str. 1 a (Schöneberg), Phone: 030/218 20 27. Not just delicious brown rice and fresh vegetables but also innovative dishes.

Natural'Mente, Schustehrusstr. 26 (Charlottenburg), Phone: 030/341 41 66.

Macrobiotic fare with ingredients from tested organic farms.

Dunkelrestaurant

unsicht-Bar Berlin, Gormannstr. 14 (Mitte), Phone: 030/24 34 25 00, www.unsicht-bar-berlin.de. Really special dining: eating in a darkened room opens your eyes to truly memorable culinary experiences.

Fast Food

Berlin is known for its prolific and varied **snack culture**. Whether you hanker for a quick grilled bratwurst early in the morning at an U-Bahn Imbiss or get cravings at night [see also p. 177] for a mini-pizza or a doner kebab. Everywhere, at all times of the day or night – hunger pangs can and must be staved off. The legendary native **Currywurst** has been facing stiff competition from international snacks for quite some time now.

Brooklyn-Sandwiches, Oranienstr. 176/ Adalbertstraße (Kreuzberg), Phone: 030/615 20 14. Celebrated for unusual sandwiches. Soufflés freshly made by Granny and delicious brownies.

Curry Imbiss Ku'damm 195, Kurfürstendamm 195 (Charlottenburg), Phone: 030/881 89 42. Berlin VIPs like to drop in here regularly for a Currywurst.

Curry & Kunst, Rosentahlerstr. 50 (Mitte), Phone: 030/28 87 38 80. Near the Hackesche Höfe classic sausages and gallery culture enter on the perfect union (Mo–Sa 11 am–4 am, Su 3 pm–midnight).

 Habibi, Goltzstr. 24 (Schöneberg), Phone: 030/215 33 32. Delicious falafel and spicy vegetable fritters are an exotic take on Oriental fast food.

Cafés

Anita Wronski, Knaackstr. 26 (Prenzlauer Berg), Phone: 030/442 84 83. A lot going on at this busy boulevard café.

Café Adler, Friedrichstr. 206 (Kreuzberg), Phone: 030/251 89 65. Café with ambience at the former Checkpoint Charlie. Has a non-smokers room.

Café am Steinplatz, Hardenbergstr. 12 (Charlottenburg), Phone: 030/312 65 89. Intellectuals and cinema fans hang out here, especially before and after film shows.

Café Einstein, Kurfürstenstr. 58 (Schöneberg), Phone: 030/263 91 90. In the style of a Viennese coffee house with a lovely

Serendipity!

A mouthwatering virtue born of necessity: postwar wurst-stall proprietress Herta Heuwer invented the **Currywurst** – purely by felicitous chance – on 4 September 1948 at her Stuttgarter Platz stall. Her husband, just back from an American prisoner-of-war camp, craved a delicacy untypical of Berlin then: spare-ribs. Herta thought it over, improvised with what she had – and served her spouse a cut-up bock wurst with Ketchup and lashings of curry. In the meantime the Currywurst has attained classic **culinary status**. The astonishing truth is: these days you

have to look around for a decent Currywurst, because the beloved old Berlin stand-by is facing stiff competition from the Turkish doner kebab. But don't despair. The Currywurst is still available – in top quality, too. Our insider tip: Some of the best Currywurst is to be had at **195 Ku'damm** (see left).

summer garden. The Villa was once owned by silent-film star Henny Porten.

Café Hardenberg, Hardenbergstr. 10 (Charlottenburg), Phone: 030/312 26 44. Café in a big hall, student hangout.

Café im Literaturhaus-Wintergarten, Fasanenstr. 23 (Charlottenburg), Phone: 030/882 54 14. Coffee and pastries combined with literature readings.

Café Kranzler, Kurfürstendamm 18 (Charlottenburg), Phone: 030/88 71 83 90. 'New edition' of the world-famous café in the Rotunda on the 2nd floor of the Neues Kranzler Eck. A tourist magnet.

This is delicious! The attractive Operncafé on Unter den Linden

Monte Video, Viktoria-Luise-Platz 6 (Schöneberg), Phone: 030/213 10 20. The breakfast menu offers a wide selection of dishes.

Morena, Wiener Str. 60 (Kreuzberg), Phone: 030/618 80 13. Young trendies like to meet here for a late breakfast.

Operncafé, Prinzessinnenpalais/Opernpalais, Unter den Linden 5 (Mitte), Phone: 030/20 26 83. Outstanding buffet breakfast and particularly good cakes and tarts.

Schlosscafé Köpenick, Schlossinsel, Phone: 030/65 01 85 85. German and Mediterranean cuisine in the elegant rooms of a Baroque palace. Su 10 am–2 pm brunch with classical music.

Cafés with a view

Aedes, Savignyplatz 599 (Charlottenburg), Phone: 030/31 50 95 35. Italian specialities, chic ambience and a gallery next door.

Alte Liebe, Havelchaussee 107 (Wilmersdorf), Phone: 030/304 82 58. Stranded Elbe-Havel boat serves coffee and cake or hearty meals.

Blockhaus Nikolskoe, Nikolskoer Weg 15 (Wannsee), Phone: 030/805 29 14. A present from Friedrich Wilhelm III to his son-in-law Tsar Nicholas and his daughter, now a restaurant serving German food for day trippers. View of the Havel, spacious terrace.

Fährhaus Caputh, Straße der Einheit 88, Caputh/Potsdam, Phone: 03 32 09/702 03. From the glassed-in porch you can view

the cable ferries plying tirelessly back and forth across the Havel.

Telecafé im Fernsehturm, Panoramastr. 1 a (Mitte), Phone: 030/242 33 33. One of the best views in Berlin.

Strandbars

Strandbar Mitte, Monbijoustr. 3 (Mitte), Phone: 030/28 38 55 88, www.strandbar-mitte.de. Fun, drinks and food on a sandy beach in Monbijou Park with a view of Museum Island (approx May–Sept. daily from 10 am)

Playa Paradiso, Goslarer Ufer 1–5 (Charlottenburg), Phone: 030/34 35 72 36. The beach provides deck chairs, beachball, BBQ, a restaurant and Th is Salsa Night with live music.

■ Festivals and Events

Public holidays

January 1 (New Years Day), April/May (Good Friday, Easter Monday), May 1 (May Day public holiday), May/June (Ascension Day), June (Whit Monday), October 3 (German Unification Day), December 25/26 (Christmas Day, St Stephen's Day)

Since Berlin is always celebrating something, the following list of festivals and events represents just a selection of the most important festivities. Calendar of events: www. berlin.de.

April/May

Frühlingsfest (Spring Festival), Kurt-Schumacher-Damm (Reinickendorf). Berlin's biggest and most bumptious fairground with all the newest gags showmen have up their sleeves.

Britzer Baumblütenfest (Tree Blossom Festival), Parchimer Allee (Neukölln), Early to mid-April, daily 2 pm–10 pm, Su from 12 noon

Neuköllner Maientage (May Days), Volkspark Hasenheide (Neukölln), Late April to mid-May

May/June

Köpeniker Sommer, Köpenicker Altstadt, Phone: 030/65 82 27 27. Traditional summer folk festival. Mid-June

Karneval der Kulturen (Carnival of Cultures), Phone: 030/60 97 70 22, www.karneval-berlin.de. Street festival and parties with bands and participants from all over the world. Whitsun

In full bloom

The reunification of Germany has made all this fun possible. When the fruit trees in the **Havel Region** orchards are in full bloom, everybody in Berlin who can get away goes to the small town of **Werder** (from Berlin by train or – particularly recommended – by excusion boat from Potsdam). Mother Nature gloriously colourful in all her spring finery shares the season with **Werderaner Obstwein** (fruit wine). A good opportunity to sample this heady libation to Spring is the Baumblütenfest, **Tree Blossom Festival**, which is celebrated in Werder around 1 May. In 1879 an enterprising fruit farmer opened a stall in his orchard to promote the sale of his fruit wine. Year after year attendance grew until the little tavern under the flowering trees turned into a **large-scale folk festival**. Nowadays the annual Tree Blossom Festival transforms the little island town, the old centre of Werder, into a sprawling fair-grounds, where all sorts of crafts products and tempting regional culinary specialities are sold.

June/July

Deutsch-Französisches Volksfest (German-French Festival), Kurt-Schumacher-Damm (Reinickendorf), Phone: 030/213 32 90, www.schausteller verbandberlin.de. One of Berlin's biggest folk festivals. Mid-June to mid-July

CSD – Christopher Street Day, Phone: 030/21 75 06 72, www.csd-berlin.de. Gay and Lesbian parade in the centre of Berlin. Late June

July/August

Loveparade, Phone: 030/30 88 12 20, www.loveparade.de. World-famous Techno parade. It is uncertain whether it will again be held from 2006. Mid-July

Deutsch-Amerikanisches Volksfest (German-American Festival), Clayallee (Zehlendorf), Phone: 030/401 38 89. Late July to mid-August

Internationales Berliner Bierfestival (Beer Festival), Karl-Marx-Allee (Friedrichshain), Phone: 030/508 68 22. Early August

Berliner Gauklerfestival (Juggler and Acrobatics Festival), Unter den Linden (Mitte), Phone: 030/247 86 11. Early August

August/September

Kreuzberger Festliche Tage, Phone: 030/43 40 79 05. Folk festival in Viktoria Park around the Kreuzberg. Late Aug. to early Sept.

October

Tag der Deutschen Einheit (German Unification Day), Phone: 030/25 00 25. Street party between the Brandenburg Gate and the Red Town Hall. 3 October

November/December

Christmas Fairs, the most popular are at Breitscheidplatz and behind Alexanderplatz as well as in Spandau Old Town at the Town Hall.

Silvesterparty am Brandenburger Tor (New Year's Eve Party at the Brandenburg Gate), Phone: 030/24 60 32 52. Germany's biggest year-end event.

■ Climate

In Berlin the bear doesn't hibernate. There is no best time to visit. On summer days the thermometer reads a mean 22–23° C; in winter temperatures average 2–3° C. Precipitation is regular but, at only 580 mm mean annual precipitation, it isn't all that frequent.

Climate data Berlin

Month	Air (°C) min./max.	Sunshine (hrs/d)	Rainy days
January	– 2/ 2	2	8
February	2/ 4	3	7
March	2/ 11	4	7
April	6/16	6	7
May	11/22	8	9
June	14/26	9	9
July	16/28	9	6
August	15/27	8	7
September	12/23	7	5
Oktober	7/16	5	7
November	3/ 8	2	9
December	– 1/ 3	1	8

■ Culture live

Current information on the numerous cultural events taking place in Berlin is available from tourist offices [see p. 163] and the daily press.

And…– action!

Every year in February Berlin gets a whiff of **Hollywood ambience**. Autograph hunters queue up in front of luxury hotels, the Berlinale Palast (Stella Musical Haus) at Marlene-Dietrich-Platz, is flooded with première spotlights, while cafés and restaurants are teeming with artists and journalists. Since 1951 the **Internationalen Filmfestspiele Berlin**, the Berlin International Film Festival, has been a magnet for actors, film-makers and journalists from all over the world. The coveted prize: the **Golden Bear**.

The Berlinale is not just for the professionals. Many of the city's cinemas show the **competing films** to the public at large. There are also retrospectives and special showings.

Tickets for the whole show can be purchased at the **Zentrale Vorverkaufsstelle** on the 1st floor of the Europa-Center (Kurfürstendamm) and at **Kino International** (Karl-Marx-Allee 33). Tickets for individual films can be bought either three days before a showing at the Europa-Center or, on the day it is shown, at the cinema. The Film Festival programme is usually confirmed two weeks before the festival begins. For further information: Phone: 030/25 92 00, www.berlinale.de

Tickets

Berlin Tourismus Marketing, Concert and theatre tickets, Phone: 030/25 00 25

Showtime, in 9 branches of Karstadt, Wertheim, KaDeWe, Phone: 030/80 60 29 29, www.showtimetickets.de

Theaterkasse Centrum, Meinekestr. 25 (Charlottenburg), Phone: 030/882 76 11

Hekticket, Hardenbergstr. 29 d/am Zoo (Charlottenburg), Phone: 030/230 99 30; Karl-Liebknecht-Str. 12/Alexanderplatz (Mitte), Phone: 030/24 31 24 31, www.heckticket.de. On the day of the performance tickets are available from 3 pm with up to 50 % discount.

Calendar of Events

February

Internationale Filmfestspiele Berlin (Berlinale), Potsdamer Str. 5 (Mitte), Phone: 030/25 92 00, www. berlinale.de. Film competition for the Golden Bear.

March

maerzmusik, Phone: 030/25 48 90, www.maerzmusik.de. International festival for contemporary music.

May

Theatertreffen Berlin, Phone: 030/25 48 92 33, www.berlinerfestspiele.de. Shows what German-language theatres can achieve. With platforms for innovation and aspiring actors.

May–September

MuseumsInselFestival, Phone: 030/20 62 87 78, www.museumsinselfestival.info. Culture marathon on Museum Island, at the Kulturforum and the Museumskomplex Dahlem with non-stop concerts, musicals, theatre, cinema and dance.

June

Fête de la Musique, www.fetedela musique.de. A world-embracing project: 500 bands from 100 countries play all across the city in June.

August

Internationales Tanzfest, Phone: 030/259 00 40, www.hebbel-theater.de. The stars of contemporary dance and the experimental avant-garde perform at the country's biggest dance festival.

September

Berliner Festwochen, Phone: 030/25 48 91 00, www.berlinerfestspiele.de. Concerts and guest performances take place at several theatres in the city. Sept. to mid-Nov.

Internationales Literaturfestival, Phone: 030/27 87 86 45, www.literaturfestival.com. The city's biggest literary event.

September/October

Art Forum Berlin, Messegelände, Phone: 030/30 38 18 33, www.art-forumberlin.de. International fair for contemporary and avant-garde art. Late Sept./early Oct.

November

JazzFest Berlin, Phone: 030/25 48 91 00, www.berlinerfestspiele.de. Jazz as world music. Early Nov.

Music

Concert halls

Berliner Dom, Am Lustgarten (Mitte), Phone: 030/20 26 91 36

Konzerthaus Berlin – Schauspielhaus am Gendarmenmarkt, Gendarmen-

markt 2 (Mitte), Phone: 030/203 09 21 01,
www.konzerthaus.de.

Philharmonie und Kammermusiksaal,
Herbert-von-Karajan-Str. 1 (Tiergarten),
Phone: 030/25 48 89 99, www.berlin-
philharmonic. com.

Sendesaal des SFB, Masurenallee 8–14
(Charlottenburg), Phone: 030/30 31 12 00

Opera and ballet

Deutsche Oper Berlin, Bismarckstr. 35 (Charlottenburg), Phone: 07 00/
67 37 23 75 46, www.deutsche-oper-
berlin.de

Staatsoper Unter den Linden,
Unter den Linden 7 (Mitte), Phone: 030/
20 35 45 55. www.staatsoper-berlin.de

Komische Oper, Behrenstr. 55–57
(Mitte), Phone: 030/20 26 00,
www.komische-oper-berlin.de

Neuköllner Oper, Karl-Marx-Straße 131–
133 (Neukölln), Phone: 030/68 89 07 77,
www.neukoellneroper.de

Tanzfabrik Berlin, Möckernstr. 68
(Kreuzberg), Phone: 030/786 58 61,
www.tanzfabrik-berlin.de

Musicals and operettas

Theater des Westens, Kantstr. 12
(near Ku'damm), Phone: 018 05/44 44,
www.stage-entertainment.de

Wintergarten, Potsdamer Str. 96
(Schöneberg), Phone: 030/25 00 88 88,
www.wintergarten-variete.de

Jazz, Rock and Pop live

Arena, Eichenstr. 4 (Treptow), Phone:
030/533 20 30, www.arena-berlin.de. Former bus terminal, 8000 m² for concerts,
theatre productions and other events.

*Sainted entertainers: a performance at the
Komische Oper*

Knaack Klub, Greifswalder Str. 224
(Prenzlauer Berg), Phone: 030/442 70 60,
www.knaack-berlin.de

KulturBrauerei, Knaackstr. 97 (Prenzlauer Berg), Phone: 030/44 31 51 52,
www.kulturbrauerei.de

Kulturzentrum Tacheles, Oranienburger
Str. 54–56 a (Mitte), Phone: 030/282 61 85,
www.tacheles.de

Quasimodo, Kantstr. 12 a (Charlottenburg),
Phone: 030/312 80 86, www.quasimodo.de

Tempodrom, Am Anhalter Bahnhof,
Möckernstraße 10 (Kreuzberg), Phone:
030/263 99 80, www.tempodrom.de

Tränenpalast, Reichstagufer 17
(Mitte), Phone: 030/20 61 00 11,
www.traenenpalast.de

Open-air events

**Freilichtbühne an der Zitadelle
Spandau**, Zitadelle Spandau
(Spandau), Phone: 030/333 40 22,
www.freilichtbuehne-spandau.de

Freilichtbühne Weißensee,
Große Seestr. 9 (Weißensee),
Phone: 030/24 72 78 03

Freiluftkino Friedrichshain, Volkspark
(Friedrichshain), Phone: 030/29 36 16 29,
www.freiluftkino-berlin.de

Freiluftkino Hasenheide,
Volkspark Hasenheide (Neukölln),
Phone: 030/283 46 03

Freiluftkino Kreuzberg, Mariannenplatz
2 (Kreuzberg), Phone: 030/24 31 30 34

Freiluftkino Museumsinsel, Bodestraße
(Mitte), Phone: 030/20 62 87 78

Freinachtkino Podewil, Klosterstr.
68–70, Phone: 030/24 74 97 77

Waldbühne, Am Glockenturm (Charlottenburg), Phone: 030/305 81 23

Theatres

Berliner Ensemble, Theater am
Schifferdamm, Bertolt-Brecht-Platz 1
(Mitte), Phone: 030/28 40 81 55,
www.berliner-ensemble.de

**Deutsches Theater, Kammerspiele
und Baracke**, Schumannstr. 13 a
(Mitte), Phone: 030/28 44 12 25,
www.deutsches-theater.berlin.net

Hebbel am Ufer, Phone: 030/25 90 04 27,
www.hebbel-am-ufer.de; 3 theatres in
Kreuzberg: Hebbel-Theater, Strese-
mannstr. 29; Theater am Halleschen
Ufer, Hallesches Ufer; Theater am Ufer,
Tempelhofer Ufer 10

Calling all senses: theatre in the Schaubühne at Lehniner Platz

Maxim Gorki Theater, Am Festungs-graben 2 (Mitte), Phone: 030/20 22 11 15, www.gorki.de

Renaissance Theater, Knesebeckstr. 100 (Charlottenburg), Phone: 030/312 42 02, www.renaissance-theater.de

Schaubühne am Lehniner Platz, Kur-fürstendamm 153 (Wilmersdorf), Phone: 030/89 00 23, www.schaubuehne.de

Schlosspark Theater, Schlossstr. 48 (Steglitz), Phone: 030/70 09 69 15, www.schlossparktheater.de

Theater am Kurfürstendamm & Komödie, Kurfürstendamm 206 (Char-lottenburg), Phone: 030/88 59 11 88, www.theater-am-kurfuerstendamm.de

Tribüne, Otto-Suhr-Allee 18 (Charlottenburg), Phone: 030/341 26 00, www.tribuene-berlin.de

Vagantenbühne, Kantstr. 12 a (Charlot-tenburg), Phone: 030/312 45 29, www.vaganten.de

Volksbühne, Rosa-Luxemburg-Platz 2 (Mitte), Phone: 030/247 67 72, www.volksbuehne-berlin.de

Children's and teen theatres

Theater an der Parkaue, Parkaue 29 (Lichtenberg), Tel 030/55 77 52 52, www.parkaue.de

Zaubertheater Igor Jedlin, Roscher Str. 7 (Charlottenburg), Phone: 030/323 37 77, www.zaubertheater.de

Puppet theatres

Die Schaubude – Puppentheater Berlin, Greifswalder Str. 81–84 (Prenz-lauer Berg), Phone: 030/423 43 14, www.schaubude-berlin.de

Figuren Theater Grashüpfer, Puschkinallee 16 a (Treptow), Phone: 030/53 69 51 50, www.theater-grashuepfer.de

Hans Wurst Nachfahren, Gleditschstr. 5 (Schöneberg), Phone: 030/216 79 25, www.hans-wurst-nachfahren.de

Kindertheater dell'arte, Drakestr. 49 (Steglitz), Phone: 030/84 31 46 46, www.dellarte.bitcreation.com

Narrenspiegel, Erich-Weinert-Str. 27 (Prenzlauer Berg), Phone: 030/81 29 83 65, www.narrenspiegel.de

Puppentheater Firlefanz, Sophien-str. 10 (Mitte), Phone: 030/283 35 60, www.puppentheater-firlefanz.de

Variety theatres and cabarets

Bar jeder Vernunft, Schaperstr. 24 (Wilmersdorf), Phone: 030/883 15 82, www.bar-jeder-vernunft.de

BKA, Berliner Kabarett Anstalt, Mehringdamm 34 (Kreuzberg), Phone: 030/20 22 00 44, www.bka-theater.de

Chamäleon Varité, Hackesche Höfe, Rosenthaler Str. 40–41 (Mitte), Phone: 030/282 71 18, www.chamaeleonberlin.com

Die Distel, Friedrichstr. 101 (Mitte), Phone: 030/204 47 04, www.distel-berlin.de

Friedrichstadtpalast, Friedrichstr. 107 (Mitte), Phone: 030/23 26 23 26, www.friedrichstadtpalast.de

Kabarett 'Die Stachelschweine', Europa-Center (Charlottenburg), Phone: 030/261 47 95, www.die-stachelschweine.de

Kabarett Kartoon, Kochstr. 50, Axel-Springer-Passage (Kreuzberg), Phone: 030/72 61 68 80, www.kabarettkartoon.de

Metamorphosis included: Varieté Chamäleon

Kabarett-Theater 'Die Wühlmäuse', Pommernallee 2–4 (Charlottenburg), Phone: 030/30 67 30 11, www.wuehlmaeuse.de

UFA Fabrik, Viktoriastr. 10–18 (Tempelhof), Phone: 030/75 50 30, www.ufafabrik.de

Wintergarten Varieté, Potsdamer Str. 96 (Tiergarten), Phone: 030/25 00 88 88, www.wintergarten-variete.de

Cinemas

CinemaxX, Potsdamer Str. 5 (Tiergarten), Phone: 018 05/24 63 62 99, 030/25 92 21 11. 19 auditoriums

CineStar IMAX, Sony-Center, Potsdamer Str. 4 (Tiergarten), Phone: 030/26 06 64 00

Colosseum, Schönhauser Allee 123 (Prenzlauer Berg), Phone: 030/44 01 81 80. 10 auditoriums.

Cubix-UFA-Palast, Rathausstr. 1, Alexanderplatz (Mitte), Phone: 030/ 257 61 10. Ultra-modern and comfortable.

Odeon, Hauptstr. 116 (Schöneberg), Phone: 030/78 70 40 19. Films in English.

UCI Kinowelt Zoo Palast, Hardenbergstr. 29 a (Charlottenburg), Phone: 030/25 41 47 77. 9 auditoriums.

UFA Kino in der KulturBrauerei, Schönhauser Allee 36 (Prenzlauer Berg), Phone: 030/44 35 40. Modern technology.

■ Museums, Memorials, Palaces

SchauLust Museen Berlin. This 3-day museum pass for 15 € enables you to visit over 70 Berlin collections. For further information: www.berlin-tourist-information.de.

Lange Nacht der Museen, Phone: 030/902 69 94 44, www.lange-nachtdermuseen. de. On one night each in Jan./Feb. and Aug. about 120 Berlin museums offer an interesting evening cultural programme.

Memorials

In addition to those covered in the main text:

Erinnerungsstätte Notaufnahmelager Marienfelde, Marienfelder Allee 66–80, (Marienfelde), Phone: 030/75 00 84 00, www.enm-berlin.de, Tu–Su 10 am–6 pm, guided tours We, Su 3 pm. Exhibition on

the German-German refugee migration in the camp built in 1953, through which 1.35 million refugees passed.

Gedenkstätte Normannenstraße, Ruschestr. 103, Haus 1 (Lichtenberg), Phone: 030/553 68 54, Mo–Fr 11 am–6 pm, Sa/Su/hols. 2 pm–6 pm. Exhibition dealing with GDR history. The site includes the office of former Stasi head Erich Mielke.

Gedenkstätte Hohenschönhausen, Genslerstr. 66, (Hohenschönhausen), Phone: 030/98 60 82 30, www.stiftunghsh.de, visit with guided tour only Mo–Fr 11 am and 1 pm, Sa/Su 10 am–4 pm every hour, also by appointment; temporary exhibitions daily 9 am–6 pm. Former Soviet special internment camp and Stasi interrogation and detention centre operated by the ministry of State Security (GDR).

Museum

In addition to those covered in the main text:

Labyrinth Kindermuseum Berlin, Fabrik Osloer Straße, Osloer Str. 12 (Wedding), Phone: 030/49 30 89 01, www.labyrinthkindermuseum.de, Tu–Sa 1 pm–6 pm, Su 11 am–6 pm, hols open Mo–Fr 10 am–6 pm, Sa 1 pm–6 pm, Su 11 am–6 pm. The children's museum mounts interactive exhibitions and events based on playing, reading and learning.

Palaces

In addition to those covered in the main text:

Schloss and Park Biesdorf, Alt-Biesdorf 55 (Marzahn), Phone: 030/514 37 36, Mo–Th 9.30 am–7 pm, Fr 9 am–2 pm, Sunday opening for groups by prior arrangement.

Schloss and Park Britz, Alt-Britz 73 (Neukölln), Phone: 030/60 97 92 0, www.schloss-britz.de, Schloss: guided tours We 2 pm–5.30 pm, rotating exhibitions from May 2006 Tu–Th 2 pm–6 pm, Fr 2 pm–8 pm, Sa/Su/hols. 11 am–6 pm; Park: daily 9 am to sunset

■ Nightlife

Berlin by night – no problem, this city has a staggeringly multi-faceted club scene. The operative locales are Mitte, Prenzlauer Berg, Friedrichshain and Kreuzberg.

The city magazines [see p. 163] will help you to find the most interesting night-spots. Also check: www.berlinatnight.de

Bars

Bar am Lützowplatz, Lützowplatz 7 (Schöneberg), Phone: 030/262 68 07. The 17-m-counter is the focal point of this bar. Kevin Costner has been sighted at it. A variety of classic cocktails, excellent choice of malt whiskys and champagne.

Dante beim Hackeschen Markt, Am Zwirngraben 8–10 (Mitte), Phone: 030/24 72 74 01. Wide selction of cocktails and a vast dance floor.

Würgeengel, Dresdner Str. 122 (Kreuz-berg), Phone: 030/615 55 60. Cocktails at the 'Angel exterminador' bar, hors d'œuvres and tapas at the tables.

Zoulou Bar, Hauptstr. 4 (Schöneberg), Phone: 030/70 09 47 37. American bar, much frequented late at night.

Discos and clubs

Adagio, Marlene-Dietrich-Platz 1 (Mitte), Phone: 030/312 94 93. Soul, Funk, R'n B and packed with beau-tiful people in a Baroque setting replete with putti and ceiling paintings.

Far Out, Lehniner Platz/Kurfürsten-damm 156 (Charlottenburg), Phone: 030/32 00 07 24, www.farout-berlin.de. Well established disco with a colourful mix of music.

Golgatha, Dudenstr. 48–64 (Kreuzberg), Phone: 030/785 24 53, www.golgatha-berlin.de. Disco with charts and rock hits. The large beer garden provides a big TV-screen.

Meet Mao at the bar on Lützowplatz

h2o-Club, Dircksenstr./Karl-Lieb-knecht-Str. (Mitte), Phone: 01 63/315 05 80, www.h2o-club.com. Black music from HipHop and Rap to Reggae and Dancehall in a quirky interior.

Icon, Cantainstr. 15 (Charlottenburg), Phone: 030/48 49 28 78, www.iconberlin. de. The scene club in the vaulted cellar hits the right note with Drum'n'Bass to HipHop.

Pubs and scene venues

Aedes, Hackesche Höfe, Rosenthaler Str. 40–41, Phone: 030/285 82 75. Frequented in the evenings by architects, gallery proprietors and tourists.

Atlantic, Bergmannstr. 100 (Kreuzberg), Phone: 030/691 92 92. Lots of glass, chrome and light, cool, stylish and chic.

Badeschiff Spreebrücke, Eichenstr. 4 (entrance: Flutgraben, Köpenick), Phone: 030/53 32 03 40. Bar and lounge on an old barge on the Spree, with a big heated swimming pool. On shore is a manmade sandy beach with hammocks (May–Oct.).

Dicke Wirtin, Carmerstr. 9 (Charlotten-burg), Phone: 030/312 49 52. Typical Berlin beer joint; serves home-cooked casseroles.

Diener, Grolmannstr. 47 (Charlotten-burg), Phone: 030/881 53 29. Rustic pub, an artist hangout, founded by the leg-endary boxer Franz Diener.

Kumpelnest 3000, Lützowstr. 23 (Schöne-berg), Phone: 030/261 69 18. Shady plush décor in a former brothel, all kinds of music and denizens from drag queens to Lagerfeld. Always packed.

Madonna, Wiener Str. 22 (Kreuzberg), Phone: 030/611 69 43. A Kreuzberg insti-tution, loud, smoke-filled and crowded. Sacral appointments include hundreds of devotional pictures and statues of the Virgin.

Roter Salon und Grüner Salon in der Volksbühne, Rosa-Luxemburg-Platz (Mitte), Red: Phone: 030/24 06 58 06, Green: Phone: 030/925 25 76. The Red Salon provides a cosy plushy setting and (avant-garde) live music. The Green Salon is noted for dance and chanson evenings. Night time is often party time.

Tanzwirtschaft Kaffee Burger, Torstr. 60 (Mitte), Phone: 030/28 04 64 95, www.kaffeeburger.de. Nostalgia for East Germany, literary forum and party venue, location of the legendary Russian disco, etc (Mo–Th from 9 pm, Fr/Sa from 11 pm, Su from 7 pm).

Zillemarkt, Bleibtreustr. 48a (Charlottenburg), Phone: 030/881 70 40. Once a big garage, now a restaurant with pub and courtyard.

Food for night owls

Nearly all Berlin snack-bars are open until midnight at least. In addition, itinerant traders provide night owls in particular night spots with baguettes, spring rolls, fishballs and other snacks.

Fressco, Zossener Str. 24 (Kreuzberg), Phone: 030/69 40 16 13. Italian delicacies and smoke-free zone.

Konnopke's, Schönhauser Allee 44 a (Prenzlauer Berg), under the elevated train tracks, Mo–Fr 6 am to midnight. Superlative Currywurst!

Schwarzes Café, Kantstr. 148 (Charlottenburg), Phone: 030/313 80 38. Scene venue, showing its age a bit, serves hot food until long past 1 am.

Witty's, Wittenbergplatz (directly across from KaDeWe), daily 11 am to midnight.

■ Sports

Berlin provides numerous and varied kinds of activities for sportsmen and sportswomen. In addition, many national and international **sporting events** take place here, such as the *Berlin Marathon* (Germany's biggest with 40 000 participants), the ISTAF for track and field sports and the finals of the DFB football championships. The Berlin Olympic Stadium has been rebuilt and is now state-of-the-art. And the Max-Schmeling-Halle in Prenzlauer Berg as well as the cyclodrome and the indoor swimming pool in Landsberger Allee have added three new multi-purpose facilities to those Berlin already had.

Sportservice Berlin,
Phone: 030/90 26 50 50. Information on sports activities and clubs.

Swimming pools, spas and workouts

Almost every section of the city has spas and workout studios, an indoor swimming pool and most also have an open-air swimming pool, not to mention the bathing beaches on the lakes and riversides in and around Berlin. Before going

Berlin is tops

Berlin is Germany's biggest city, has the longest underground rail network, the zoo with the largest variety of species, has the biggest fleet of sports boats and the most dog-loving households. The first person to lift off into the air did so in Berlin, pictures learnt motion here, the first radio reporter made announcements and Christo wrapped his first German building here: the Reichstag.

No other city in Europe has as many trees as Berlin – about 400 000 of them. And the city has more bridges – 1662 – than even Venice. It has even more pubs – supposedly about 7000.

to one of the more than 40 public swimming pools, you should confirm the opening hours:

Berliner Bäderbetriebe,
Phone: 018 03/10 20 20,
www.berlinerbaederbetriebe.de

Indoor swimming pools

blub Badeparadies, Buschkrugallee 64 (Neukölln), Phone: 030/606 60 60. Jacuzzis solarium, sauna, fitness centre.

Solf-Sauna, Bundesallee 187 (Wilmersdorf), Phone: 030/854 50 14. Swimming pool, jacuzzi, sauna, solarium.

Stadtbad Charlottenburg, Krumme Str. 10 (Charlottenburg). Berlin's oldest indoor swimming pool, opened in 1898. Notable for its decorative tiling.

Stadtbad Neukölln, Ganghoferstr. 3–5 (Neukölln). Praised as Europe's most beautiful indoor swimming pool when it opened in 1914.

Thermen am Europa-Center, Nürnberger Str. 7 (Charlottenburg), Phone: 030/257 57 60. Thermal pool, steam bath and sauna, also fitness, massage and solarium. Restaurant.

Open-air swimming pools

Freibad Wendenschloss, Möllhausenufer 30 (Köpenick), Phone: 030/651 71 71

Kombibad Gropiusstadt – Sommerbad, Lipschitzallee 27–33 (Buckow), Phone: 030/60 97 19 22

Prinzenbad, U-Bahnhof Prinzenstraße (Kreuzberg), Phone: 030/616 10 80

Sommerbad Wilmersdorf,
Forckenbeckstr. 14 (Wilmersdorf),
Phone: 030/897 74 10

**Sommerbad am Insulaner Munster-
damm**, Munsterdamm 80 (Steglitz),
Phone: 030/79 41 04 13

Strandbad Müggelsee, Fürsten-
walder Damm 838 (Rahnsdorf),
Phone: 030/648 77 77

Strandbad Wannsee, Wannseebadweg
25 (Wannsee), Phone: 030/70 71 38 30

Ice-skating

Sportpark Neukölln, Oderstraße 182
(Tempelhof), Phone: 030/62 84 40 07

**Eisstadion Wilmersdorf (Horst-Dohm-
Eisstadion)**, Fritz-Wildung- Str. 9
(Wilmersdorf), Phone: 030/824 10 12,
030/823 40 60 (recorded message)

Golf

There are about 16 golf courses around
Berlin, most of them set in beautiful scenery. For further information:

Golfverband Berlin-Brandenburg,
Forststr. 34 (Steglitz),
Phone: 030/823 66 09, www.gvbb.de

Horses

Horse Races

Galopprennbahn Hoppegarten,
Goetheallee 1 (Dahlwitz-Hoppegarten),
Phone: 0 33 42/389 30. Race course
opened in 1868, the main grandstand
is an historic monument.

Sailing fun at the beach on Wannsee

Trabrennbahn Karlshorst,
Treskowallee 129 (Lichtenberg),
Phone: 030/50 01 70. Trotting races.

For equestrians

Reiterhof Lübars, Alt-Lübars 5
(Reinickendorf), Phone: 030/40 39 76 64,
www.reitsport-luebars.de

Reiterverein Onkel Toms Hütte,
Onkel-Tom-Str. 172 (Zehlendorf),
Phone: 030/813 20 81. Dressage, jumping.

Reit- und Springschule am Poloplatz,
(Frohnau), Phone: 030/401 58 35

Tennis

Freizeitpark Tegel, Campestr. 11 (Tegel),
Phone: 030/434 66 66, www.tennistegel.
de. Indoor and outdoor tennis courts.

TSB City Sports, Brandenburgische
Str. 53 (Charlottenburg), Phone: 030/
873 90 97. Squash courts, tennis courts,
badminton courts, sauna.

TSF Tennis, Squash and Fitness,
Richard-Tauber-Damm 36 (Tempelhof),
Phone: 030/743 60 01, and Galenstr. 33–35
(Spandau), Phone: 030/333 40 83

Aquatic sports and boat hire

Boots-Charter Lüders, Wannsee bathing beach, own entrance (Zehlendorf),
Phone: 030/803 45 90. Canoes, rowing
boats, sailing boats and pedal boats.

**Deutscher Unterwasser Club
Berlin**, Scabellstr. 7 (Zehlendorf),
Phone: 030/05 32 42. Diving courses.

Marina Lanke Berlint, Scharfe Lanke
109–131 (Spandau), Phone: 030/362 00 90.
Yacht and motorboat hire, sailing and
motorboat school, children's play-
ground, bistro, barbecue area and a
caravan park.

M. Mühl, An der Sechserbrücke (Tegel),
Phone: 030/433 76 90. Rowing boat and
pedal boat hire, minigolf course.

Richtershorner Ruderverein, Karolinen-
hof, Sportpromenade 17 (Köpenick),
Phone: 030/675 85 50

Segel-Schule Berlin, Friederikestr. 24
(Tegel), Phone: 030/431 11 71. Rowing
boats, pedal boats, canoes and sailing
boats.

Football

Olympiastadion, Olympischer Platz
(Charlottenburg). Buy tickets in advance
at the usual ticket offices or directly
from:

Hertha BSC, Hanns-Braun-Straße, Friesenhaus 2 (Charlottenburg), Phone: 018 05/18 92 00

■ City Tours

Flights

To have a bird's-eye view of Berlin at least once, take a helicopter tour (Schönefeld Airport) or float over in a hot-air balloon (Ebertstraße/Vossstraße, near Potsdamer Platz). For further information:

Air Service Berlin CFH GmbH, Flughafen Tempelhof or Schönefeld Airport, Phone: 030/53 21 53 21, www.air-service-berlin.de, www.commander-frank.de

Walking tours and themed trips

If you want to participate in tour of the city tailored to your individual needs, apply to *Berlin Tourismus Marketing* [see p. 163]. In addition, all sorts of themed trips and tours are offered:

art:berlin, Oranienburger Str. 32 (Mitte), Phone: 030/28 09 63 90, www.artberlin-online.de. Berlin from A to Z and off the beaten track.

Berliner Geschichtswerkstatt, Goltzstr. 49 (Schöneberg), Phone: 030/215 44 50. Historical art, architecture, literary tours and boat trips. Late April to Sept., Su every 2 weeks.

Berliner Unterwelten, Phone: 030/49 91 05 17, www.berliner-unterwelten.de. Tours 1–3, tickets U-Bahn Gesundbrunnen, south concourse, exit Humboldthain, Brunnenstr. 108 a. Tour 1: U-Bahn, bunkers and Cold War, Sa, Mo 11 am, 1 pm. Tour 2: From Flak Tower to the Rubble Hill. Tour 3: Dark Worlds, Sa/Su 12 noon, 2 pm, 4 pm. Tour 4: Rohrpost Technology Monument, Oranienburger Str. 72 (tickets), across from New Synagogue, Sa/Su 11 am, 1 pm

KulturBüro Berlin, Malmöer Str. 60 (Prenzlauer Berg), Phone: 030/444 09 36, www.stadtverfuehrung.de. Guided tours of museums, city and park walks with a focus on art.

Hear We Go, Phone: 030/50 56 37 84, www.hearwego.de. Individual audio tours with headphones available for hire from: BTM Tourist Info in the south wing of the Brandenburg Gate, The Mauermuseum – Haus am Checkpoint Charlie, the Berlin Story, Unter den Linden 10.

Tours can also be downloaded for MP3 or available at shops as CD.

StaTours, Neue Kantstr. 25, Phone: 030/30 10 51 51, www.sta-tours.de. Tours in small groups to view the flats and palaces of the stars of yesteryear and today.

Stattreisen Berlin, Malplaquetstr. 5 (Wedding), Phone: 030/455 30 28, www.stattreisenberlin.de. City tours with emphasis on all aspects of history, Jewish culture, everyday life and literature.

Trabi-Safari, Phone: 030/27 59 22 73, www.trabi-safari.de. Starts at Gendarmenmarkt. Convoy reconnoitering, drive yourself in a Trabi with radio link to tour guide: through the 'Wild East' or as 'Berlin Classic' tour.

Bus tours

The main points of departure for sightseeing tours by bus that usually start hourly are Kurfürstendamm/Meinekestraße and Tauentzienstraße/Marburger Straße, other hop on, hop off spots along the way.

Berlin City Tour, Phone: 030/68 30 26 41, www.berlin-city-tour.de

Berliner Bären Stadtrundfahrt, Seeburger Str. 19 b, Phone: 030/35 19 52 70, www.bbsberlin.de

Berolina Stadtrundfahrten, Phone: 030/88 56 80 30, www.berolina-berlin.com

BVG Tour Nostalgie, Phone: 030/25 62 55 69. Good Friday to end Oct.

Severin und Kühn, Kurfürstendamm 216, Phone: 030/880 41 90, www.severin-kuehn-berlin.de

A particularly inexpensive way of touring the city is to take **Bus 100**. It leaves from the bus terminal in front of Bahnhof Zoo, goes past Schloss Bellevue, Reichstag, Brandenburger Tor and Unter den Linden to Alexanderplatz.

Boat tours

Berlin can be explored by boat via its many waterways. The main mooring points for sightseeing tours in the city centre are the Janowitz, Schloss, Hansa and Kottbusser Bridges as well as the Pergamonmuseum. For trips outside of Berlin go to the mooring points at Bahnhof Wannsee (boats to Pfaueninsel, Potsdam or Werder), Treptower Park (towards

Convoyed by Neptune! Seeing the sights by Spree boat

the south-east on the Dahme and Spree to Müggelsee and in the Teuplitzer waters) and Greenwich Promenade in Tegel (Tegeler See and Oberhavel). For further information:

Reederei Riedel, Planufer 78 (Kreuzberg), Phone: 030/693 46 46, www.reedereiriedel. de. The trips start from Hansabrücke, Märkisches Ufer, Kottbusser Brücke, Corneliusbrücke.

Stern- und Kreisschifffahrt, Puschkin-allee 15 (Treptow), Phone: 030/536 36 00, www.sternundkreis.de. Biggest Berlin pleasure-boat business with a fleet of 30 excursion steamers, 6 ferries and 80 moorings in Berlin and Brandenburg.

▮ Statistics

Status: Capital city of the Federal Republic of Germany.

Geographical facts: 52°31'12" north and 13°24'36" east. Mean elevation above sea level 34 m; highest points: Teufelsberg 115 m, Müggelberg 115 m.

Surface area: 89 182 ha, of which water: 6.7%; woodland area: 18 %; recreational area (parks, private gardens, sports facilities): 11.5%.

Length of the city boundaries: 234 km.

Population (as of 2004): 3.38 million.

Traffic network: 5334 km roads, of which 66.1 km are Autobahn, 473 km U- and S-Bahn, 1626 km bus lines, 187, 7 km tram lines. Number of people conveyed annually by inner-city public transport: U-Bahn 457 million, S-Bahn 318 million, Bus 407 million, Tram 171 million

Rail traffic: Main train stations are Bahnhof Zoologischer Garten, Ostbahnhof, Hauptbahnhof (Lehrter Bahnhof), Lichtenberg. More than 300 regional and long-distance arrivals and departures daily.

Airports: Berlin has three airports: *Tegel* is the biggest with respect to the daily number of take-offs and landings (430) as well as the number of passengers (11.3 Mio. a year). *Schönefeld* is used by 2.7 million passengers a year, it has 96 take-offs and landings a day. Is scheduled for enlargement as Berlin Brandenburg International Airport (BBI) in a few years. *Tempelhof* has had 52 take-offs and landings a day and 280 000 passengers a year. However, the Senate has decided to abandon Tempelhof Airport and demolish it but a potential operating consortium has brought an action against the Senate decision. The lawsuit is pending.

Hotels: employees: approx 56 000; bed capacity: 75 000; guests annually: 6 million; overnight stays: approx 13 million.

Economy: GDP 77.3 billion €, workforce of 1.53 million, of which ca 1 million in the service and information sector. Berlin has also developed into a film and TV city, both for film-making and as the seat of production companies and TV channels.

Administraton: 141 representatives, both men and women, in the Abgeordnetenhaus. Klaus Wowereit is the current mayor and governs with a coalition of SPD and PDS. The Berlin Town Hall is in Mitte District.

Districts: Berlin is divided into twelve districts: Charlottenburg-Willmersdorf, Friedrichshain-Kreuzberg, Lichtenberg, Marzahn-Hellersdorf, Mitte, Neukölln, Pankow, Reinickendorf, Spandau, Steglitz-Zehlendorf, Tempelhof-Schöneberg and Treptow-Köpenick.

Schools: Berlin has 21 institutions of higher learning, including three major universities (Freie Universität, Humboldt Universität, Technische Universität) and a total student body of 141 000. Berlin is, therefore, Germany's biggest university city. There are also 122 higher secondary schools (Gymnasien), 71 comprehensive schools, 83 secondary schools (Realschulen), 60 secondary modern schools (Hauptschulen) and 447 primary schools.

City coat of arms: A black bear rampant sinister on a silver ground; a five-pointed gold crown above the escutcheon.

Accommodation

Camping

The annually updated **ADAC Camping-Caravaning Guide** with CD Rom, available at booksellers and at ADAC branches, gives a selection of tested campsites. The **ADAC Stellplatzführer**, which is also published annually, is informative on staying overnight with caravans (trailers) (www.adac.de/camping).

Citycamping Hettler und Lange, Gartenfelder Str. 1 (Spandau), Phone: 030/33 50 36 33. www.hettler-lange.de, open all year round.

DCC-Campingplatz Kladow, Krampnitzer Weg 111–117 (Spandau), Phone: 030/365 27 97, open all year round.

DCC-Camping am Krossinsee, Wernsdorfer Str. 38 (Schmöckwitz), Phone: 030/675 86 87, www.dccberlin.de, open all year round.

Hostels and Guest-houses

A&O Hostel, three locations: Boxhagener Str. 73 (Friedrichshain), Joachimstaler Str. 1–3 (am Zoologischen Garten), Köpenicker Str. 127–129 (Mitte), Phone: 030/297 77 10, www.aohostels.de. Decent low-budget lodging with single, double and multiple-bed rooms.

Bogota, Schlüterstr. 45 (Charlottenburg), Phone: 030/881 50 01, Fax 030/883 58 87, www.hotelbogota.com. Large airy rooms, centrally located.

EastSeven Berlin Hostel, Schwedter Str. 7 (Prenzlauer Berg), Phone: 030/93 62 22 40, Fax 030/93 62 22 39, www.eastseven.de. Backpacker hostel with 17 rooms, most with shared bath. Garden, communal kitchen, etc.

Funk, Fasanenstr. 69 (Charlottenburg), Phone: 030/882 71 93, Fax 030/883 33 29. Popular since the 1930s, in a fine 1870s boom-era building with delightfully old-fashioned décor.

Korfu II, Rankestr. 35 (Charlottenburg), Phone: 030/212 47 90, Fax 030/211 84 32, www.hp-korfu.de. A friendly hotel right at the Gedächtniskirche.

Merkur, Torstr. 156 (Mitte), Phone: 030/282 82 97, Fax 030/282 77 65, www.hotel-merkur-berlin.de. A clean, traditional guest-house.

Kreuzberg, Großbeerenstr. 64 (Kreuzberg), Phone: 030/251 13 62, Fax 030/251 06 38, www.pension-kreuzberg.de. A neat, simple guest-house.

Hotels

*****Brandenburger Hof**, Eislebener Str. 14 (Wilmersdorf), Phone: 030/21 40 50, Fax 030/21 40 51 00, www.brandenburger-hof.com. Superlative location, elegant reception rooms in an historic setting, rooms in Bauhaus design and a gourmet restaurant, Die Quadriga (1 Michelin star). Quiet inner courtyard with a lovely Japanese garden.

*****Grandhotel Esplanade**, Lützowufer 15 (Tiergarten), Phone: 030/25 47 80, Fax 030/254 78 82 22, www.esplanade.de. This hotel deserves every one of its five stars! Just a visit to **Harry's New York Bar** in the hotel is worth every penny.

*****Hotel Adlon**, Unter den Linden 77 (Mitte), Phone: 030/250 20, Fax 030/25 02 11 09, www.hotel-adlon.de. Rich in tradition, this hotel was destroyed in the war but has been reconstructed to match its old splendour – a 'megastar'.

*****Hotel Palace**, Europa-Center, Budapester Str. 45 (Charlottenburg), Phone: 030/250 20, Fax 030/25 02 11 09, www.palace de. Modernised, with elegantly furnished and decorated suites and rooms.

*****Hotel Steigenberger**, Los-Angeles-Platz 1 (Charlottenburg), Phone: 030/212 70, Fax 030/212 71 17, www.berlin.steigenberger.de. A large hotel with 397 rooms and all luxury features, quiet though near Kurfürstenplatz.

*****Intercontinental**, Budapester Str. 2 (Tiergarten), Phone: 030/260 20, Fax 030/26 02 26 00, www.berlin.intercontinental.com. At the heart of the city.

*****Kempinski Hotel Bristol**, Kurfürstendamm 27 (Charlottenburg), Phone: 030/88 43 40, Fax 030/883 60 75, www.kempinski-bristol.de. A Member of Leading Hotels of the World, it numbers star tenor Placido Domingo and other luminaries among its guests. 301 most elegant rooms, three restaurants and the celebrated Bristol Bar.

*****Schlosshotel im Grunewald**, Brahmsstr. 10 (Grunewald), Phone: 030/89 58 40, Fax 030/89 58 48 00, www.schlosshotelberlin.com. Fashion Tsar Karl Lagerfeld not only dresses ladies – he also designed the interior of this luxury hotel, which looks back on a rich tradition.

The Regent Berlin, Charlottenstr. 49 (Mitte), Phone: 030/203 38, Fax 030/20 33 61 19, www.regenthotels.com. Highly praised luxury hotel right on Gendarmenmarkt with personal service and elegant, stylish rooms and suites.

Westin Grand Hotel Berlin, Friedrichstr. 158–164 (Mitte), Phone: 030/202 70, Fax 030/20 27 33 62, www.westin.com/berlin. The famous stair in the lobby is a catwalk for models and showcases newly-weds and acrobats.

****ackselhaus & bluehome**, Belforter Str. 21 (Prenzlauer Berg), Phone: 030/44 33 76 33, Fax 030/441 61 16, www.ackselhaus.de. This apartment hotel, a member of Charming Hotels of the World, consists in two houses with 25 themed rooms (Venice, Rome, Africa). A beautiful garden and Club del Mar restaurant.

****Bleibtreu**, Bleibtreustr. 31 (Charlottenburg), Phone: 030/88 47 40, Fax 030/88 47 44 44, www.bleibtreu.com. A hotel of uniquely reticent modern elegance.

****Dolce Berlin Müggelsee**, Müggelheimer Damm 145 (Köpenick), Phone: 030/65 88 22 00, Fax 030/65 88 22 67, www.berlin.dolce.com. Respectable modern hotel in a lovely spot directly on Großer Müggelsee.

****Estrel Residence Hotel**, Sonnenallee 225 (Neukölln), Phone: 030/683 10, Fax 030/68 31 23 45. Huge hotel with 1125 rooms.

****Golden Tulip Hotel Residenz**, Meinekestr. 9 (Charlottenburg), Phone: 030/88 44 30, Fax 030/882 47 26, www.hotel-residenz.com. Jugendstil building with lots of style and flair, especially popular with TV stars. Good restaurant.

****Hotel Seehof am Lietzensee**, Lietzensee Ufer 11 (Charlottenburg), Phone: 030/32 00 20, Fax 030/32 00 22 51, www.hotel-seehof-berlin.de. An oasis in a big city: rooms and indoor swimming pool with view of the lake and park.

****Hecker's Hotel**, Grolmanstr. 35 (Charlottenburg), Phone: 030/889 00, Fax 030/889 02 60, www.heckers-hotel.com. Friendly private hotel.

****Luisenhof**, Köpenicker Str. 92 (Mitte), Phone: 030/241 59 06, Fax 030/279 29 83, www.luisenhof.de. 27 rooms, simple 1870s elegance.

***/*Sorat Art'otel**, Joachimstaler Str. 28–29 (Charlottenburg), Phone: 030/88 44 70, Fax 030/88 44 77 00, www.sorat-hotels.com/artotel-berlin. Exciting avant-garde designer hotel near Ku'damm, decorated with art works by Wolf Vostell.

***Art Nouveau**, Leibnizstr. 59 (Charlottenburg), Phone: 030/327 74 40, Fax 030/32 77 44 40, www.hotelartnouveau.de. Stylishly themed rooms and suites in a modernised Jugendstil building near Ku'damm.

***Riehmers Hofgarten**, Yorckstr. 83 (Kreuzberg), Phone: 030/78 09 88 00, Fax 030/78 09 88 08, www.hotel-riehmers-hofgarten.de. This friendly, tastefully decorated hotel is in a fine 1870s boom-era building. The e.t.a hoffmann restaurant serves classic modern cuisine.

***Askanischer Hof**, Kurfürstendamm 53 (Charlottenburg), Phone: 030/881 80 33, Fax 030/881 72 06, www.askanischerhof.de. Spacious rooms and Jugendstil interiors.

***Frauenhotel Artemisia**, Brandenburgische Str. 18 (Wilmersdorf), Phone: 030/873 89 05, Fax 030/861 86 53, www.frauenhotel-berlin.de. This hotel presents itself as a man-free zone, with attractively decorated rooms.

***Kastanienhof**, Kastanienallee 65 (Mitte), Phone: 030/44 30 50, Fax 030/44 30 51 11, www.hotel-kastanienhof-berlin.de. Hotel-guest-house with an informal family atmosphere.

Hotel Am Anhalter Bahnhof, Stresemannstr. 36 (Kreuzberg), Phone: 030/251 03 42, Fax 030/251 48 97, www.hotel-anhalter-bahnhof.de. A modest, pleasant hotel.

Dittberner, Wielandstr. 26 (Charlottenburg), Phone: 030/881 64 85, Fax 030/885 40 46, www.hotel-dittberner.de. An elegant guest-house with an arty atmosphere.

Hotel am Scheunenviertel, Oranienburger Str. 38, Phone: 030/282 21 25, Fax 030/282 11 15, www.hotelas.com. A nice hotel near the Hackesche Höfe and Friedrichstraße.

Hotel Charlot, Giesebrechtstr. 17 (Charlottenburg), Phone: 030/327 96 60, Fax 030/32 79 66 66, www.hotelcharlot.de. Atmosphere and service are both good.

Youth hostels

Reservations: Phone: 030/262 30 24, www.djh-berlin-brandenburg.de

Jugendgästehaus am Wannsee, Badweg 1 (Nikolassee), Phone: 030/803 20 34

Jugendherberge Berlin International, Kluckstr. 3 (Schöneberg), Phone: 030/261 10 97

Jugendherberge Ernst Reuter, Hermsdorfer Damm 48–50 (Hermsdorf), Phone: 030/404 16 10

Jugendherberge Potsdam, Schulstr. 9, Potsdam, Phone: 03 31/ 581 31 00, www.jh-potsdam.de

Private lodgings

Agentur Wohnwitz, Holsteinische Str. 55 (Wilmersdorf), Phone: 030/861 82 22, Fax 030/861 82 72, www.wohnwitz.com

Euroflat Berlin Apartments, Stresemannstr. 72 (Mitte), Phone: 030/786 20 03, Fax 030/785 06 14, www.wohnung-berlin.de

Mitwohnagentur Home Company, Joachimstaler Str. 17 (Charlottenburg), Phone: 030/194 45, Fax 030/882 66 94, www.berlin.homecompany.de

Zeitraum Wohnkonzepte, Immanuel-kirchstraße 8 (Prenzlauer Berg), Phone: 030/441 66 22, Fax 030/441 66 23, www.zeit-raum.de

▍ Means of Transport

Public transport

Berliner Verkehrsbetriebe (BVG) with U-Bahn, Bus and Tram and the S-Bahn suburban rail line provide a comprehensive transport network [Plan see pp. 184/185].

Since the traffic network is liable to frequent changes, you should also get hold of an updated map on arrival or check the internet pages.

BVG Call Center, Phone: 030/194 49, www.bvg.de

S-Bahn Berlin, Phone: 030/29 74 33 33, www.s-bahn-berlin.de

Individual BVG tickets can be used interchangeably for U-Bahn, bus, tram, and S-Bahn and are valid for two hours. But it is worth your while to take advantage of special offers like the Tageskarte (day ticket: with or without surrounding region) or the day card for small groups (up to 5 persons).

The **CityTourCard** (www.citytourcard. com) for 1 person is available from BVG and at S-Bahn stations for 48 or 72 hours for price zones AB (inner city). Discounts for tourist attractions are an enticing bonus.

The **Berlin WelcomeCard** from BTM enables an adult and up to three children (to age 14) to use all public transport in Berlin and Potsdam for 72 hours. The Card also gives discounts for 105 tourist attractions. It is available from BTM [see p. 163], at hotels, airports and DB, BVG and S-Bahn ticket windows.

Bike hire

Bahrdt im Zentrum, Kantstr. 88–89 (Charlottenburg), Phone: 030/323 81 29

Icken's Fahrradshop, Pichelsdorfer Str. 96 (Spandau), Phone: 030/331 32 96

Fahrradstation (Bicycle Station), Rosenthaler Str. 40–41 (Mitte), Phone: 018 05/10 80 00, www.fahrrad-station.de, Leipzigerstr. 56, Auguststr. 29 a (Mitte), Bergmannstr. 9 (Kreuzberg), Goethestr. 46 (Charlottenburg)

potsdam per pedales e.V., Bahnhof Griebnitzsee (Potsdam), Phone: 03 31/ 748 00 57, www.potsdam-per-pedales.de

Car rental

The **ADAC Autovermietung** provides car hire at reasonable rates. Bookings (at least 3 days in advance) at all ADAC branches or by Phone: 018 05/31 81 81 (0.12 €/call).

Offices of all large international car rental firms at all three Berlin airports. City offices:

AVIS, Budapester Str. 43 (Charlottenburg), Phone: 030/230 93 70, www.avis.de

Europcar, Kurfürstenstr. 101–104, am Europacenter (Wilmersdorf), Phone: 030/235 06 40

Sixt Budget, Nürnbergerstr. 65 (Charlottenburg), Phone: 018 05/25 25 25

Taxi

Taxi, Phone: 030/21 02 02, 030/21 01 01, 030/26 10 26

Mobilcab , Phone: 030/21 02 02. For persons in wheelchairs

Velotaxi, Phone: 01 51/12 28 00 00. Through the capital with muscle power: Bike Taxi for two passengers with light luggage only.

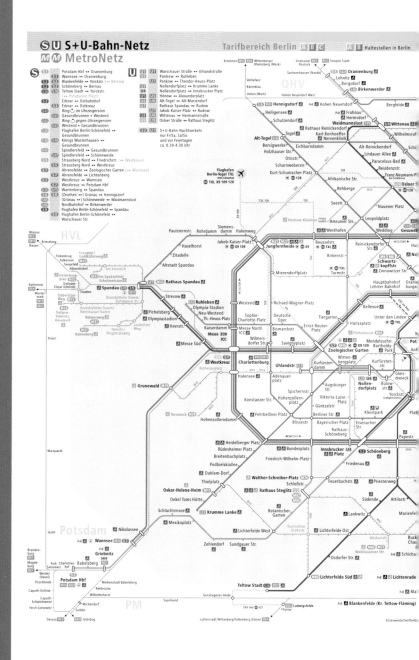

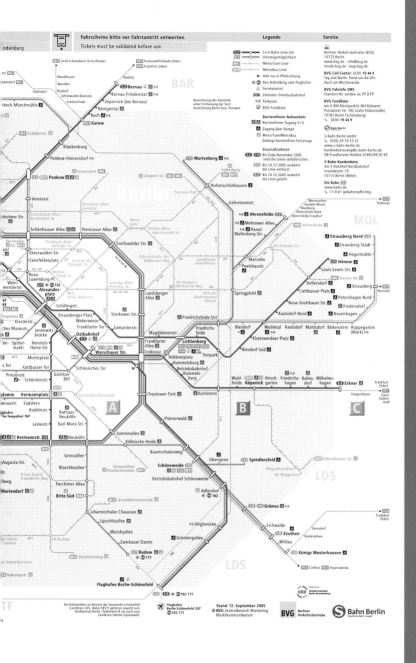

Pocket language guide

Basics

yes/no	ja/nein
please/thank you	bitte/danke
all right/agreed	in Ordnung/einverstanden
Excuse me!	Entschuldigung!
Pardon?	Wie bitte?
I only speak a little German.	Ich spreche nur wenig Deutsch.
Can you help me, please?	Können Sie mir bitte helfen?
open/closed	geöffnet/geschlossen
straight on/left/right /back	geradeaus/links/rechts/ zurück
near/far	nah/weit
How far is it?	Wie weit ist es?
Where is/are ...	Wo ist/sind ...
Is this the way to ...?	Ist das der Weg nach ...?
I (don't) like that	Das gefällt mir (nicht).
I would like ...	Ich möchte ...
Do you have ...?	Haben Sie ...?
Is there ...?	Gibt es ...?
How much is that?	Wie viel kostet das?
Can I pay by credit card?	Kann ich mit Kreditkarte bezahlen?
Could you please recommend a hotel/ Bed & Breakfast?	Können Sie mir bitte ein Hotel/eine Pension empfehlen?
Where is a good/ inexpensive restaurant?	Wo gibt es ein gutes/ günstiges Restaurant?
The bill, please.	Die Rechnung, bitte.

Greetings and introductions

Good morning!	Guten Morgen!
Good morning!/ Good afternoon!	Guten Tag!
Good evening!	Guten Abend!
Good night!	Gute Nacht!
What's your name, please?	Wie ist Ihr Name, bitte?
My name is ...	Mein Name ist ...
I come from England/ from the US.	Ich bin aus England/ aus den USA.
Wie geht es Ihnen?	How are you?
Good bye!	Auf Wiedersehen!
See you!	Tschüs!

Days of the week

Monday	Montag
Tuesday	Dienstag
Wednesday	Mittwoch
Thursday	Donnerstag
Friday	Freitag
Saturday	Samstag
Sunday	Sonntag

Months of the year

January	Januar
February	Februar
March	März
April	April
May	Mai
June	Juni
July	Juli
August	August

Numbers

0	null	17	siebzehn
1	eins	19	neunzehn
2	zwei	20	zwanzig
3	drei	21	einundzwanzig
4	vier	22	zweiundzwanzig
5	fünf	30	dreißig
6	sechs	40	vierzig
7	sieben	50	fünfzig
8	acht	60	sechzig
9	neun	70	siebzig
10	zehn	80	achtzig
11	elf	90	neunzig
12	zwölf	100	einhundert
13	dreizehn	200	zweihundert
14	vierzehn	1000	eintausend
15	fünfzehn	2000	zweitausend
16	sechzehn	1 000 000	eine million

September	September
October	Oktober
November	November
December	Dezember

Time

What time is it?	Wie viel Uhr ist es?
yesterday/today/ tomorrow	gestern/heute/ morgen
in the morning/ in the afternoon	am Vormittag/ am Nachmittag
in the evening/at night	am Abend/ in der Nacht
at one o'clock/ at two o'clock ...	um 1 Uhr/ um 2 Uhr
at a quarter to (past) ...	um Viertel vor (nach) ...
at ... thirty	um ... Uhr 30
minutes/hours	Minuten/Stunden
days/weeks	Tage/Wochen
months/years	Monate/Jahre

Pronunciation tips

a	like 'ah', eg: ah
ai, ei	like 'eye', eg: either
ä	like 'e', eg: bed
o	like 'oh' and like 'aw', eg: oh, awful
ö	like 'er', eg.: peu, deux in French, 'Er, can I ...'
u	like 'ou', eg: you
ü	like 'ue', eg: French rue, avenue
c	before 'e' and 'i' like 'ts', eg: nuts
c	before 'a' and 'o' like 'k', eg: call,
ch	after vowels like soft 'kyh'
e	like 'eh' and 'ay', eg: bed and day
h	aspirated, eg: hall
g	hard before vowels, except at end of word eg: guard, young
i	like 'e' and like 'ih' eg: eve and inn
s	like 's' before 'i','e', 'a', 'o' 'u' but usually like 'sh' before consonants
sch	like 'sh' eg: ship
v	like 'f', eg: fine
w	like 'v', eg: very
z	like 'ts', eg: nuts

Index

Photo credits

Cover: Pariser Platz, Brandenburg Gate and Reichstag
Photo: *laif, Köln (Langrock/Zenit)* (from p. 10/11)

Frontispiz
Top: Inside the Reichstag dome. Photo: *Ralf Freyer, Freiburg*
Centre: Insel der Jugend in Treptower Park (from p. 81 bottom)
Bottom: Bar am Lützowplatz (from p. 176)

AKG, Berlin: 118, 139 top, 145, 146 top – *Constantin Beyer, Weimar*: 31, 85 – *Fotostudio Ulf Böttcher, Potsdam*: 157,
161 – *Ralf Freyer, Freiburg*: 4 (3. from top), 6 left, 30, 38, 41 top, 72, 74, 76 top, 78, 79, 80, 81 top, 92, 106 bottom,
139, 144 (2), 162 (5), 176, 180 – *Hans Christian Glave, Berlin*: 2 (2. v. top), 25, 26, 45 (2), 49 bottom, 52, 58/59, 60, 62
top, 97, 98, 99 bottom, 108, 109, 116 (2), 126, 131 bottom, 134, 147, 149, 166, 174 top – *Rolf Goetz, Stuttgart*: 73, 76
bottom, 81 bottom – *ADAC Archives*: 13 top, 13 centre, 14, 15 top, 146, 155 – *Bildagentur Huber, Garmisch-Par-
tenkirchen*: 9 bottom, 15 bottom (Wh. von 133), 22/23 (Gräfenhain), 27, 64 (F. Damm), 105/106 (Mader), 106/107
(Bleyl), 140 bottom, 133 (Gräfenhain), 152 (F. Damm) – *laif, Köln*: 7 top (Kirchner), 7 bottom (Zielske), 8 centre
(Wh. von 115) (Galli), 8 bottom (Wh. von 108) (Galli), 9 top (Galli), 10/11 (Langrock/Zenit), 11 bottom (Neumann), 16/17
(Zielske), 19 (Galli), 21 (Adenis/Gaff), 28 (Galli), 32/33, 35 (Kirchner), 37, 40 (Galli), 43 top (Paul Hahn), 43 bot-
tom, 46, 47 (Nascimento/Rea), 48 (Maecke/Gaff), 50 (Baltzer/Zenit), 51 (Boening/Zenit), 53 (Kirchner), 56 top
(Adenis/Gaff), 56 bottom (Galli), 62 bottom (Biskup), 65, 66 (Maecke/Gaff), 68 (Hoefe), 70/71, 82/83, 88 (Neu-
mann), 94/95 (Kirchner), 94 (Frei), 96, 100, (Kirchner), 102 top (Craig/Rea), 108 (Galli), 110 (Babovic), 112 bottom
(Galli), 112/113 (Kirchner), 114 bottom (Neumann), 115 (Galli), 120 (Geilert/Gaff), 121 (Kirchner), 122/123 (Riehle),
127 (2) (Gerhard Westrich), 130/131 (Kirchner), 136, 137, 142/143, 156 bottom, 158 top (Neumann), 160 (Junge-
blodt), 169 (Neumann), 170 (Decoux/Rea), 174 bottom – *LOOK, München*: 20 (Rainer Martini), 24, 92 top (Max
Galli) – *Mauritius, Mittenwald*: 59 bottom (Latza), 29, 153 (Elsen), 57, 69, 119 (Schnürer), 150 (Hackenberg) –
Neumeister Photographie, München: 55, 132, 158 bottom, 159 – *Erhard Pansegrau, Berlin*: 110 top, 148 – *Günter
Schneider, Berlin*: 44, 49 top, 86 (2), 87, 89, 99 top, 110 bottom, 117, 123 bottom, 135 top, 140 top, 141, 156 top, 167,
173, 175 top – *Claudia Schwaighofer, München*: 91 – *Staatliche Museen zu Berlin–Preußischer Kulturbesitz, Berlin*: 13 bottom (Kunstbibliothek), 39 left (Ägyptisches Museum), 39 right, 41 bottom (Antikensammlung), 124
(2) (Museum für Vor- und Frühgeschichte/Verlag Postel, Berlin/Strüben) – *Süddeutscher Verlag/Bilderdienst
(DIZ), München*: 12, 13 top left – *Tierpark Friedrichsfelde, Berlin (Klaus Rudloff)*: 70 bottom – *Ullstein Bild, Berlin*:
125 – *Verwaltung der Staatlichen Schlösser und Gärten, Berlin*: 135 bottom – *Ernst Wrba, Wiesbaden*: 63, 93,
114 top

ADAC Travel Guides published in this series (german editions):

Imprint

Editorial: Carin Pawlak
Editorial english edition: Carlo Lauer & Partner, Aschheim
Translation: Joan Clough, München
Updating: Dagmar Walden
Maps: Huber Kartographie, München
Production and design: Martina Baur
Author Treptow-Koepenick: Rolf Goetz, Stuttgart

Advertising partner: Kommunalverlag
GmbH & Co KG, MediaCenterMünchen,
Phone: 089/92 80 96-44

Printed in Germany
Printed on paper free of chlorine bleach

ISBN 3-89905-300-1

First edition 2006
© ADAC Verlag GmbH, München
© of works shown by Alexander Calder,
Corbusier, Rainer Fetting, Georg Kolbe, Ludwig
Mies van der Rohe, Dimitrij Vrubel: VG Bild-Kunst,
Bonn 2006

Readers' forum

Our readers' opinion is important to us, thus
we are pleased to hear from you. If this travel
guide appealed to you or if you have important remarks on the contents – proposals for
supplements and improvements, tips and
corrections – please write to:

**ADAC Reiseführer Redaktion,
ADAC Verlag GmbH
81365 München
verlag@adac.de**

* also available as ADAC Travel Guide Plus
  with CityMap or RegionalMap

■ A Day in Berlin

You should reserve the morning for a stroll down **Kurfürstendamm** or a shopping tour through the glitzy emporia in **Friedrichstraße** or **Potsdamer Platz**. Old and modern buildings make any shopping tour a quickie

course in the history of architecture. In the afternoon you can queue up with other tourists who want to go on an official tour of the city. Taking the No. 100 bus, however, is just as interesting, and – depending on the bus driver you get – just as informative. Leaving from **Bahnhof Zoo**, it passes the **Victory Column**, **Schloss Bellevue**, the Government buildings in the **Regierungsviertel**, the **Reichstag** and the **Brandenburg Gate** before driving down **Unter den Linden** boulevard to **Alexanderplatz**. In short, a brief tour through Berlin history. To sweeten your farewell to Berlin: enjoy delicious cakes and pastries served at the **Operncafé** in the former Prinzessinnenpalais, Unter den Linden. The **Tadschikische Teestube** in the nearby Palais Am Festungsgraben has an Oriental flavour.

■ A Weekend in Berlin

Friday: On arriving, stroll up and down the **Ku'damm**, window-shopping and making purchases from the many boutiques and department stores in the quarter around the boulevard. Afterwards you'll be ready for a cup of coffee at **Café Einstein** or **Café Kranzler** or be feeling like lunch at **KaDeWe**, with its tempting gourmet floor and restaurant with a view. In the afternoon you'll be off on a **tour of the city**, an absolute must, before exploring different sections of the city: **Prenzlauer Berg**, **Kreuzberg** and **Friedrichshain** are the best places for soaking up some typical Berlin ambience. If you prefer history served up with elegance, you should visit the

Nikolaiviertel in Berlin-Mitte. There is a broad range of evening entertainment: boulevard comedies, theatre, cinema or cabarets and musicals.

Saturday: Devote this day to the finer things of life – for instance, lingering at the **Flea Market** along Straße des 17. Juni is sure to be rewarding. Whether it's bed linen, antique lamps or fine china you're after: you're bound to find some bargains. Another must is a visit to at least one of the many Berlin **Museums**. Several famous collections are on the **Museumsinsel** in Berlin-Mitte, including the Perga-

monmuseum, the Alte Nationalgalerie and the Altes Museum, where lovely Ne-

fertete stays. The **Kulturforum** just off Potsdamer Platz lures visitors with paintings at the Gemäldegalerie. No matter what museum you opt for, you'll find plenty worth seeing. After so much uplifting culture, a lucullan repast will restore you in the evening. Perhaps at **REmake**, a gourmet restaurant in Berlin-Mitte?

Sunday: If the weather is good, an excursion to **Wannsee** is recommended. From there you can take a boat trip to Potsdam or **Pfaueninsel**. A scenic footpath runs from the Peacock Island along the banks of the Hav-

el to **Schloss Kleinglienicke**. An excellent place to take a break for refreshment is **Blockhaus Nikolskoe**. If the weather isn't co-operating, a visit to Berlin's **Schloss Charlottenburg** with its magnificent rooms is a sumptuous alternative.